# THE ART LOVER'S GUIDE TO
# AMSTERDAM

# THE ART LOVER'S GUIDE TO
# AMSTERDAM

## ANGELA YOUNGMAN

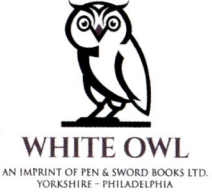

**WHITE OWL**

AN IMPRINT OF PEN & SWORD BOOKS LTD.
YORKSHIRE ~ PHILADELPHIA

First published in Great Britain in 2025 by
White Owl
An imprint of
Pen & Sword Books Ltd.
Yorkshire - Philadelphia

Copyright © Angela Youngman, 2025

ISBN 978 1 39900 187 8

Printed and bound in India by Replika Press Pvt. Ltd.
Design: SJmagic DESIGN SERVICES, India.

Pen & Sword Books Ltd. incorporates the imprints of Pen & Sword
Books: After the Battle, Archaeology, Atlas, Aviation, Battleground,
Discovery, Family History, History, Maritime, Military, Politics,
Select, Transport, True Crime, Fiction, Frontline Books, Leo Cooper,
Praetorian Press, Seaforth Publishing, Wharncliffe and White Owl.

For a complete list of Pen & Sword titles please contact

PEN & SWORD BOOKS LIMITED
George House, Beevor Street, Off Pontefract Road, Hoyle
Mill, Barnsley, South Yorkshire, England, S71 1HN.
E-mail: enquiries@pen-and-sword.co.uk
Website: www.pen-and-sword.co.uk

or

PEN AND SWORD BOOKS
1950 Lawrence Rd, Havertown, PA 19083, USA
E-mail: uspen-and-sword@casematepublishers.com
website: www.penandswordbooks.com

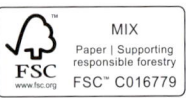

# CONTENTS

Introduction..................................................6

1 The Netherlands....................................9

2 Amsterdam..........................................10

3 Dutch Art Movements......................19

4 Key Artist Profiles...........................29

5 Artist's Amsterdam..........................41

6 Exploring Amsterdam's Art............44

7 Within Easy Reach of Amsterdam...................107

Further Reading.................................159

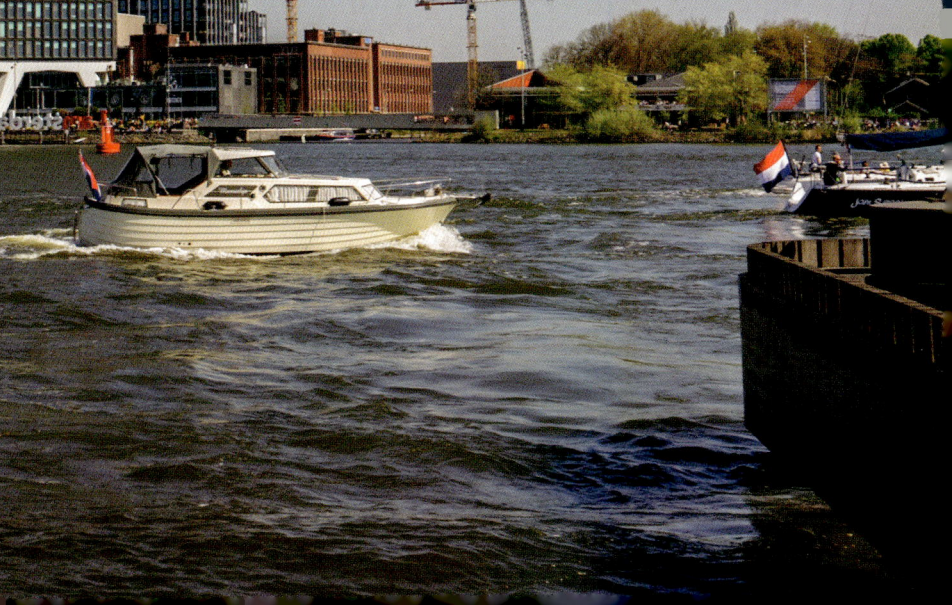

# INTRODUCTION

Amsterdam is an art lover's Mecca. Thousands flock to see the Rijksmuseum and Van Gogh Museum every day, eagerly exploring the vast array of art on display. Yet these are only two of the fantastic museums and art galleries to be found in and around Amsterdam. The Netherlands has an impressive art history that includes Rembrandt, Vincent Van Gogh, Hieronymus Bosch, Piet Mondrian, Frans Hals, Willem van de Velde and Rachel Ruysch. It has inspired artists for centuries leading to the development of major art movements like the Dutch Golden Age artwork, or the work of the De Stijl artists that have influenced artists worldwide. It has resulted in the creation of distinctive applied arts such as the characteristic blue and white Delftware still produced today.

The Dutch are very proud of their artistic heritage. Many towns and cities throughout the Netherlands are named after artists, including lesser-known ones. Amsterdam has a Johannes Vermeerstraat and Rembrandtsplein as well as Adriaen Van Ostadestraat, Hobbemakade and Moreelsestraat. In Leiden streets are named after artists like Jan Van Goyen and Gerard Dou, while Zwolle honours Gerard ter Borch and Utrecht Joachim Wtewael and Hendrik ter Brugghen.

Art is visible everywhere in Amsterdam. Parks are filled with eye-catching art such as the giant puppy

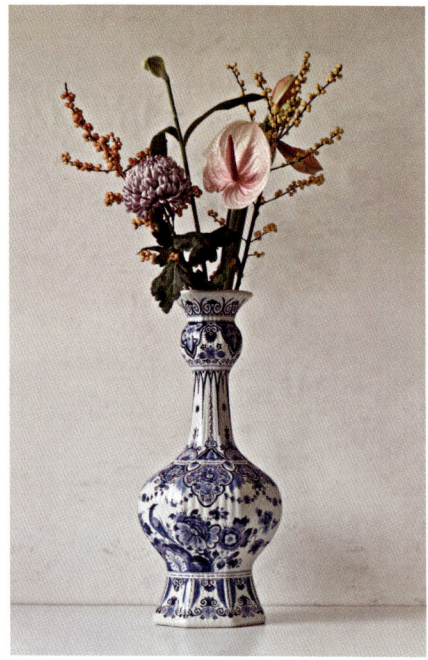

▲ *A classic Royal Delft baluster vase.* (Royal Delft)

sculptures peeking over the bridge on Postjesweg on Rembrandtpark, while a sleeping rabbit made from artificial grass can be seen on top of the Nieuwe Bibliotheek. In Erasmuspark, a marble polar bear attracts attention while in Vondelpark there is a sculpture by Picasso. One of the most popular outdoor sculptures is the Blue Violin Player on Tweede Marnixplantsoen.

Visit in spring if you are intent on exploring the colour and beauty of the bulb fields that attracted Monet, but there is much to see at other times, too. Winter brings its own charm to Amsterdam's landscape, as does the autumn hues. Visiting out of season can

make it easier to access some of the museums and galleries.

Check out the annual Amsterdam Art Weekend (www.amsterdamart. com) offering an opportunity to discover contemporary art in galleries and art institutes. Apart from special exhibitions, there are performances, artist talks and small-scale art fairs.

Most people head automatically for the most well-known art venues, so queues can be long. Book tickets in advance. Exploring beyond the well-known locations can offer unexpected delights – how about funeral art, fluorescent art, a Van Gogh-style picture that includes diamonds, Second World

▼ *Violet and white tulips bloom near windmills and houses beside a canal.*

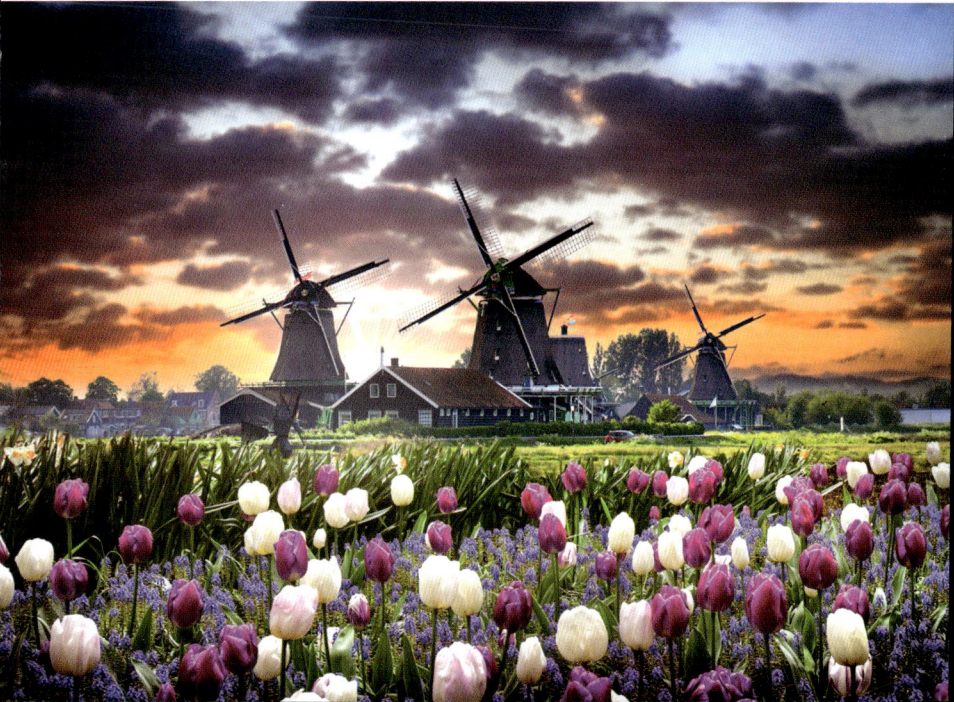

War Resistance Art, gargoyle sculptures, cat-related artworks and artworks in flower. Those are just a few of the many possibilities worth exploring, plus there are numerous art-related destinations available within a short distance. Amsterdam is keen to attract visitors who enjoy art, culture, history and museums.

The Netherlands is a compact country with good transport facilities, making it easy to combine Amsterdam with Haarlem, Rotterdam, Den Bosch, Delft or Utrecht, Volendam and Amstelveen. Amsterdam has always played a central role in Dutch art, but artists have frequently sought work in, trained in or been inspired by other cities.

# 1

# THE NETHERLANDS

There is a Dutch saying that 'God created all the world except Holland, which was created by the Dutch.' This is a low-lying country, mostly reclaimed from the sea.

Much of the region was part of the Duchy of Burgundy, until it was passed through marriage to the Habsburg family and the Holy Roman Empire. In 1555, Emperor Charles V handed the low country states forming modern-day Belgium, Luxembourg and the Netherlands to his son, Philip of Spain.

Philip's personal priority was Spain and the Roman Catholic Church. He authorised the Inquisition to deal with all Protestant heretics and to 'burn, strangle or bury alive all unrepentant heretics'.

This led to a revolt in Antwerp (now part of Belgium) that spread northwards. Led by William of Orange, civil war resulted in the Protestant northern regions forming the United Provinces republic in 1609. War with Spain continued until 1648.

Opposition to monopolies operated by the Dutch East Indies and West Indies companies resulted in a series of Anglo-Dutch wars. By 1799, the French Emperor Napoleon had conquered the region. Independence was regained in 1813, and since 1814 the Netherlands has been a constitutional monarchy.

Seventeenth-century records refer to artists travelling by barge, dining in one city and returning home the same day. One artist, David Beck, frequently took one and a half hours to travel between The Hague and Delft, returning within a few hours.

▼ A classic Dutch low-lying polder landscape.

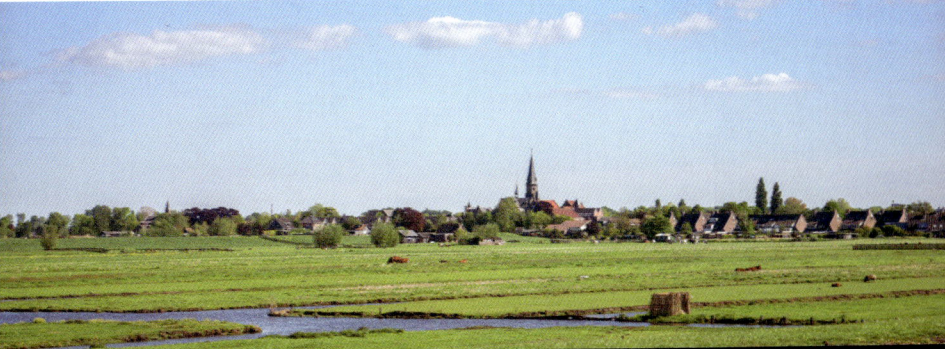

# 2

# AMSTERDAM

Located in the North Holland province of the Netherlands, Amsterdam is the biggest city in the Netherlands. A major cultural hub and tourist destination, it is the centre of the diamond industry and a global financial centre.

It is the capital city of the Kingdom of the Netherlands, although the Dutch government is actually based in The Hague. Schiphol Airport is one of the busiest airports globally. Within the metropolitan area of Amsterdam are the provinces of North Holland and Flevoland together with the municipalities of Aalsmeer, Almere, Amstelveen, Amsterdam, Beemster, Beverwijk, Blaricum, Bloemendaal, Diemen, Edam-Volendam, Gooise Meren, Haarlem, Haarlemmermeer, Heemskerk, Heemstede, Hilversum, Huizen, Landsmeer, Laren, Lelystad, Oostzaan, Ouder-Amstel, Purmerend, Uitgeest, Uithoorn, Velsen, Waterland, Weesp, Wijdemeren, Wormerland, Zaanstad and Zandvoort.

A flat city built on land over 2m below sea level, Amsterdam's extensive canal network with its more than 1,200 bridges is a UNESCO World Heritage Site.

▼ *A panoramic view of Amsterdam showing its canals and urban landscape.*

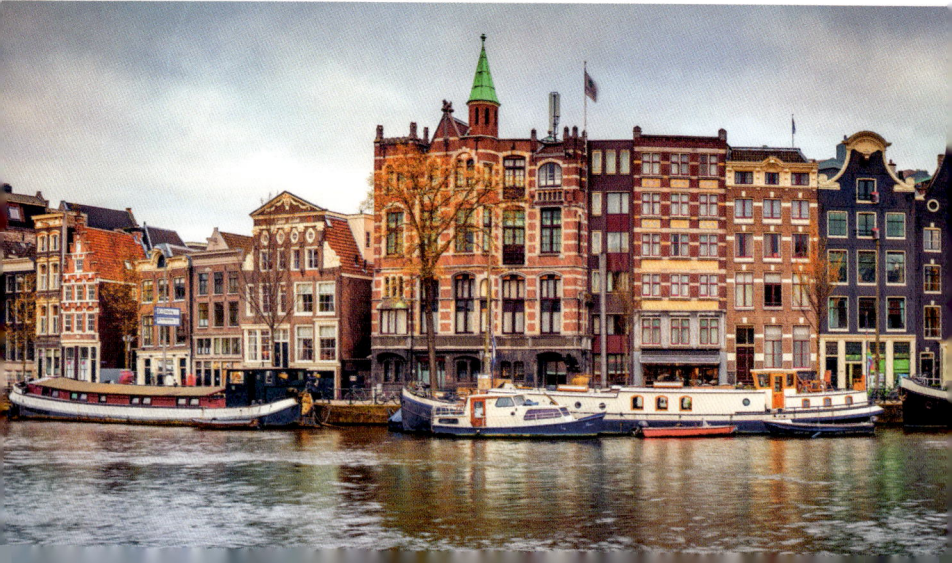

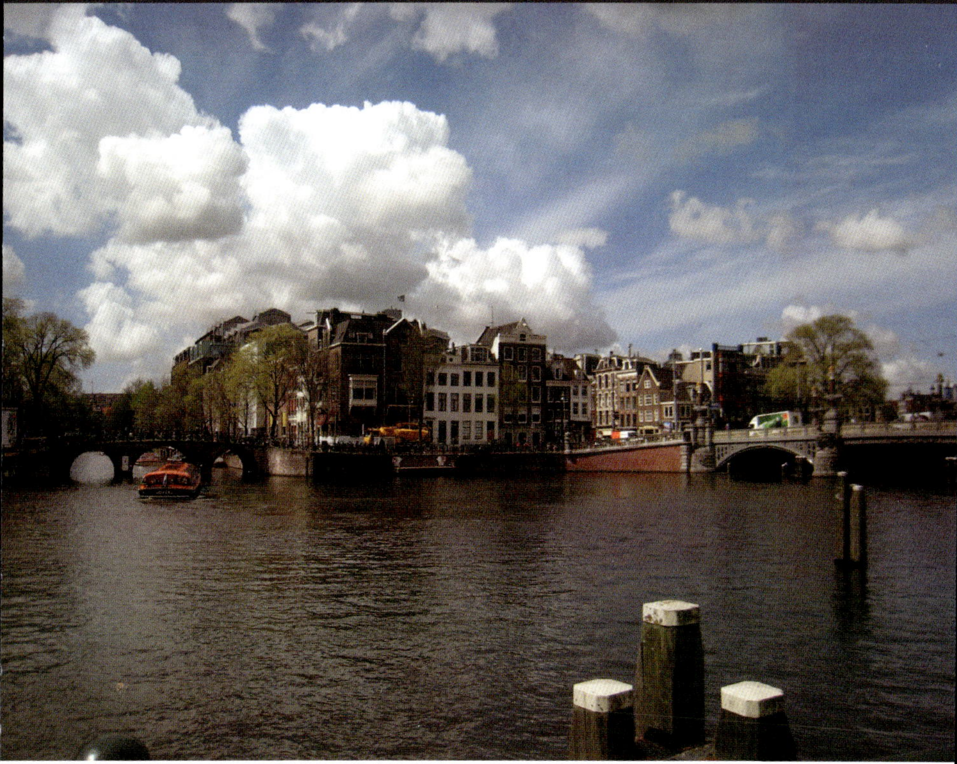

▲ *A typical canal scene within Amsterdam.* (Angela Youngman)

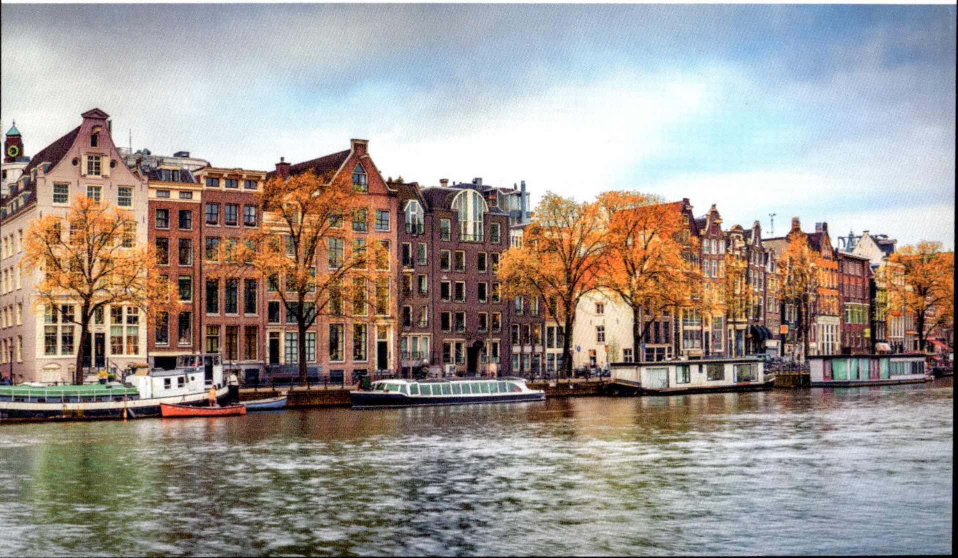

The reasons for its important role in art development and the creation of superb art collections lie in the city's landscape and history.

The earliest historical record referring to Amsterdam is a 1275 document granting 'the people who live near the Amstel dam exemption from tolls for transporting goods'. The Amstel Dam had been built in 1240 on the site of what is now Dam Square, joining two banks of the Amstel River estuary. By the sixteenth century, it had grown to become a walled city of around 12,000 people trading with the Baltic countries, where it sourced cargoes of grain, fur and timber. Some of this was exported to France, Portugal and Spain, the ships returning with spices, wine and salt. Ships from Amsterdam were a familiar sight in every European port.

The outbreak of war between the United Provinces and Spain in the late sixteenth century enabled Amsterdam to gain pre-eminent status. At the start of the rebellion, the city had around 30,000 inhabitants. Fifty years later it had grown to more than 100,000. Jewish diamond cutters and merchants sought refuge in Amsterdam following the fall of Antwerp in 1565. Trade and commerce developed rapidly and the city expanded steadily. Three circular canals were built – the Herengracht, Keizersgracht and Prinsengracht – linked by numerous smaller ones along which long rows of tall, thin, gabled houses were built.

In 1594, Amsterdam merchants began making voyages to the Far East. This led to the creation of the Dutch East India Company in 1602.

This venture was granted a trading monopoly by the United Provinces for all areas east of the Cape of Good Hope. A similar venture, the West India Company, covered all trade west of the Cape of Good Hope. Most of the financial backing for both ventures came from Amsterdam, the remainder from other Dutch towns. These ventures were built into the largest trading organisations the world had ever seen complete with trading plantations, ports, warehousing and merchandise. Amsterdam became Europe's trading capital. Profits were consistently high, and in very good years could be 50 per cent or more of share value. The sheer scale of trade passing through Amsterdam encouraged ever greater commercial development, including the creation of paper money, a stock exchange and the first exchange bank to allow people to pay debts by credit transfer.

Amsterdam merchants became rich, likewise the majority of the population and other regional cities. They sought ways of spending their money. Art was the solution. Even the wealthier peasants could afford paintings and decorative items that could beautify their homes and record their achievements. Merchants and civil groups commissioned group portraits such as Rembrandt's The Night Watch. The symbols of the guilds involved are always clearly marked. Demand was so high that, along with the development of specific types of paintings, it became known as the Dutch Golden Age of art.

Amsterdam's townscape was a popular subject for paintings. Johannes Lingelbach painted Dam Square in 1656 portraying the construction of the Town Hall, a building that later became the Royal Palace. Seascapes by Willem van de Velde and his son, Willem van de Velde the Younger, show Amsterdam harbour full of tall masts against the background of Prins Hendriks Quay and the Schreierstoren tower.

Amsterdam possesses a seventeenth-century ambiance, with tall, gabled canal-side buildings that artists like Rembrandt would recognise. It is a landscape that continues to provide artistic inspiration as no two buildings are the same.

The main architectural style to be seen around Amsterdam is Dutch Renaissance/Baroque in Dam Square and former merchants' houses along the canals.

Also common are buildings constructed in the Expressionist Amsterdam School style, which existed between 1910 and 1930. These brick buildings were characterised by

▼ *Traditional Dutch canal-side houses.*

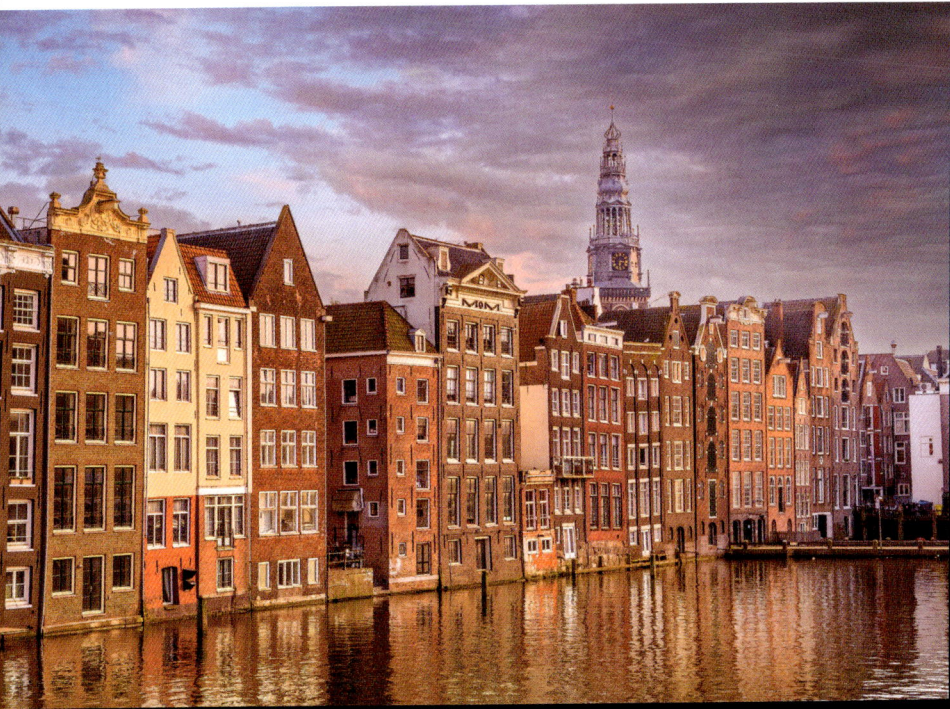

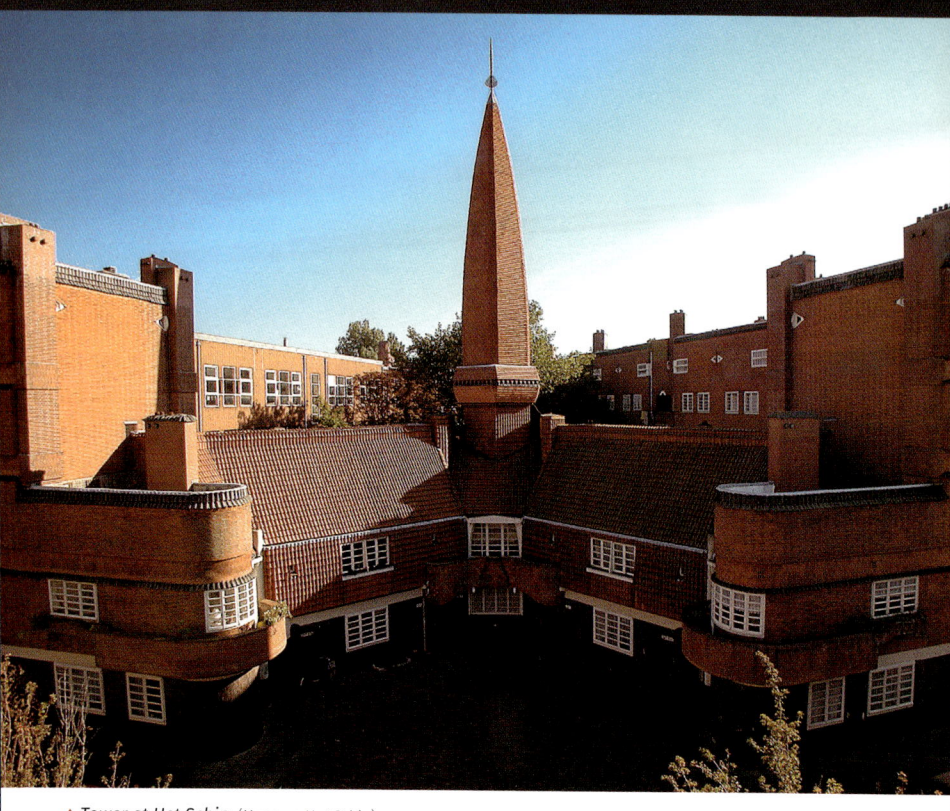

▲ *Tower at Het Schip.* (Museum Het Schip)

decorative masonry, art glass, wrought ironwork, exterior sculptures and spires or windows with iron bars. A typical example is the Amsterdam School Museum and public housing complex on Oostzaanstraat designed in 1919 by architect Michel de Klerk. The design resembles that of a ship, hence its nickname of The Ship.

## Travelling to Amsterdam

Amsterdam is extremely accessible by air, train and road.

Schiphol International Airport (www.schiphol.nl) is one of the top airports in Europe, catering for more than 50 million passengers each year. There are frequent international and national flights to and from Schiphol to destinations worldwide. It is the busiest airport in the Netherlands and 5.6 miles (9km) from the centre of Amsterdam.

Direct trains from Schiphol into Amsterdam Centraal Station take around twenty minutes. Bus services take about twenty minutes to reach Duivendrecht station, just south of the city centre.

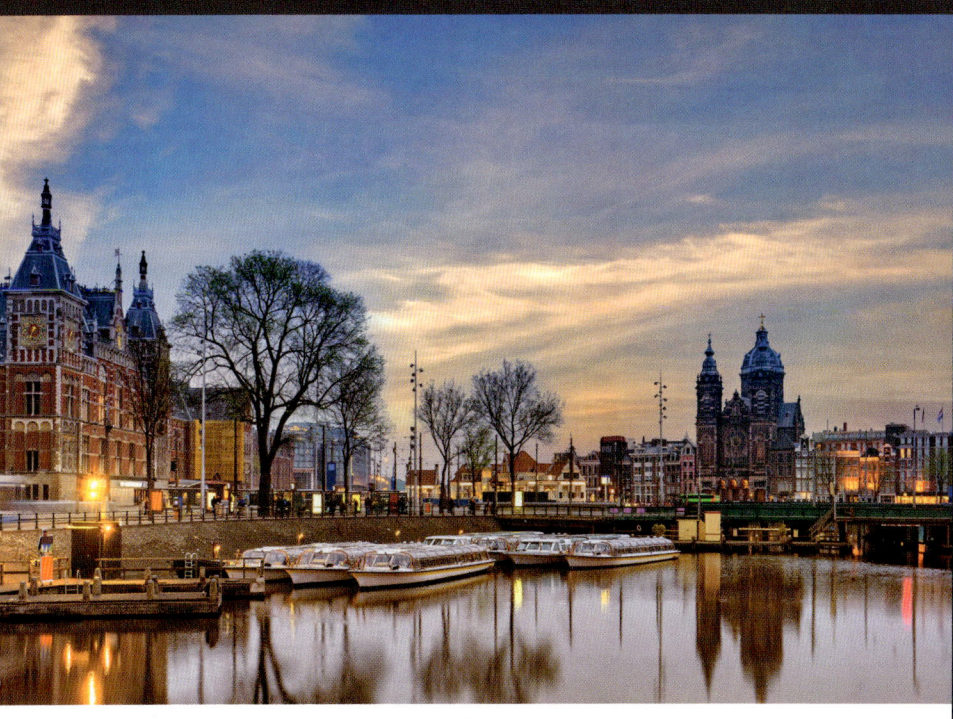

▲ *Amsterdam Centraal Station and nearby Basilica of Saint Nicholas.*

Amsterdam Centraal Station is a major railway station located to the north of the city centre, with connections to most European cities such as Paris and Brussels. There are regular services to cities including Haarlem, Rotterdam, The Hague, Utrecht and Den Bosch. Trains are fast, reliable and numerous, making it an extremely easy way to travel within the Netherlands. The station is served by taxis, buses, metro and trams.

There is a direct Eurostar service between London St Pancras and Amsterdam via Rotterdam, taking visitors direct from city centre to city centre. Additional services are available via Eurostar to Brussels, changing to the Thalys train to Amsterdam.

Numerous coach services link Amsterdam with cities and towns across Europe. National Express, Flixbus and Eurolines are among coach operators providing daily direct journeys from London to Amsterdam.

If travelling by car, there are ferries available from Newcastle to Amsterdam, Hull to Rotterdam, Harwich to Hook of Holland as well as routes from Dover to Calais. It takes around three and a half hours to drive from Eurotunnel Calais to Amsterdam.

## Getting Around Amsterdam

Amsterdam is a very pedestrian-friendly city, and it is extremely easy to find your way around. Most Amsterdammers travel by cycle and there are thousands on the roads each day.

Avoid King's Day (27 April) unless you plan to join in the festivities since all transport closes down. King's Day is an annual Dutch holiday, celebrating King Willem-Alexander's birthday. Amsterdam becomes a positive riot of orange, with almost everyone wearing something in the colour. Buildings are covered in flags and orange confetti is everywhere, forming a city-wide street party, with concerts, children's activities, music, food and drink, markets and a boat parade passing along the canals.

Trams are the most common form of public transport. The system is fast, frequent, extensive and reliable, criss-crossing the entire city. Some trams have conductors, others require you to pay the driver, or you can buy day passes. Check in and out by showing tickets to the on-board machine.

▼ *Bikes in Amsterdam.* (Angela Youngman)

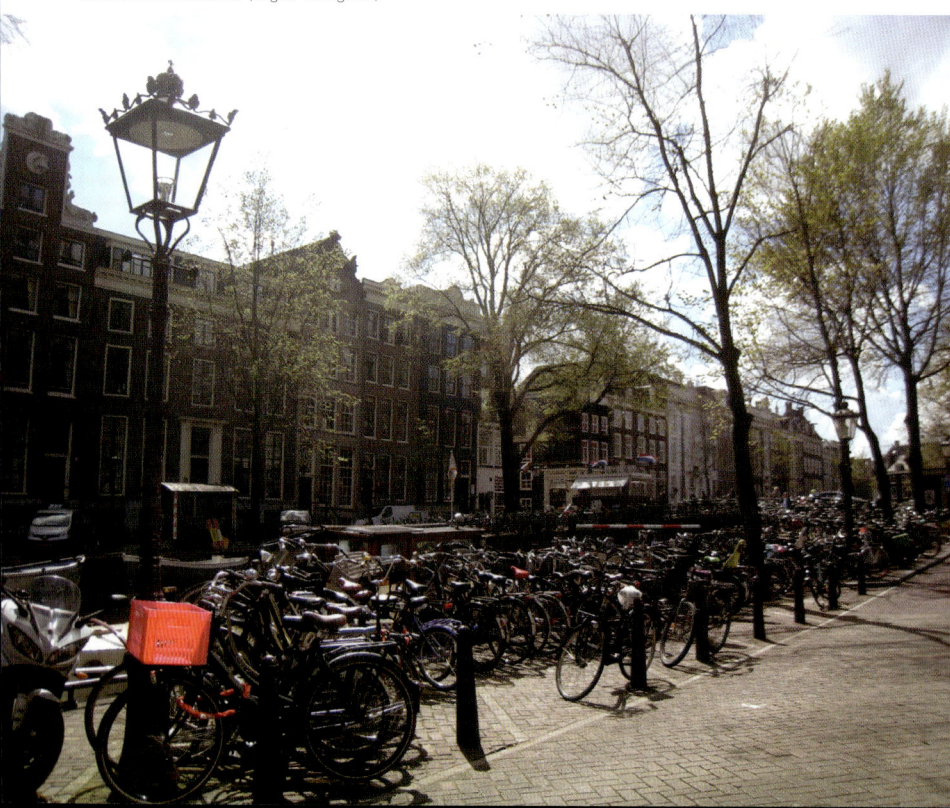

The metro is a light rail network with four routes radiating out from Centraal Station to outlying districts including Amstelveen and Dieman.

A night bus network operates when all other transport systems stop in the late evening.

The Canal Bus network offers a hop on, hop off facility covering the main canal routes through the city, with a stop close to the Rijksmuseum.

Travel passes can be purchased at the Amsterdam Visitor Centre close to Centraal Station, as well as from any tram conductors. The unlimited ride passes are available from one to seven days in length, and can be used on trams, metro and some bus routes.

The iAmsterdam City Card is ideal for visitors, providing unlimited access to public transport and free entry to most attractions, including museums and art galleries such as the Rijksmuseum. It can be linked to the Amsterdam and Region Travel Ticket covering Haarlem, Rotterdam, Zaanse Schans, Keukenhof, Volendam and Edam, all of which are within a short distance of Amsterdam.

▼ *Travelling by boat around Amsterdam.* (Angela Youngman)

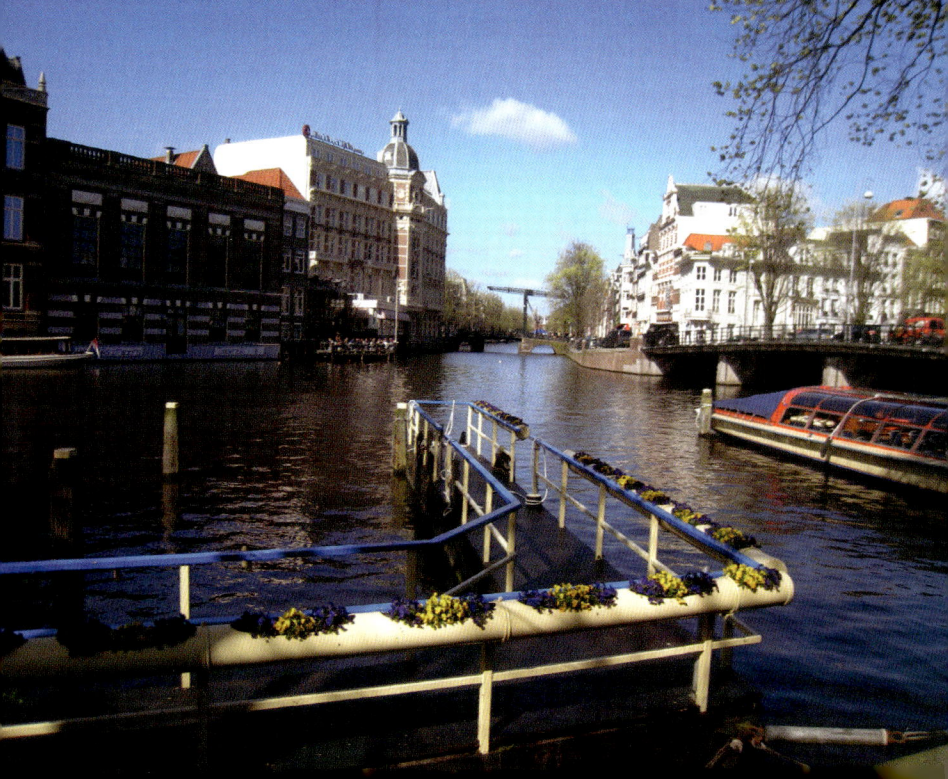

**Tourist Information Centre**
iAmsterdam Visitor Centre
Stationsplein 10,
Amsterdam

Located outside the Amsterdam Centraal railway station, it provides help with travel, activities and accommodation. It sells the iAmsterdam visitor card and travel passes. Queues can be long, so take a number when you walk into the centre.
**www.iamsterdam.com**

**iAmsterdam Visitor Centre Schiphol**
This unit is located at the Arrivals 2 hall. Staff can deal with queries, accommodation, travel passes and the iAmsterdam visitor card.

**3**

# DUTCH ART MOVEMENTS

## Early Northern Renaissance / Early Netherlandish Painting

During the late medieval and Renaissance periods, northern artists including Jan van Eyck excelled at representing flowers, jewels and fabrics. Described as the inventor of oil painting, van Eyck created images that mirrored nature. Other prominent artists include Lucas van Der Leydon and Jan Gossaert.

## The Dutch Golden Age of Painting

The Reformation led to a major change in artists' work since religious art was prohibited. Artists sought alternative styles and their skill in detail provided the answer.

Aristocrats, wealthy merchants and civic guilds wanted portraits that could be sent as gifts or hung on walls, reflecting their power and prestige. Merchants wanted to have their portraits painted for posterity showing off their insignia of office, while militias, bands and councils wanted group portraits

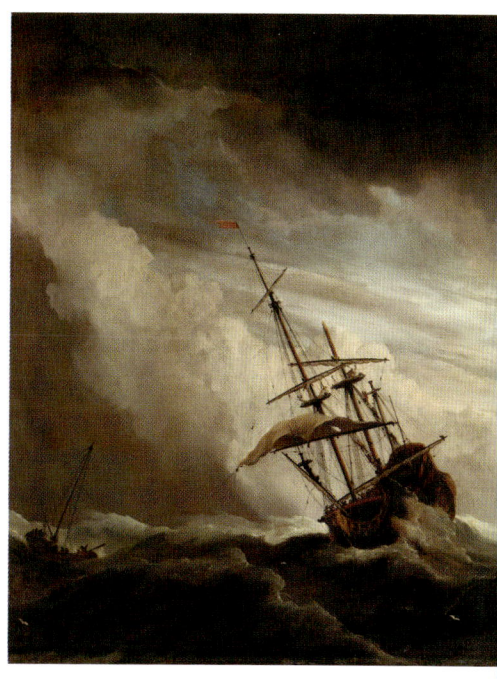

▲ *Typical Dutch seascape of the period. Used with permission of the Rijksmuseum.* (Rijksmuseum)

for their meeting places. Allied with this demand for portraiture, there was a demand for landscapes, townscapes, seascape, maritime and history paintings.

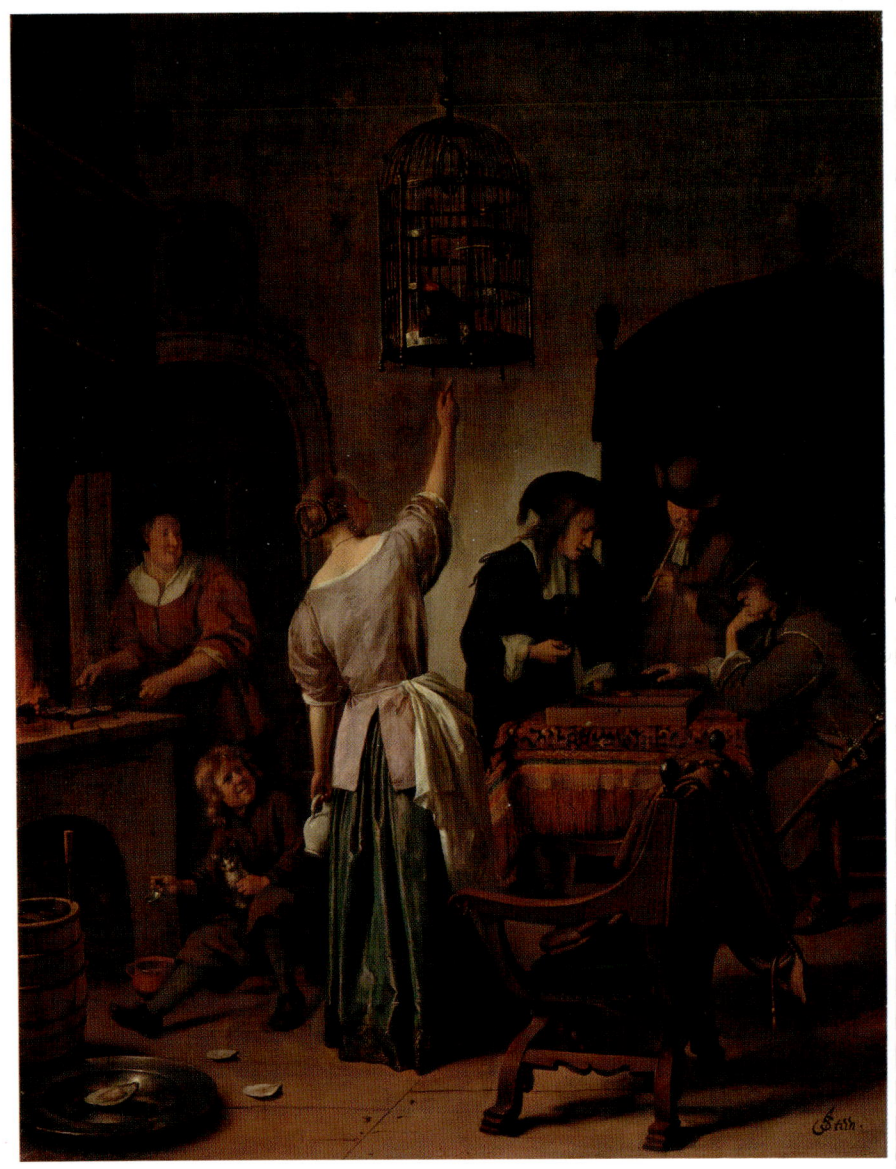

▲ *Interior with a Woman Feeding a Parrot, known as The Parrot Cage, by Jan Steen in the Rijksmuseum. Used with permission of the Rijksmuseum.* (Rijksmuseum)

Out of this developed a style of painting in which the Dutch excelled – genre paintings showing ordinary life such as house interiors, still life and flowers, tavern scenes, celebrations, hunting parties and skating scenes. Artists discovered the beauty of the sky, water, fields and trees, while others such as Jan Steen included their portraits within paintings, or created self-portraits. Rembrandt painted more than forty self-portraits during his lifetime.

Demand for paintings, engravings and applied arts spread throughout all

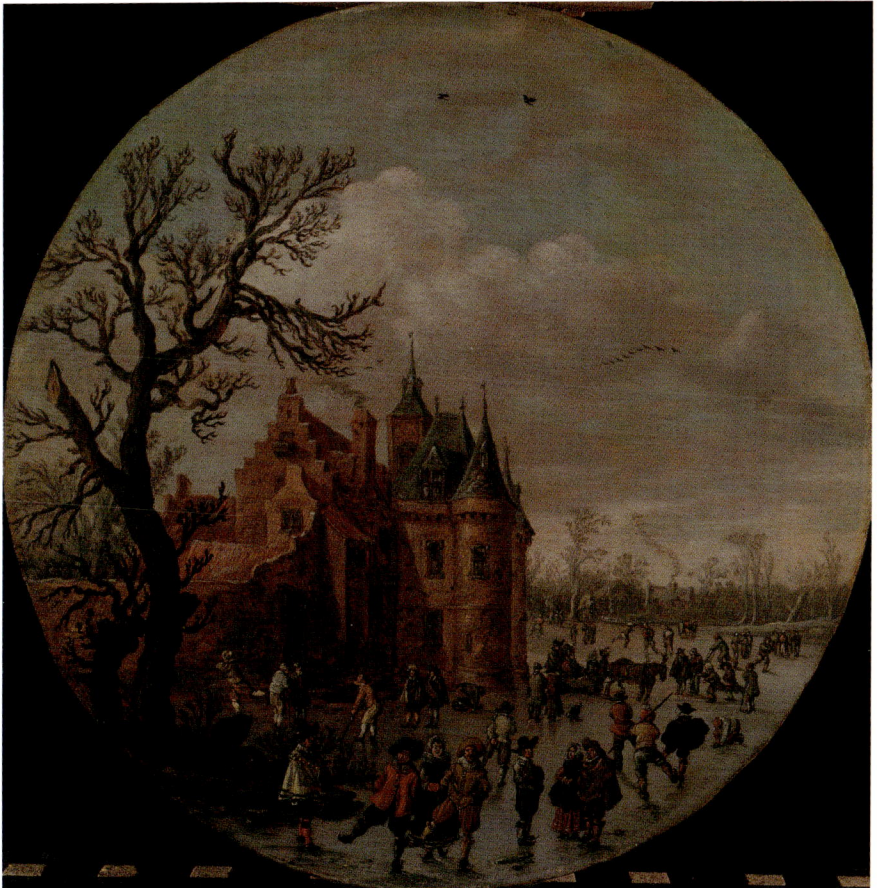

▲ *Winter landscape by Jan van Goyen in the Rijksmuseum. Used with permission of the Rijksmuseum.*
(Rijksmuseum)

levels of society. English and French travellers commented that even peasants had paintings on the walls of their homes. Some paintings were said to have cost less than household linen. Many pieces of art were sold via auctions held in taverns organised by professional dealers.

Between five and ten million paintings were created. This was the period in which some of the greatest artists flourished, such as Rembrandt, Vermeer and Frans Hals.

Individual talents flourished. Hendrick Avercamp focused on painting wintery days, especially scenes reflecting life on the ice; Adriaen Coorte became an expert in small groups of objects in a ghostly light. Some architectural painters concentrated on just one detail: Anthonie de Lorme

painted the Church of St Lawrence in Rotterdam, while Jan van der Vucht calculated the price of a painting on the number of columns involved in the painting of a church. Melchior d'Hondecoeter specialised in birds and Quirijn van Brekelenkam painted tradespeople. Jacob van Ruisdael specialised in landscapes, while Willem van de Velde focused on maritime paintings such as the Arrival of the Admiral's Ship Gouden Leeuw (Golden Lion).

Other painters including Rembrandt and Adriaen van Nieulandt created portraits, landscapes, kitchen scenes, still life and history paintings.

The seventeenth century marked the development of applied arts including characteristic blue and white Delftware in which delicate ceramics and tiles

▼ *Enjoying the Ice Near a Town, Hendrick Avercamp. Used with permission of the Rijksmuseum.* (Rijksmuseum)

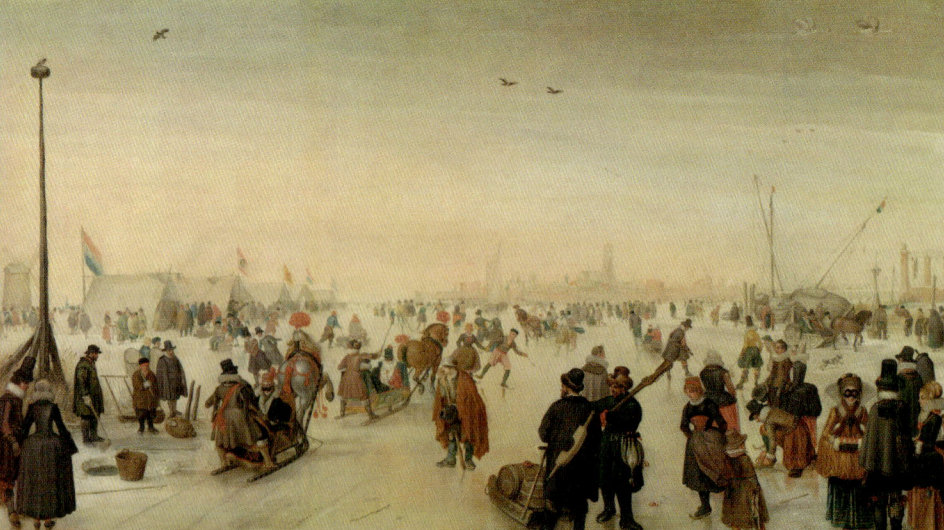

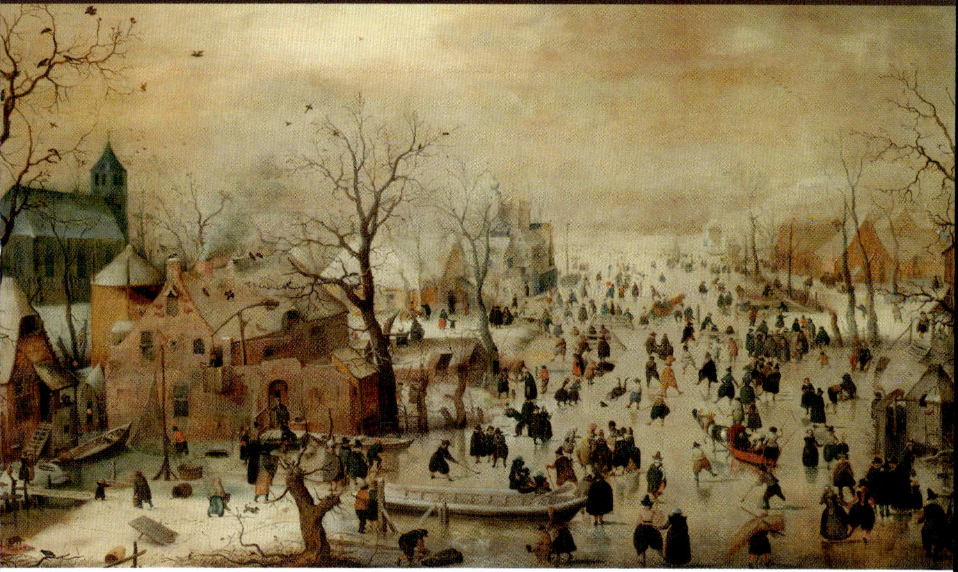

▲ *Example of a winter scene genre painting. Used with permission of the Rijksmuseum.* (Rijksmuseum)

▼ *Classic Dutch images on blue and white Delft tiles.* (Angela Youngman)

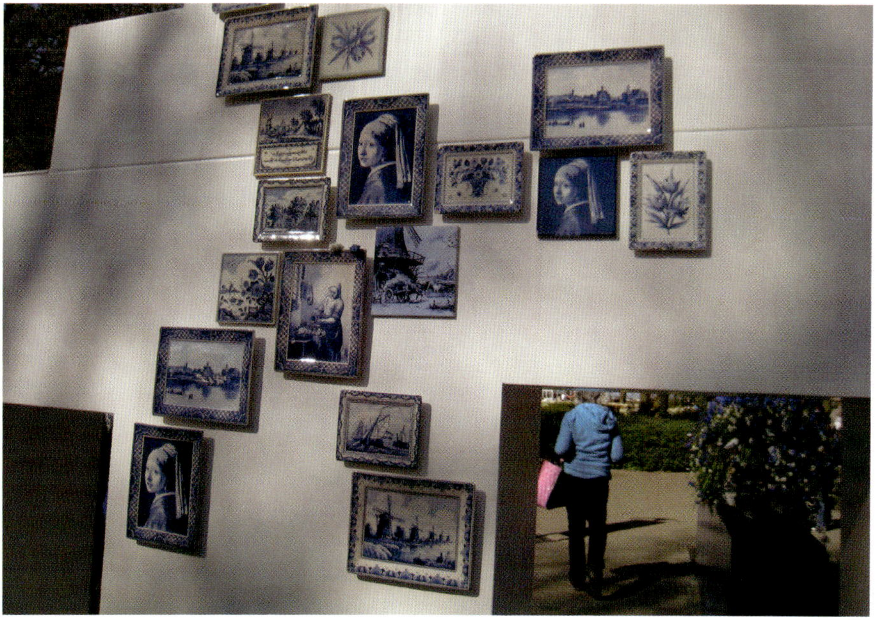

were painted with detailed bouquets of flowers, battle scenes, seascapes, townscapes, countryside and people. Highly engraved silverware was popular, as were items such as the Nautilus Cup to be seen in the Gemeente Museum, Delft.

## Dutch Flower Painting

Flowers have always formed a prominent part of Dutch art. Intricate tulip flowers appeared in paintings, embroidered on dresses, woven into tapestries and painted on to porcelain.

In 1590, the oldest botanical garden in Europe, the Hortus Botanicus in Leiden, began breeding and cultivating tulips. Such programmes resulted in colourful and unusual flowers such as frilled petalled ones known as parrot tulips or versions that had streaks and flames across the petals.

Frilly tulips are known as Rembrandt tulips due to the frequency with which they appear within his paintings. In 1634 Rembrandt painted his wife Saskia as Flora, goddess of spring and flowers, wearing a crown of flowers, including tulips.

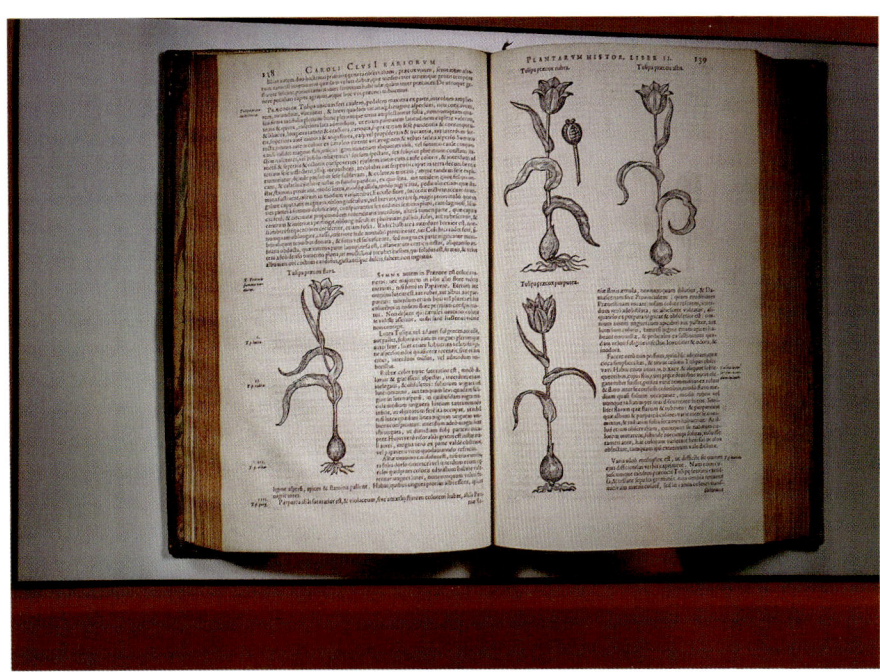

▲ *Botanical book illustrations, 1601.* (Tulip Museum)

Two Dutch painters are renowned for their skill in flower painting: Rachel Ruysch and Jan van Huysum.

Born in 1664, the daughter of botanists, Ruysch gained international fame for her work. She created a unique style of paintings, placing tulips and flowers against dark backgrounds using delicate colours and meticulous detail. Ruysch was the first woman to be offered membership of the Confrerie Pictura in The Hague (an exclusive club for artists and academics). Her paintings sold for 750–1,200 guilders, compared with the 500 guilders or less paid to Rembrandt. Examples of her work are in the Rijksmuseum and the Mauritshuis.

Van Huysum succeeded Ruysch as the tulip and flower specialist. Born in Amsterdam in 1682, his artistic skills were developed by his father, Justus, who was also a flower painter. Van Huysum's first dated work was in 1706.

## The Hague School

This term refers to a group of painters active in The Hague between 1860 and 1890, sometimes also known as the Grey School due to their use of grey paint. Artists including Jozef Israels, Anton Mauve, Gerard Bilders and Hendrik Willem Mesdag were influenced by the Barbizon style and wanted to paint what they saw in a realistic fashion. Hague School painters worked outside *en plein air* to capture light and atmosphere.

The Hague School was most influential in 1870–88. Artists collaborated in holding exhibitions, initially focusing on gloomy, greyish tints expanding into lighter palettes and looser brushwork under the influence of French Impressionism. Jacob Maris added vivid brushwork into his Amsterdam town views, while Willem Maris focused on the image of sunlight sparkling on water surrounded by summer meadows. Johan Hendrik Weissenbruch turned to brightly coloured beach scenes and landscapes in an almost abstract manner.

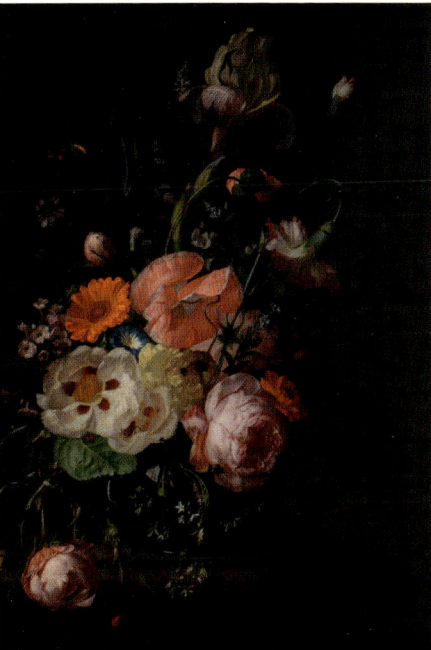

▲ *Rachel Ruysch: Still Life with Flowers on a Marble Tabletop. Used with permission of the Rijksmuseum.* (Rijksmuseum)

By the mid-1880s the Hague School came to an end, partly due to the fact that the city's growth led to artists leaving to continue painting the countryside.

Piet Mondrian started painting in the style of the Hague school, while Vincent Van Gogh received his first training as an artist from Anton Mauve.

Examples of work by the Hague School of Artists can be found in numerous art galleries and museums. Typical examples in the Rijksmuseum Amsterdam include:

Fishing Pinks in Breaking Waves by Hendrik Willem Mesdag

Morning Ride Along the Beach by Anton Mauve

Woodland Pond at Sunset by Gerard Bilders

## Amsterdam Impressionists

The Amsterdam impressionists were an offshoot of the Hague School, focusing mainly but not exclusively on everyday urban life. Influenced by French Impressionism, participants aimed to create impressions using rapid, fast brushstrokes. Key artists included George Hendrik Breitner, Isaac Israels and Willem Bastiaan Tholen. Breitner was one of the most prominent members, regarding himself as 'the people's painter', creating paintings of ordinary people, street scenes, industrial sites and canals in the rain using photography to capture atmospheric effects.

Typical examples of the work of the Amsterdam impressionists include:

De Schelpenvisser by Jan Toorop, Rijksmuseum

Market with Flower Stalls by Floris Arntzenius, Rijksmuseum

Two Servants by George Hendrik Breitner Teylers, Museum Haarlem

## De Stijl

A twentieth-century Dutch art movement, led by Piet Mondrian and Theo van Doesburg. The term 'De Stijl' means 'the style', referring to an abstract, very pared-down aesthetic focusing on geometric forms – straight lines, squares and rectangles – together with primary colours. It was regarded as a universal visual language for the modern era.

It offered social and spiritual redemption in the wake of the horrors of the First World War. In 1918, Gerrit Rietveld inscribed a poem on the underside of his Red and Blue Chair stating, 'When I sit, I do not want to sit as my seated flesh likes, but rather as my seated spirit would sit, if it wove the chair for itself.' Rietveld's Red and Blue Chair, together with the philosophy it expressed within the poem, became a canonical part of the De Stijl movement.

Over the next few years, artists could be seen following De Stijl's ideas within all aspects of art, including fine and applied arts, sculpture, industrial design, typography and architecture, helping to give rise to the International style of the 1920s and '30s, and the Bauhaus movement.

The Stedelijk Museum Amsterdam and the Germeente Museum in The Hague are the main locations for De Stijl paintings, while the Germeente has a comprehensive Piet Mondrian collection.

## CoBrA

Although a short-lived art movement, it proved very influential. CoBrA combined Dutch group Reflex, Danish group Host and the Belgian Revolutionary Surrealist group. The name was created from the first letters of the cities in which the founding members lived and reflected the animal imagery often seen in CoBrA paintings.

Founding members included Karel Appel, Asger Jorn, Constant Nieuwenhuys (known as Constant), Corneille Beverloo, Christian Dotremont and Joseph Noiret. In November 1948, they issued a manifesto entitled 'La cause était entendue' (The Case Was Settled) with Appel commenting, 'We wanted to start again like a child.'

Experimental, expressive and spontaneous, the CoBrA art style was based on complete freedom of colour, form, primitive art, tribal and folk art, graffiti, children's art, Marxism and modernism.

CoBrA is regarded as a significant milestone in the development of European abstract expressionist art. Christie's describes it as 'the last true Avant-Garde movement of the 20th century'.

Examples of CoBrA art can be seen at the CoBrA Museum Amstelveen, and at the Rijksmuseum, which contains examples of Appel's work.

## Street Art

Street art is very popular. Moco Museum, Amsterdam, includes street art within its contemporary art remit, describing it as the 'voice of the streets'. There are several specialist street art museums, notably in Amsterdam, Rotterdam and Utrecht. Among the most famous examples of street art in Amsterdam are the rare Keith Haring mural, the Blue Violin player statue that arrived anonymously on Tweede Marnixplantsoen in the 1980s, and the ten large-scale murals installed on apartment buildings surrounding Platanenweg in Amsterdam. Most famously, a massive mural of Anne Frank entitled Let Me Be Myself created by Eduardo Kobra smiles down on visitors as they step off the ferry.

Graffiti and street art has had a tremendous impact on art, fashion,

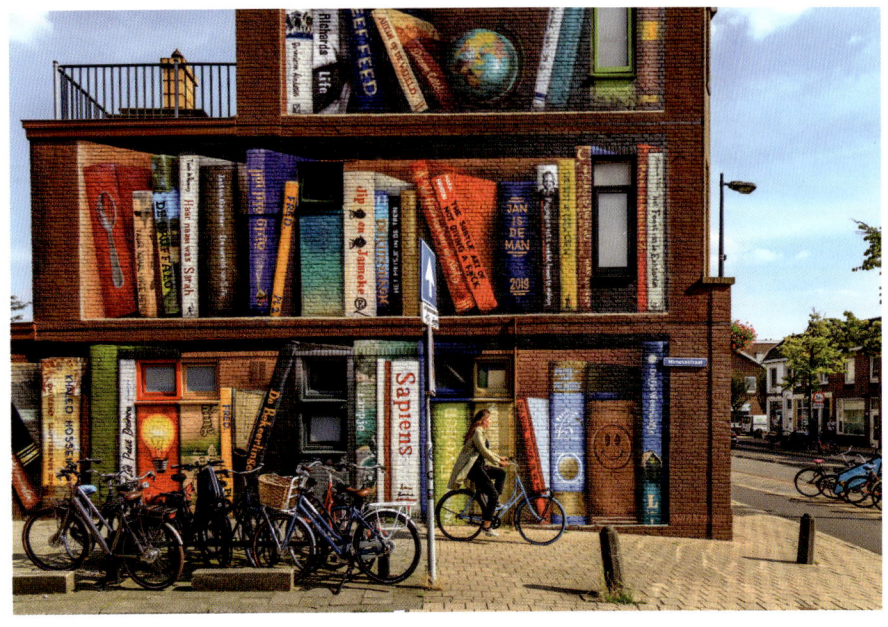

▲ *Street art in Utrecht.* (Utrecht Marketing)

design, advertising and culture within Amsterdam, with numerous artists taking centre stage such as Rafael Sliks, Jan Is De Man, Inkie, TWOONE and Jenny Sharaf.

Museums devoted to street art include:

STRAAT Amsterdam
Street Art Museum Amsterdam
Street Art Museum Rotterdam

**4**

# KEY ARTIST PROFILES

## Hieronymus Bosch

Hieronymus Bosch is one of the most imaginative of all Dutch artists. Born around 1450 in the city of S-Hertogenbosch, Brabant, he came from a family of painters. His father was Anthonius van Aken, artistic advisor to the Illustrious Brotherhood of Our Blessed Lady. Early in his career, Hieronymus began signing his work Jheronimus Bosch, taking his surname from his birthplace, s-Hertogenbosch

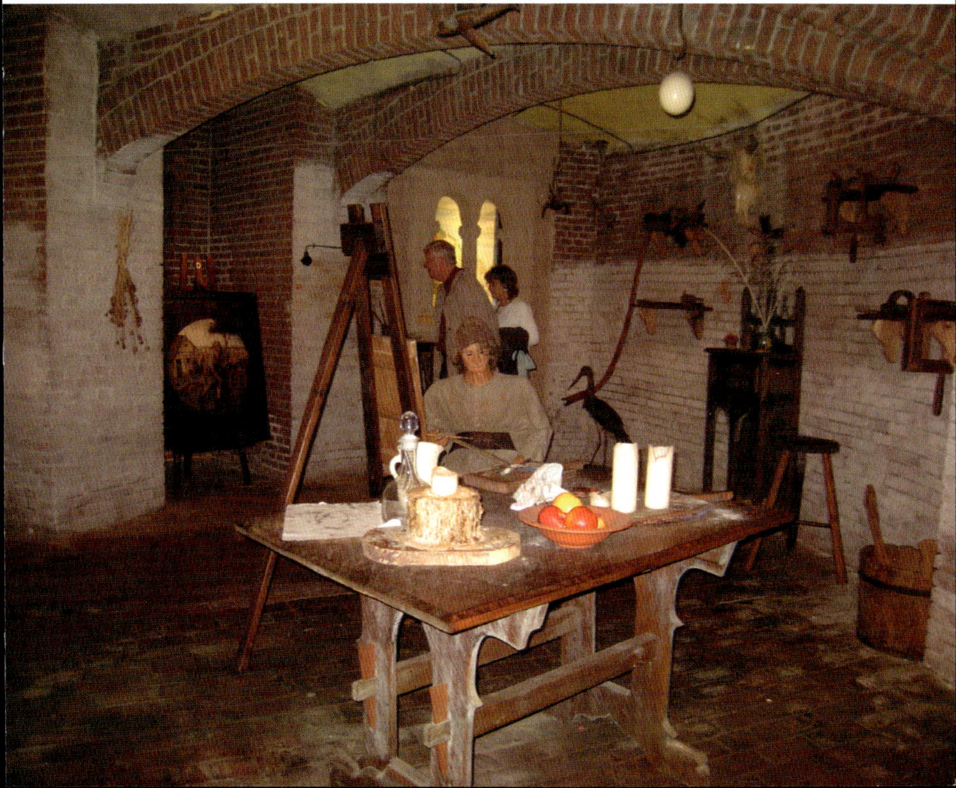

▼ *Bosch workshop replica in Den Bosch.*
(Angela Youngman)

(Duke's Forest), which is usually shortened to Den Bosch (the forest). Bosch became a prominent citizen, with his studio and his family home in the central marketplace. In 1486/87 he joined the Brotherhood of Our Lady, a devotional lay confraternity of around forty influential citizens of Den Bosch.

His work is idiosyncratic and individual. It was imaginative rather than realist.

Bosch worked on oak panels using a small range of oil-based paint colours.

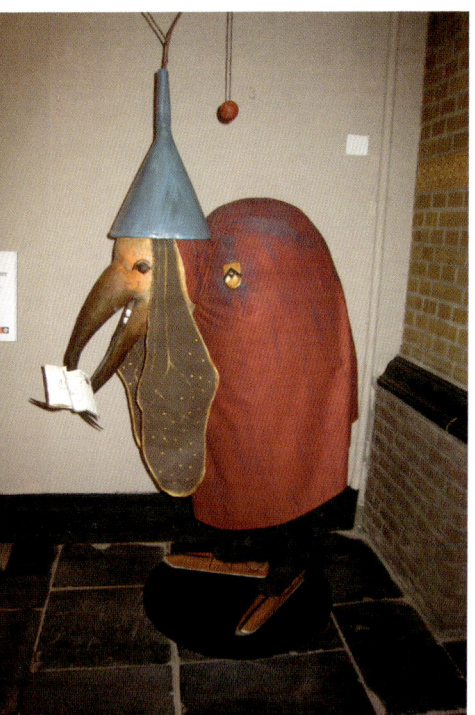

▲ *Model based on a Bosch character.*
(Angela Youngman)

He created incredible scenes of heaven and hell, peopled by exotic animals, hybrid characters and terrifying demons that are part animal, part human and part machine, sometimes with one eye or two, possessing strange-looking heads and bodies that are elongated and twisted. Only a small number of his works have survived, but are widely available as reproductions. Bosch was a major influence on many sixteenth-century northern painters such as Pieter Bruegel the Elder as well as on the surrealist movement of the twentieth century.

Works by Bosch can be seen in:

Museum Boijmans Van Beuningen Rotterdam, which has a Diptych as well as a couple of paintings: the Marriage Feast at Cana and St Christopher carrying the Christ Child.

The Noordbrabants Museum, Den Bosch, has a copy of the Adoration of the Child on loan from the Rijksmuseum, Amsterdam.

## Jan van Eyck

Born around 1380–90 most likely in Maaseik, Limburg, Jan van Eyck began working in The Hague in 1422. He was painter to John III the Pitiless, ruler of Holland and Hainault, later working for the Duke of Burgundy. While in Holland, van Eyck was involved in redecorating the Binnenhof palace, The Hague.

His style was extremely influential among successive generations of painters within Flanders and the Netherlands, helping to establish a Northern Renaissance Dutch style of painting.

Van Eyck is particularly important due to the fact that he devised a new form of preparing paints using oils in glossy colours for slower, more accurate work, applied in a series of transparent layers and glazes giving depth and shadow, as well as adding glittering highlights using a pointed brush.

## Frans Hals

A painter of the Dutch Golden Age, Frans Hals played a major role in the development of seventeenth-century group portraiture. Highly skilled in the use of quick, deft brushwork, he captured a moment in time for a sitter, freezing them in the act of holding a glass or pipe.

Born around 1580–81 in Antwerp, his Protestant family moved to Haarlem. Hals remained in the Netherlands for the rest of his life.

He trained as a painter under Karel van Mander and by the time he was 27 had become a member of Haarlem's Painters' Guild of St Luke. By 1616, he was well known as an artist, creating a life-size group portrait known as The Banquet of the Officers of the St George Militia Company. He served in a military guild, a *schutterij*, as part of the Dutch War of Independence and as chairman of the Painters' Corporation of Haarlem.

Hals married twice, firstly to Anneke Hamensdochter, who died after the birth of their third child, and then Lysbeth Reyniers, with whom he had eight more children. Three of his sons became painters.

Financial problems resulted in him working as a painter, art dealer and restorer. Eventually, Hals had to sell all his belongings in order to settle a debt with a baker, leaving him destitute. In 1664, the municipality of Haarlem granted him a small annuity. He died in 1666 and is buried in St Bavo Church, Haarlem.

As an artist, Frans Hals illustrated society – banquets, meetings, groups of guildsmen, merchants, burgomasters, gentlefolk, people in taverns as well as itinerant players and singers. He created many group portraits, plus many individual ones. He liked to capture daylight and silvery tones in his work, using a delicate range of colour to highlight expressions and personality using a very fluid painting technique.

There are around 220 known works ascribed to Hals and the Frans Hals Museum, Haarlem, contains more than 100. Many of these were originally owned by the City of Haarlem.

Examples of his work can be seen at the Rijksmuseum, Amsterdam, where The Merry Drinker is popular with visitors. This lively painting shows a well-dressed man wearing a lace collar and cuffs, holding a glass of white wine.

Other examples include:

The Smiling Boy, Mauritshuis, The Hague

Man and his wife, Rijksmuseum

Officers of the Civic Guard of St Hadrian at Haarlem, Frans Hals Museum, Haarlem

## Piet Mondrian

A renowned painter and art theoretician, Piet Mondrian is one of the giants of modern art. His name is sometimes spelt with two 'a's, reflecting the traditional Dutch spelling.

Mondrian was born in Amersfoort, a town within the province of Utrecht, in 1872. His father was a drawing teacher and his uncle studied with the Hague School of Artists. As a child, Piet often went drawing with his father and uncle. By 1882, he had already qualified as a primary school teacher but was keen to further his art practise. In 1882, he entered the Academy of Fine Art in Amsterdam. Initially interested in impressionist-style landscapes, he became more abstract with works such as Avond (1910) emphasising the importance of primary colours.

In 1911, Mondrian moved to Paris, where he discovered cubism. During his

▼ *The Mondrian house in Amersfoort, Utrecht.*

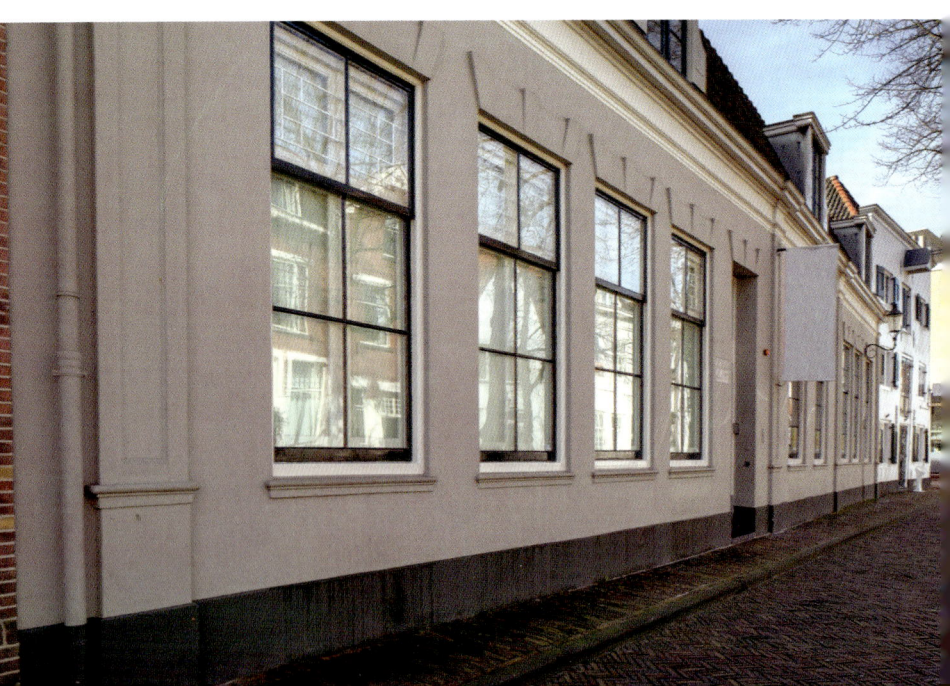

time in Paris he dropped the second 'a' in his surname. He stayed in Paris until 1914, when he returned to the Netherlands until the end of the First World War, before going back to Paris. Fearing the onset of war in 1938, he moved to London and then to New York, where he died in 1944.

Mondrian aimed to include spiritual awareness and philosophical thought within his art. He joined the Theosophical Society in 1909, and from then on his work was mainly inspired by his search for spiritual knowledge.

In same year, he wrote a letter to H.P. Bremmer explaining his art style. 'I construct lines and colour combinations on a flat surface, in order to express general beauty with the utmost awareness ... though horizontal and vertical lines constructed with awareness, but with calculation, led by high intuition, and brought to harmony and rhythm, these basic forms of beauty, supplemented if necessary by other direct lines or curves, can become a work of art, as strong as it is true.'

Mondrian began composing his characteristic grid-based paintings in late 1919, and by 1921 the style had become clear with thick black lines separating areas, many of which were left white or painted in blocks of primary colours. He continued to evolve this style for the rest of his life, eventually creating paintings using lines sometimes made from coloured tape rather than paint, with small shimmering rectangles of colour, which leap out of the canvas.

Mondrian became one of the most influential artists of the twentieth century, especially in the fields of abstract expressionism, minimalism, colour field painting, as well as in design, architecture and fashion. Ultimately Mondrian was regarded as equalling modernism. His influence has continued past his death. Mondrian has become synonymous with geometric styles using lines and coloured blocks.

In 2021, The Hague officially opened a road tunnel named in honour of Mondrian's greatest work, Victory Boogie Woogie. The tunnel is part of Rotterdamsebaan, running from the Ypenburg Junction (A4 and A13) to the Binckhorst Business Park.

His work can be seen at:

Stedelijk Museum, Amsterdam, has numerous drawings and paintings, including Composition with Blue, Yellow, Red, Black, Grey, 1922.

The Kunstmuseum, Den Haag, which has the largest collection of Mondrians in the world, items covering all stages of his artistic development such as Woods near Oele, 1908; Tableau 1, 1921; and his final masterpiece, Victory Boogie Woogie, 1944.

The Mondriaan House, Amersfoort, contains a number of Mondrian paintings, e.g. Pollard Willows on a Ditch outside Amsterdam, Watercolour, 1905, and Chrysanthemum Flower, 1908.

Museum Boijmans Van Beuningen Depot, Rotterdam, has paintings such as Chrysanthemum in a Glass, A Rose, Composition No. 11 and Composition with Colour Fields.

## Rembrandt

One of the greatest of all Dutch painters, Rembrandt enjoys worldwide renown for his artistic skill, mastery of dramatic light and shade (chiaroscuro) and storytelling abilities. His career is inextricably intertwined with seventeenth-century Amsterdam.

Born in Leiden on 15 July 1606, Rembrant Harmenzon van Rijn's family took their name from the Rijn Mill, on the River Rijn. His father, Harmen Gerritzoon van Rijn, was a miller, his mother, Neeltgen Willemsdochter van

▼ *Rembrandt's The Night Watch in the Rijksmuseum, Amsterdam. Used with permission of the Rijksmuseum.* (Rijksmuseum)

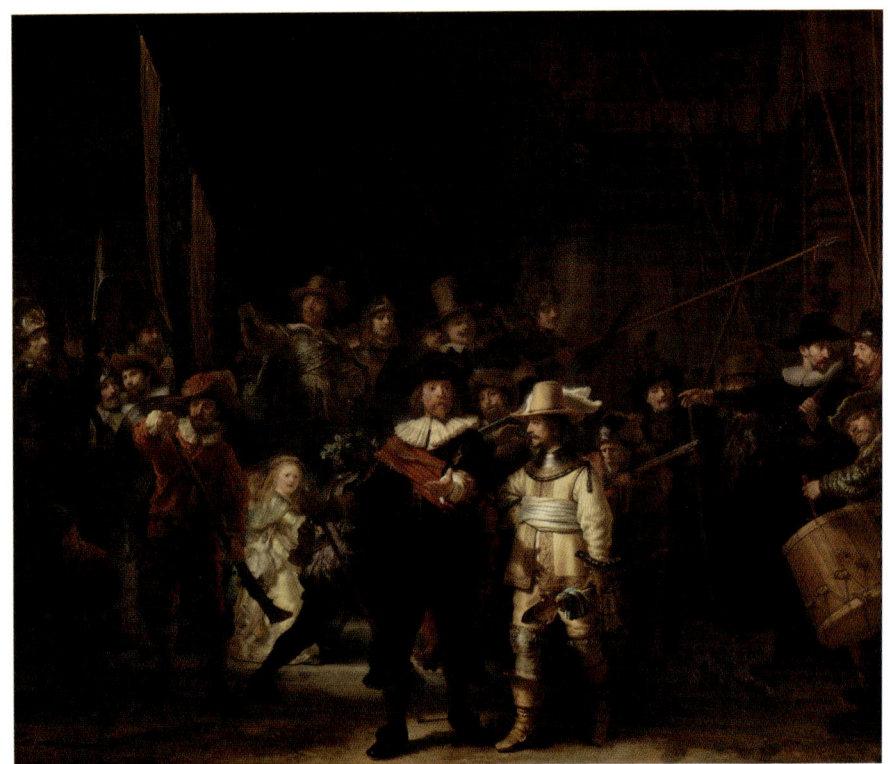

Zuythbrouck, was the daughter of a baker. He entered Leiden University in 1620 but soon realised his skills lay elsewhere and he became apprenticed to a painter, Pieter Lastmann. Rembrandt moved to Amsterdam in 1631/32.

The name Rembrandt is unusual, and the way in which he signed his work changed throughout his career. Initially, he signed his work RH, then from 1626 changed to RHL, with the L standing for Leiden. In 1632, he used the monogram RHL van Rijn before changing to Rembrant. It was early in 1633 that he finally adopted the spelling with which he is most associated – Rembrandt.

Rembrandt became the most popular painter in Amsterdam, joining the Guild of St Luke in 1634 and marrying a wealthy bride, Saskia van Uylenburgh. Rembrandt worshipped her. She became his model for numerous drawings, etchings and paintings. Although he began painting her portrait soon after their marriage, he never completed the picture until after her death in 1642.

Rembrandt was a prolific artist and etcher. He painted all types of material, including landscapes, portraits, story paintings and historical subjects, but was most popular as a portraitist. Rembrandt created numerous self-portraits, one of the first artists ever to do so. His skill in using light and shade to create drama was unequalled.

During the 1640s he became more focused on religious paintings, less flamboyant and more introspective, possibly resulting from the death of his mother in 1640, followed by the death of Saskia two years later. Landscape painting captured his attention rather than lucrative portraits. His income decreased and domestic problems surfaced. One of his mistresses sued him for breach of promise. He developed a relationship with his servant, Hendrickje Stoffels, but could not legalise it due to Saskia's will, which required him to forfeit his share of her estate if he remarried.

Desperate to pay for his expensive house on the prestigious St Anthoniesbreestraat, Rembrandt used loans to pay off loans. In 1656, he auctioned his objects collection and transferred ownership of the house to his son, Titus. Declared insolvent, he avoided bankruptcy by being granted an 'accession bonorum', allowing him to sell his goods as long as he could convince the court of his good faith. In 1658, the house was finally sold, although he did not move out until 1660. To protect him from creditors, Hendrickje and Titus formed a business partnership, making Rembrandt their employee, thus enabling him to keep the earnings from his work. Titus acted as his father's art dealer.

After 1660, Rembrandt and his family lived modestly in rooms located within the Rozengracht. His work output increased and in 1661 he produced more dated paintings than in any year since the early 1630s. Hendrickje died in 1663, and Titus in 1668. During Rembrandt's final years he lived with his daughter Cornelia, enjoying a very simple lifestyle. He continued producing masterpieces. Rembrandt died on 4 October 1669 and was buried in Amsterdam's Westerkerk beside Hendrickje and Titus.

Throughout his career, Rembrandt's artistic output was prodigious. Apart from his mastery of shade, he used an etching needle like a pen to create rich, sombre effects.

The Night Watch is his greatest work and more than 2.2 million people annually visit the Rijksmuseum just to see it. Officially known as Militia Company of District II under the Command of Captain Frans Banninck Cocq, it gained the name of Night Watch after it was covered in dark varnish. Over the years, this varnish layer became so thick it protected the canvas from a knife attack in 1911! Restoration in 2019 revealed that the painting was actually much lighter and brighter than people thought. The Night Watch was extremely innovative when Rembrandt created it. Although similar civic group paintings were common, Rembrandt was the first to create a group portrait that could be seen as a history painting, with characters caught in motion as though they are about to march out of the painting. It was also extremely large – the painting we know today was actually cut down in 1715 to enable it to fit between doors

when being moved to a new location at Amsterdam Town Hall.

Another famous painting is The Anatomy Lesson of Dr Nicolaes Tulp painted in 1632, which established his reputation as an artist in Amsterdam. It reflected his innovative portrait approach in the way he posed a group, and his use of light and shadow showing the doctor conducting an autopsy. The portrait revitalised the way artists painted portraits.

Typical examples of his work include:

The Night Watch, Rijksmuseum

The Anatomy Lesson of Dr Nicolaes Tulp, Mauritshuis, The Hague

The Jewish Bride, Rijksmuseum

Peter's Denial, Rijksmuseum

Landscape with a Stone Bridge, Rijksmuseum

## Jan Steen

Lively tavern scenes were Jan Steen's specialty, creating colourful, humorous scenes that make the viewer smile instantly. A typical example is 'The Merry Family', showing an exuberant, uproarious group of people including a boisterous elderly man raising his glass, a flute player stretched out along a bench and a baby waving a spoon.

It was a world with which he was very familiar, as he worked as both a brewer and an artist. He had a ready supply of material constantly at hand.

Jan Steen was born in Leiden to a wealthy family of brewers in 1626, and attended Leiden University in 1646. He trained as an artist in Utrecht and Haarlem and married the daughter of landscape artist Jan van Goyen in 1648. He worked in The Hague, before moving to Delft and later back to Leiden, where he was licensed to keep an inn in 1672.

He became one of the leading painters of the genre style popular in the Dutch Golden Age, producing detailed vibrant scenes of domestic life as well as some religious and mythological paintings. The term 'a Jan Steen household', referring to a lively, chaotic gathering, became a Dutch proverb: *een huishouden van Jan Steen*. Members of his family were often used as models, as well as including self-portraits. Some paintings featured cats, such as Children Teaching the Cat to Read and The Cat's Medicine.

Jan Steen died in 1679. A prolific artist, it is known that he produced around 800 paintings, of which approximately 350 have survived.

Typical examples of his work include:

La Toilette, Rijksmuseum

The Merry Family, Rijksmuseum

The Feast of St Nicholas, Rijksmuseum

Children Teaching a Cat to Dance (The Dancing Lesson), Rijksmuseum

The Way you Hear it, Mauritshuis

Girl Shucking Oysters, Mauritshuis

While the Old People Sing, Mauritshuis

## Vermeer

Born Johannes Janszoon in 1632, Vermeer was the son of a weaver turned innkeeper and art dealer. His father, Reynier Janszoon, rented the Flying Fox, located on the Herengracht, Delft, using the premises to sell drink and paintings. This was not unusual as art

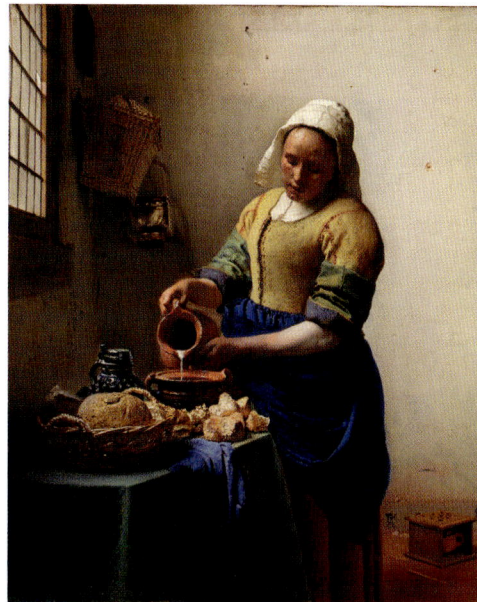

▲ *The Milkmaid by Johannes Vermeer on display in the Rijksmuseum. Used with permission of the Rijksmuseum.* (Rijksmuseum)

auctions often took place in taverns. By 1640, Janszoon had changed his name to Vermeer. Johannes Vermeer helped his father in the buying and selling of art, and continued to do so after his father's death in 1652. A year later, he married Catherina Bolnes against her mother's wishes. They had fifteen children, of which four died young.

Vermeer seems to have been mainly self-taught, although art historians think that he studied with Carel Fabritius and was certainly friends with another prominent Delft artist, Gerard ter Borch.

In 1653, Vermeer joined the Guild of St Luke as a master painter. As an artist, he created calm, serene Dutch interiors featuring one or two people, plus some landscapes and portraits. Typical examples of his work include The Girl with a Pearl Earring and Woman in Blue Reading a letter. The Milkmaid is a very typical Vermeer, showing a woman concentrating on pouring milk from a jug into a bowl within a gold, blue, brown colour scheme.

Vermeer became a member of the Delft Civil Militia in 1664. This was mainly ceremonial with an occasional night of watch duties around the town while maintaining law and order.

In 1672, the death of his sister and mother resulted in a modest inheritance, so he rented out the inn and concentrated purely on painting. This did not prove to be a good decision since it coincided with a change in painting style to large mythological canvasses. He took a long time to complete each work. Vermeer borrowed large sums of money, which included 1,000 guilders from lenders in Amsterdam. He died in January 1675, leaving his widow with crippling debts. A short time after Vermeer's death, his widow had to sell two paintings just to settle a debt with the baker. By March, all his possessions and remaining paintings had been auctioned off to repay his debts. Vermeer is buried in the Oude Kerk, Delft.

The Rijksmuseum Amsterdam contains numerous examples of his work such as Woman in Blue Reading a Letter, The Milkmaid, Street in Delft and The Love Letter.

## Vincent Van Gogh

Born in Brabant, Zundart, Vincent was the eldest son of a Protestant minister, Theodorus van Gogh, and Anna Carbentus. Vincent was particularly close to his brother, Theo. He developed a love of nature at an early age, walking and exploring the countryside around Brabant. When he was 16 years old, his uncle found him a trainee job working at The Hague branch of international art dealers, Goupil & Cie. In 1873, Vincent moved to the London office, where he became a frequent visitor to the National Gallery and British Museum, developing a liking for works of art by François Millet and Jules Breton. Deciding to become a minister, he

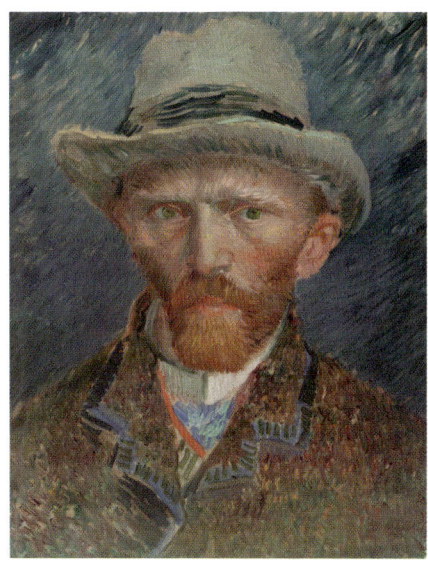

began working as a lay evangelist but his contract was not renewed.

Van Gogh took some lessons in The Hague from Anton Mauve and it was here that he painted his first watercolours. After a short stay in Antwerp, he and Theo moved to Paris, where Van Gogh experimented with pointillism and Impressionism.

In February 1888, he moved to Provence attracted by the bright, colourful scenery. Van Gogh made his

◄ *Vincent Van Gogh picture on display in Rijksmuseum. Used with permission of the Rijksmuseum.* (Rijksmuseum)

▼ *The Potato Eaters.* (Kroller-Muller Museum Otterlo)

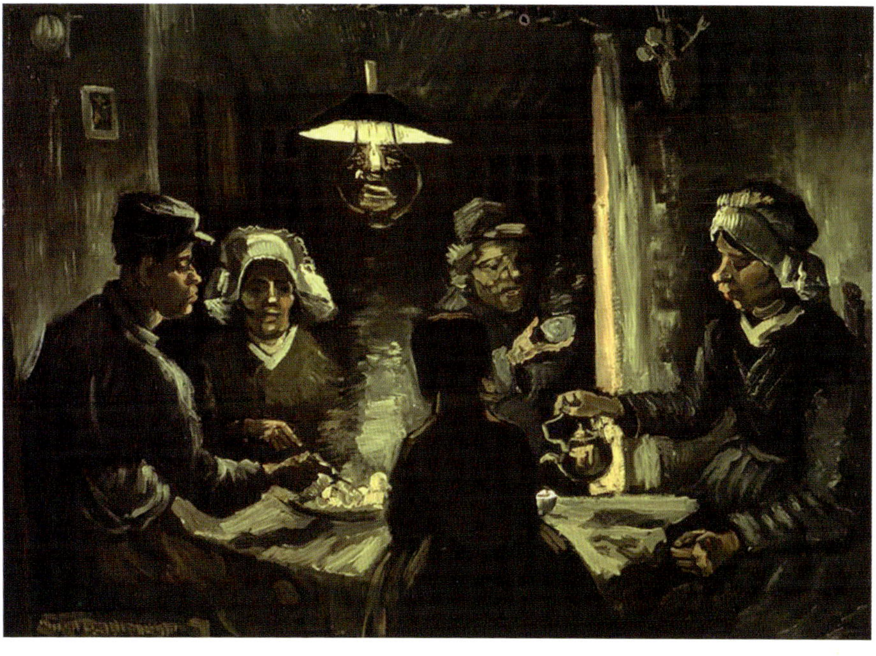

home in Arles, where he worked at a frantic pace creating paintings of the landscape, irises, sunflowers, as well as the interior of his bedroom. It was here that he cut off his left ear, and was admitted to hospital. Later, he admitted himself voluntarily to an asylum in Saint-Rémy-de-Provence, where he painted the hospital gardens and local scenes.

Moving back to Auvers, a village 20 miles from Paris, Van Gogh lived under the care of Doctor Paul Ferdinand Gachet. During his final seventy days of life, Van Gogh worked intensely, creating seventy-five paintings and fifty drawings. In July 1890, he shot himself and returned home fatally wounded. He died the next day with Theo at his side. Theo Van Gogh died soon afterwards and is buried alongside his brother at Auvers.

Van Gogh produced around 2,000 works of art, of which more than ninety were paintings. A large proportion of these works, including famous ones such as Sunflowers, The Bedroom at Arles, The Pink Peach Tree, The Sower and many self-portraits, can be seen in Dutch galleries.

The Netherlands contains the largest collections worldwide of Van Gogh's works. These are primarily located at the:

Van Gogh Museum, Amsterdam
The Rijksmuseum, Amsterdam
Kröller-Müller Museum, Otterlo

# 5

# ARTIST'S AMSTERDAM

Artists wanting to sketch and draw have a plethora of potential locations. Strolling around the city highlights many buildings and scenes that would have been familiar to artists of the Dutch Golden Age. Quite apart from sketching and drawing material on view in the museums and art galleries, there are many stunning vistas and buildings to draw. There are lots of hidden details on houses and buildings, such as this image of Christiaan Huygens.

The colourful houses at Zevenlandenhuizen near the Vondelpark

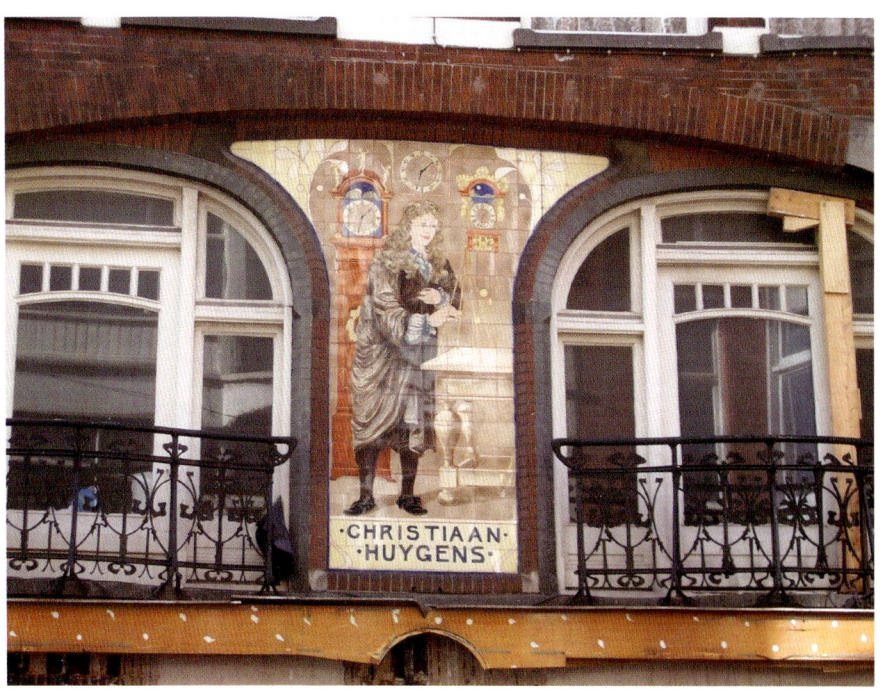

▲ *Christiaan Huygens.* (Karis Youngman)

are very eye-catching, being inspired by the architectural styles of seven different nations including Spain, France and Russia. Many are pink and white striped, possessing triangular balconies or circular, arched, inset windows.

Amsterdam's canals offer lots of inspiration. The Prinsengracht offers great views from any of the canal bridges, or on the canal side of a watery landscape. Over on the Singel Canal is the world's only floating flower market, the Bloemenmarkt.

Vondelpark is a great place for vistas, autumn colours, a rose garden and lots of people to sketch.

Museumplein, with its lively ambiance and stunning architecture, includes the Rijksmuseum and the Van Gogh Museum.

Platanenweg's eye-catching murals showcase street art with bright, graphic designs such as Leon Keer's image of childish objects and toys in a red box with a hammer underneath.

Check out rooftops as you meander around the city. There is a vast array of different styles, as well as the unexpected in the form of the gargoyles at Huis met de Kabouters.

Not far from Amsterdam are scenes that inspired Monet in

▼ *Bloemenmarkt floating flower market in Amsterdam.*

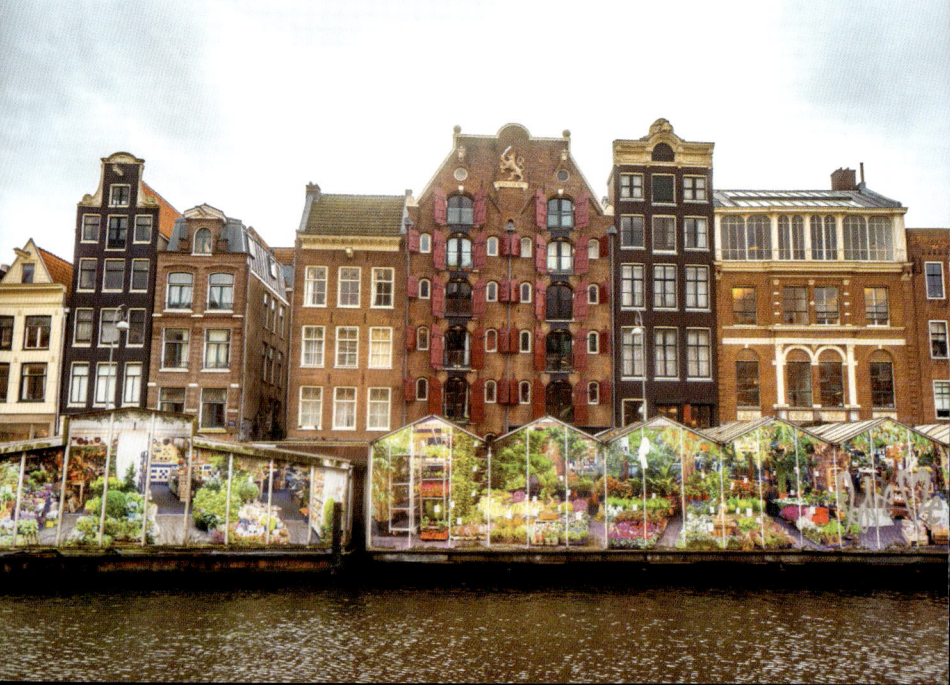

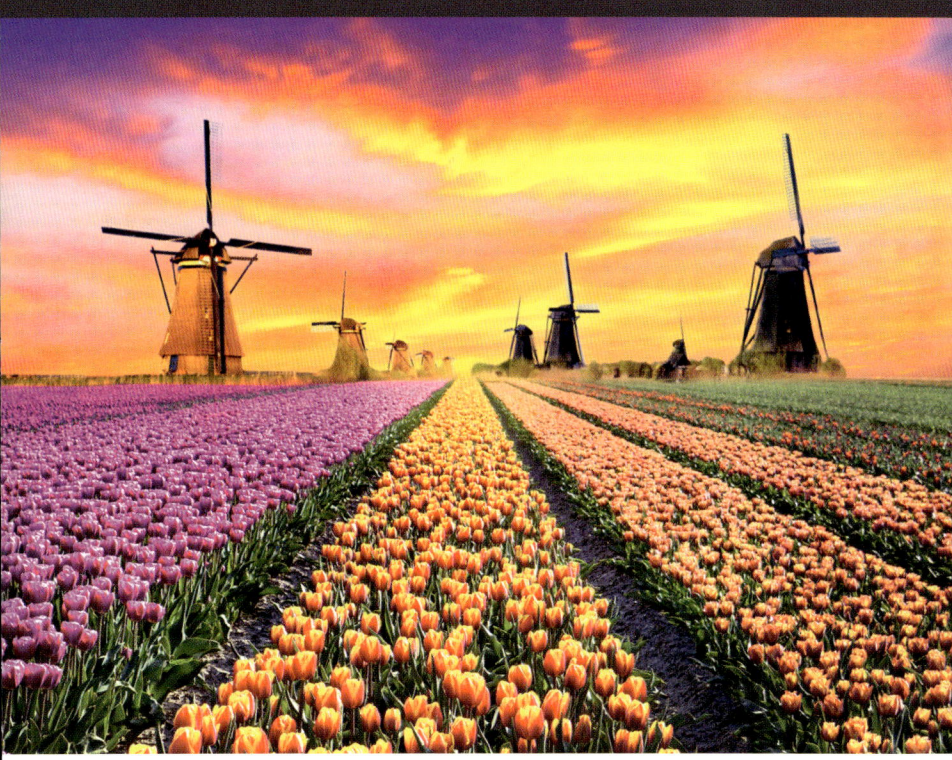

▲ *Typical landscape with bulb fields.*

Volendam or around the Keukenhof, while elsewhere you can follow in the footsteps of Piet Mondrian or Van Gogh.

Artists needing to top up supplies while in Amsterdam can seek out:

### Van Beek Art Supplies

Stadhouderskade 63, 1072 AD Amsterdam
**www.vanbeekart.nl**

### Van der Linde

Rozengracht 38, 1016 NC Amsterdam (four minutes from the Anne Frank House)
**www.vanderlindewebshop.com/nl**

### Henxs Amsterdam Montana Shop

Sint Antoniesbreestraat 138, 1011 HB Amsterdam
(one minute from the Rembrandt House Museum)
**www.henxs.com**

# EXPLORING AMSTERDAM'S ART

## Bos En Lommer and De Baarsjes

Erasmuspark
Jan van Galenstraat, 1056 Amsterdam

Named after the Dutch writer
Desiderius Erasmus (1467–1536),
the Erasmuspark was created as
a municipal park in 1926. It was
refurbished in 2000 and redesigned
in Mondrian style, stressing harmony
between colour and the lines of paths,
trees and grass. The Miracle Garden,
created by Amsterdam visual artist
Elspeth Diederix, was designed to
bring the world of plants and flowers
closer to people.

There are numerous sculptures
on display including the white Polar
Bear sculpted by Italian artist Simona
Vergani made from one large piece of
Italian marble. Other statues include
a bronze dog on a quay wall by Linda
van Boven, a statue of Leda and the
Swan by Han Rädecker, abstracts by
Berend Peter Esch and Renze Hettema,
as well as a Tiger and Polar Bear by Jan
Trapman. The park includes a series
of four statues created by Hilda Krop

depicting the cardinal points of the
compass: Eskimo with Weapon flanked
by Igloo and Walruses; African Hunter
with Spear and Shield plus lions;
Chinese Stevedore and Pagoda; and

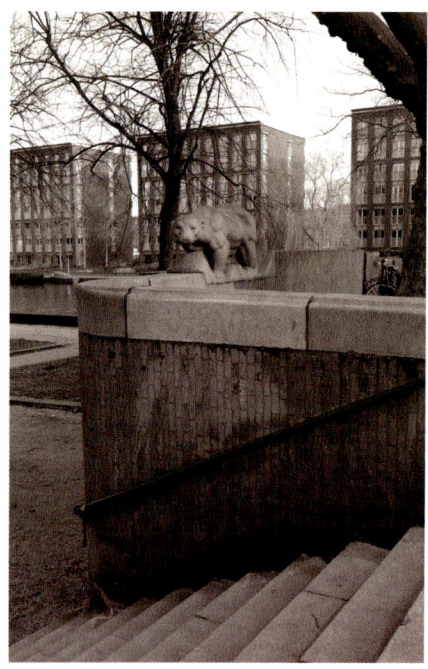

▲ *Polar bear sculpture at Erasmuspark.*

American Stock Trader on the phone trading quotes.

**Nearby attractions:** Rembrandt Park, Keith Haring Mural.

### Keith Haring Mural

View from parking space,
Willem de Zwijgerlaan 334
1055 RD Amsterdam

In 1986, Keith Haring was in Amsterdam for a solo exhibition at the Stedelijk Museum. He decided to paint a mural on the wall of what was then the Depot of the Stedelijk Museum, on the site of the Central Market Hall in West Amsterdam. The white mural shows an imaginary sea monster with a fish-style tail, ridden by a man bearing a St Andrew's cross on his chest. Measuring 12 × 15m, this is a rare example of Haring's work, one of the few surviving examples in existence. It is also the largest he created in any public space within Europe. The artist's signature can be seen on the right below the mural, together with three St Andrew's crosses taken from the Amsterdam coat of arms.

In 1988, building problems caused by moisture resulted in the Stedelijk Museum installing a protective wall, hiding the mural from view. In 2014, plans to redevelop the Central Market Hall site led artist Mick La Robb to head a campaign to make the mural visible again. Additional lobbying by the Keith Haring Foundation and the Stedelijk Museum, together with the willingness of the construction company to co-operate, led to the aluminium panels being removed in 2018. Restoration of the mural took place in 2020.

The artwork is only partially visible to the public via the parking space on Willem de Zwijgerlaan road near Karel Doormanstraat.

**Nearby attraction:** Erasmuspark.

### Rembrandtpark

Postjesweg 1057 Amsterdam

Named after Rembrandt van Rijn, this park was laid out in the early 1970s. It is located within the Bos en Lommer and De Baarsjes neighbourhoods in western Amsterdam. An elongated park, it includes various viaducts over roads including the A10, Postjesweg, Jan Evertsenstraat and Cornelis Lelylaan. Sited on either side of the Postjesweg viaduct are the Twee Hondjes (Two Dogs) created by Marjolijn Mandersloot. These supersized playful puppy sculptures look down on to the road, and have a slight cartoonish ambiance. The Twee Hondjes were installed in 2002 and reflect how the park is a popular meeting place for dogs and their owners.

Slightly further north within the park is REMBO, a 3.2m-high green statue of a human figure, looming out between the trees. Sculpted by Bastienne Kramer, it was installed in 2005.

**Nearby attraction:** Erasmuspark.

## Centrum

Allard Pierson Museum
University of Amsterdam
Oude Turfmarkt 127-129,
1012 GC Amsterdam
**www.allardpierson.nl**

Explore 10,000 years of cultural history from the Nile to the Amstel river at the Allard Pierson Museum with artefacts covering every aspect of art and culture from books, ancient pottery and religious artwork to performing arts set designs, Jewish cultural history, graphic design, paintings, maps and botanical illustrations. These include a Feast of the Tabernacles painting by Dirk van Santen, drawings for a Dick Bos cartoon, decorative examples of nineteenth-century typography and a Roman mummy portrait of a young girl. The Allard Pierson is a university museum, and contains all the heritage collections owned by the University of Amsterdam. There are frequent special exhibitions related to the collections with the museum.

**Nearby attractions:** Schuttersgalerij (Civic Guards Gallery), Rembrandt House Museum.

## Amsterdam Centraal

Stationsplein,
1012AB Amsterdam

Designed by Pierre Cuypers (the designer of the Rijksmuseum), the building was opened in 1889. Built in Gothic–Renaissance style, it is an

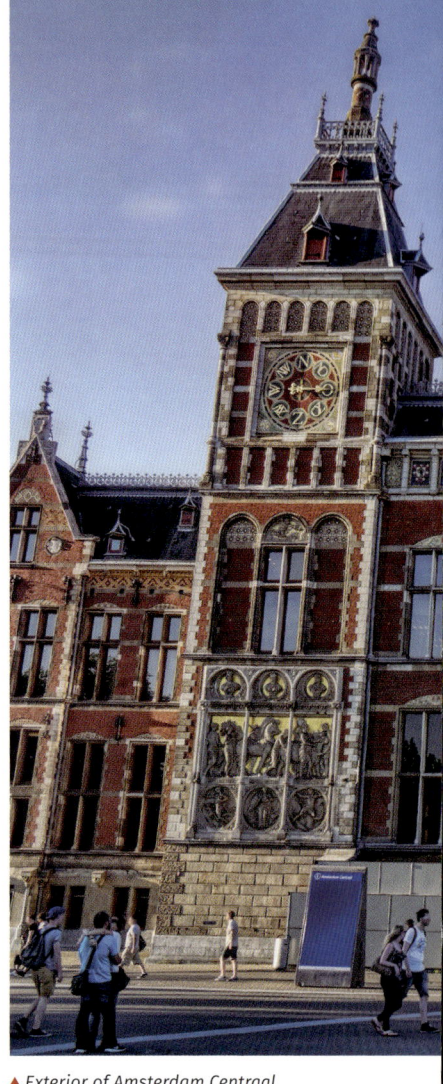

▲ *Exterior of Amsterdam Centraal.*

imposing building, with twin towers marking the central entrance, and distinctive terracotta and cream stonework. Amsterdam Centraal is a massive railway station that serves

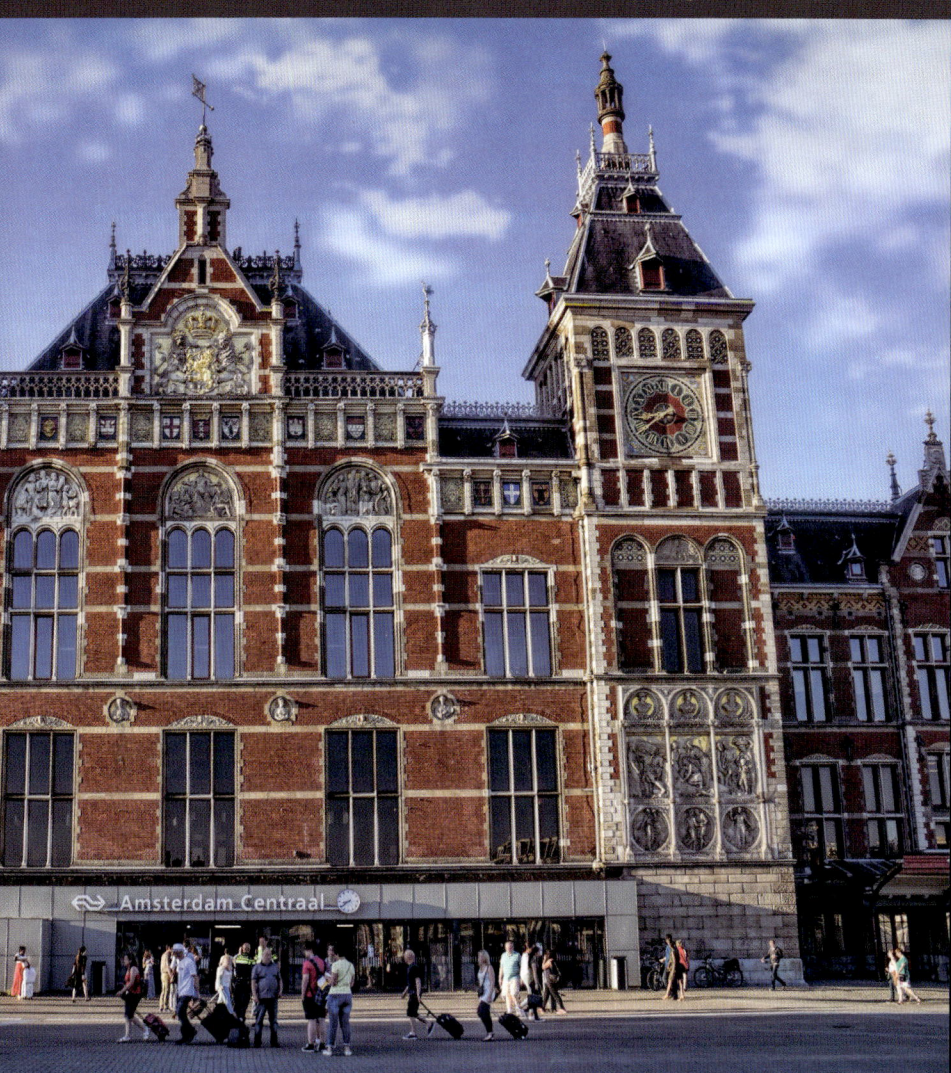

national and international locations. Amsterdam Centraal has been a national state monument since the 1970s.

**Nearby attractions:** Art'otel, Bers van Berlage, St Nicholas Kerk, STRAAT Museum.

**Amsterdam Illusions**
Oudezijds Voorburgwal 143 H,
1012 ES Amsterdam

An interactive collection of installation art containing more than thirty paintings created by contemporary Dutch artists. The subject matter is varied. Many of the paintings focus on Dutch traditions, history and culture while others are wider subjects such as the sinking of *Titanic*. Visitors can ride a bike through a field of tulips, discover why the Dutch wore clogs, slide down a stream of lava from an erupting volcano or save the universe.

**Nearby attractions:** Civic Guard Museum, Koninklijk Paleis.

### Amsterdam Museum on the Amstel
Amstel 51,
1018 DR Amsterdam
**www.amsterdammuseum.nl**

The Amsterdam Museum presents exhibitions and displays telling the story of Amsterdam and highlighting its art and heritage. It holds more than 100,000 objects collected over five centuries, such as portraits, cityscapes, landscapes, porcelain, decorative arts, street organs, clothing, architectural drawings and sculptures. Many of the paintings on display show the general development of the city and how it has changed over the centuries, along with the people depicted within the various artworks. Some of the paintings such as Abraham de Vries's painting of the Regents of the Old City Orphanage link to the history of the museum building when it was an orphanage. Among the more unusual artefacts is a replica of Café 't Mandje, a pub in the Red Light

district, and a 1960s environmentally friendly vehicle known as the Witcar.

**Nearby attractions:** Jewish Museum, Hermitage Museum, Outsider Art.

### Amsterdam Pipe Museum
Prinsengracht 488
1017 KH Amsterdam
**www.pipemuseum.nl/en**

A unique museum devoted to the culture of pipe smoking. On display are numerous pipes, many of which are carved with detailed, complex designs showing faces and landscapes, while others have designs painted on porcelain or ceramic. There are numerous artworks related to the history of pipe smoking, dealing with people involved in the industry, characters and scenes showing people smoking with pipes from around the world, period cartoons, decorative labels and posters, and advertising literature. The museum is the result of a private collector's lifetime interest in the subject, and is now managed by a foundation.

**Nearby attractions:** Huis Marseille, Rembrandt's Amsterdam, Rijksmuseum, Vondelpark.

### Anne Frank's House
Prinsengracht 267, 1016 GV Amsterdam
**www.annefrank.org**

The tragic story of Anne Frank is well known. Prior to the outbreak of the

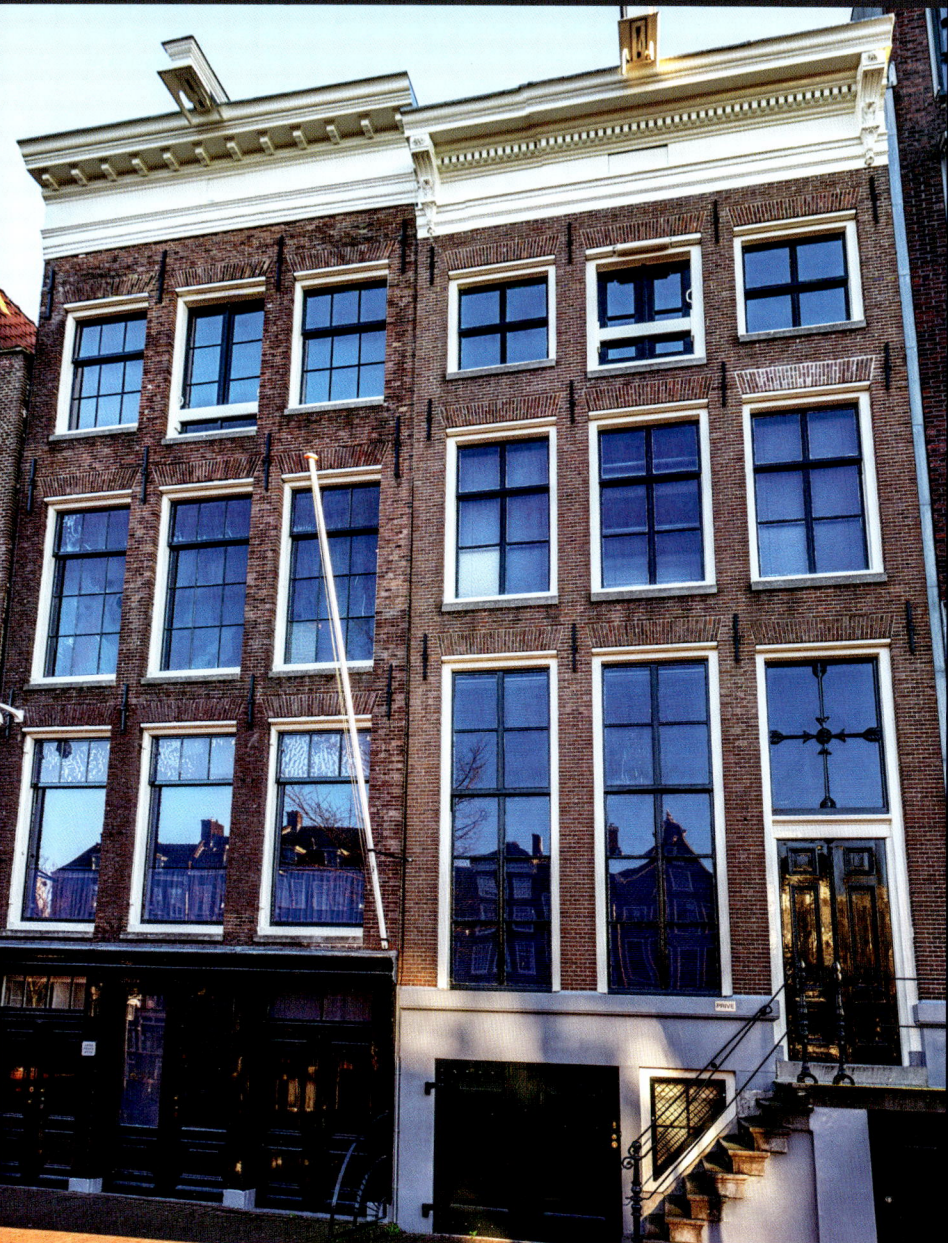

▲ *Anne Frank's House.*

Second World War, Anne and her family lived in the annex of a building on Prinsengracht 263. Soon after the Germans invaded the Netherlands, Otto Frank made arrangements for his family to go into hiding, creating a hidden annex within the building. Two other Jewish families joined them – van Peis and Fritz Pfeffer. Access to the hidden annex was concealed behind a moveable bookcase, with food and other necessities provided by the office staff. In August 1944, the hiding place was betrayed to the police, and all the family members were deported to concentration camps. Otto Frank survived, Anne did not. Visitors have flocked to Anne Frank's House ever since her diary talking about growing up and her life in this hidden annex was published. Among the material on display are illustrations and drawings that she made while in hiding. Booking in advance is recommended as this is a very small, compact space and access is limited.

**Nearby attraction:** Electric Ladyland.

### Art'otel

Prins Hendrikkade 33,
1012 TM Amsterdam
www.artotelamsterdam.com

Describing itself as a 'seamless fusion of art and life', Art'otel represents a new generation of hotels incorporating art within its buildings.

Part of the Radisson hotel group, Art'otel Amsterdam has worked with Dutch sculptor Joep van Lieshout to create its unusual artistic concept. Modern contemporary art from the Atelier van Lieshout can be found throughout the public areas, dining and meeting facilities as well as within the bedrooms. Within the hotel, 120 pieces of art from Lieshout follow the theme of the Course of Life, referring to all the different steps and stages in human life. Each room features a unique piece of art. Lieshout's work combines art, design and architecture, using themes reflecting conception, social, functional and non-functional elements and visions. Lieshout has been described as one of the top Dutch contemporary artists, with work displayed in museums and art collections worldwide.

Members of the public can explore the art on view within any of the public areas, as well as within the hotel's art gallery. The 300 sq metre gallery hosts a rotating calendar of exhibitions by varying artists. It can be accessed from the hotel's upper floor through a signature 12m, two-storey art curtain displaying a continuous programme of video art.

Art'otel is located directly opposite Amsterdam's Centraal Station.

**Nearby attractions:** Amsterdam Centraal Station, Beurs van Berlage, St Nicholas Kerk, STRAAT Museum.

## Beurs van Berlage

Damrak 243,
1012 ZJ Amsterdam
**www.beursvanberlage.com**

A major conference centre and exhibitions venue within the heart of Amsterdam, it has held countless art exhibitions including studies of Banksy, Renée Stotijn, and a retrospective about Audrey Hepburn. The building began life as a stock exchange in the late nineteenth century and has been described as the first example of modern architecture within the Netherlands. Worth noting are the exterior statues, decorative keystones and the detailed relief beside the main entrance as it shows all aspects of international trade from boats, pack animals to goods and people, highlighting the way in which transport brings people together.

**Nearby attractions:** Amsterdam Centraal, Art'otel, Hash, Marijuana and Hemp Museum, Rembrandt House.

## Bloemgracht

1015 Amsterdam

The Bloemgracht is a seventeenth-century canal reaching from the

▼ *The Bloemgracht canal and its adjacent houses.*

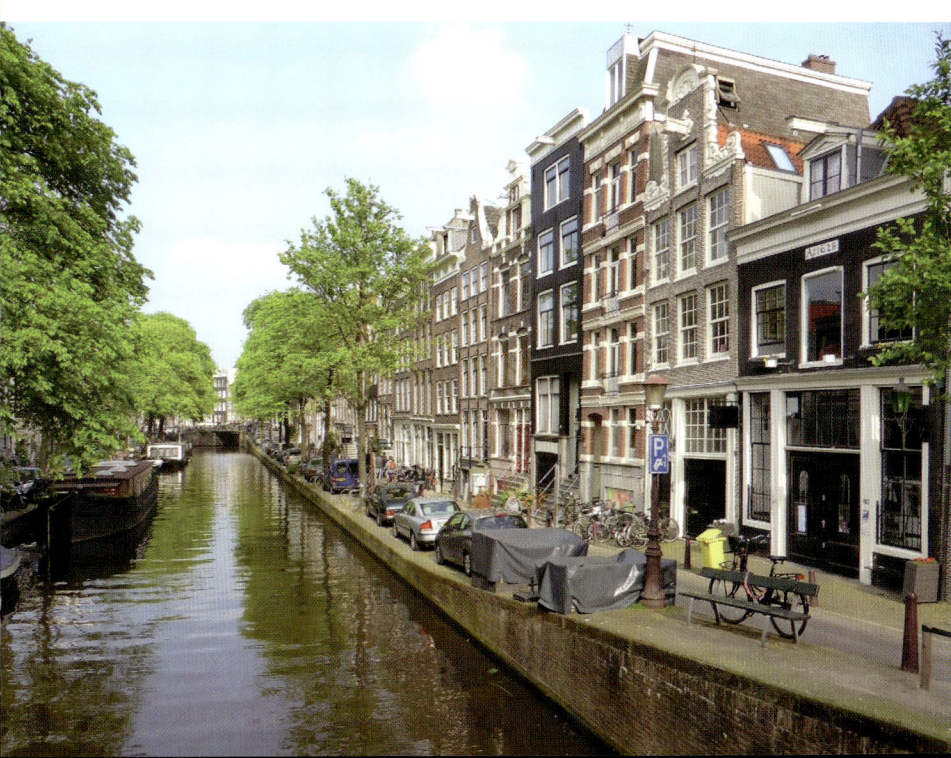

Prisengracht to the Lijnbaansgracht and was once the centre of artistic activity, home to many artists and paint factories. Rembrandt van Rijn had a studio in the area, as did cartographer Willem Blaeu, while Jurriaan Andriessen lived here. It is a very picturesque street complete with tall gabled houses and windows often overflowing with flowers overlooking the tree-lined canal in the centre.

**Nearby attractions:** Electric Ladyland, Anne Frank's House, Blue Violin Player.

## Blue Violin Player

Tweede Hugo de Grootstraat, 1015 ZP Amsterdam

An eye-catching bright blue metal statue of a running figure wearing a long coat, carrying a violin case and raising a hat in one hand – but it has no head. The statue appeared on site in 1982. No one knows who created it. There are reports that the city council received the work on the basis that the artist's name remained unknown. Other reports say that it was totally anonymous, appearing overnight, and local residents had to convince the city council to leave it in place following attempts to remove it. The statue is located close to the Raampoort bridge.

**Nearby attraction:** Electric Ladyland.

## Civic Guards Gallery (Schuttersgalerij)

Kalverstraat 92,
1012 PH Amsterdam
**www.amsterdammuseum.nl**

Managed by the Museum of Amsterdam, the Civic Guards Gallery is a fascinating portrait gallery containing historic portraits of the wealthy citizens of Amsterdam who formed the City Guard. In general the City Guard used to focus on practising musket drill and enjoying a social life. The portraits were commissioned on an annual basis in order to commemorate their City Guard commitments and charity work. Citizens portrayed in the paintings had to pay for their involvement. Artists employed by the Civic Guard to create these paintings included Rembrandt and Frans Hals. Numerous modern portraits are included featuring contemporary celebrities such as Dutch ballet choreographers, Ajax football players as well as ordinary people like policemen and Moroccan immigrants. Worth noting within the gallery is the presence of a huge seventeenth-century wooden statue of Goliath, plus smaller sculptures of David and his shield bearer.

**Nearby attractions:** Allard Pierson Museum of Antiquities, Huis Marseille, Museum for Photography, FOAM.

**Electric Ladyland**
Tweede Leliedwarsstraat 5,
1015 TB Amsterdam
**www.electric-lady-land.com**

Totally unique, this is the only museum of its kind worldwide as it is devoted to the subject of fluorescent art in every shape and form. This is where you can find out about every aspect of the form, including fluorescent minerals and manufactured items that fluoresce under ultraviolet light. What makes this museum even more unusual is the fact that visitors can see the various lights and artefacts illuminated. During guided tours, visitors experience 'Participatory Art' as they become part of the art environment depending on the way people move. The museum is divided into what it describes as 'Fluorescent Participatory Environments'. One of the areas relates to The Magic Land of Lights, Sounds and Dimensions / Sister Mary Bernadeth Grotto. The area is totally blank and without colour, until the visitor begins creating through movement. Demonstrations are provided for a variety of items including fluorescent mineral artworks dating from the 1950s, and advertisements dating back to 1932. Other examples on display include items relating to fluorescence as it occurs in astronomy, geology and oceanography as well as many common items that possess fluorescent properties.

Among the artistic elements to be seen in this exhibition are mineral artworks created by three 1950s American artists: Miera (the Japanese Man) and Mr and Mrs Philips. A typical example of fluorescent art made by Mrs Philips is a scene showing Boats at Sea, which transforms into three different images depending on the type of light being used: daylight, night scene and a brilliantly coloured mixture.

The name of the art gallery and the museum is derived from a recording studio built by Jimi Hendrix in 1970, known as the Electric Lady Studios in New York.

Electric Ladyland is located in the basement of the building on Tweede Leliedwarsstraat, with an Electric Lady Art Gallery above. Access to the museum is by appointment only, so contact it first before arriving.

**Attractions nearby:** The Blue Violin Player.

**FOAM**
Keizersgracht 609,
1017 DS Amsterdam
**www.foam.org**

An international, multifaceted photography museum, FOAM explores all aspects of artistic photography including fashion, documentary, and themed work. Above all, the museum sets out to challenge accepted views of the role of photography and to showcase exceptional photographical talent. It holds a changing programme of exhibitions, debates and talks as well as publishing an international photography magazine. Examples of exhibitions held here include Staging Resistance, Bill Brandt on The Beautiful and the Sinister. At least three exhibitions are always open to the public at the same time, and these can involve well-known names as well as young talent within smaller exhibitions. FOAM acts as a creative hub where photographers can take part in special forums.

**Nearby attractions:** Hermitage Amsterdam, Kattenkabinet, Outsider Art Museum.

### Hash, Marihuna & Hemp Museum
Oudezijds Achterburgwal
148 Amsterdam
**www.hashmuseum.com**

▲ *Exterior of the FOAM museum.* (FOAM/Christian Van der Kooy)

This is the oldest museum worldwide dedicated to one plant – cannabis. It is the collection of Ben Dronkers, a prominent cannabis entrepreneur and owner of the world's largest cannabis seed producer, Sensi seeds. He and his colleague, Ed Rosenthal, founded the Cannabis Info Museum in Amsterdam in 1987, within what was then termed the Red Light District. The immediate reaction from the justice minister was to decide it was promoting illegal activities, and ordered its closure. It reopened the next day following a legal challenge by the duo. Eventually the museum was renamed the Hash, Marihuana & Hemp Museum. The building is a former canal house complete with gabled roof. Within the museum are countless rare items related to all aspects of cannabis history and culture, from ritual to cultivation, medicine to film. Among the collection are illustrations from 1930s anti-marijuana propaganda films and books, posters and artwork relating to the 1960s counterculture, photographs highlighting agricultural scenes showcasing the growing of hemp and its uses, a large collection of unusual paintings, prints, drawings and photographs of people smoking as well as old master paintings by seventeenth-century Dutch artists like David Teniers the Younger and Adriaen Brouwer showing scenes with taverns and 'smoking houses'. Displays within the Amsterdam museum represent only a proportion of the full collection, since the owners also run a similar museum gallery in Barcelona.

A few minutes' walk leads you to the associated Hemp Gallery, which includes exhibitions dealing with sustainability and the role of hemp, as well as a changing programme of displays such as tattoo art and cannabis.

**Nearby attractions:** Allard Pierson Museum of Antiquities, Beurs van Berlage.

### Huis Marseille
Keizersgracht 401,
1016 EK Amsterdam
**www.huismarseille.nl**

Amsterdam's first photography museum, it possesses a collection of modern, national and international images. In addition to this collection, Huis Marseille

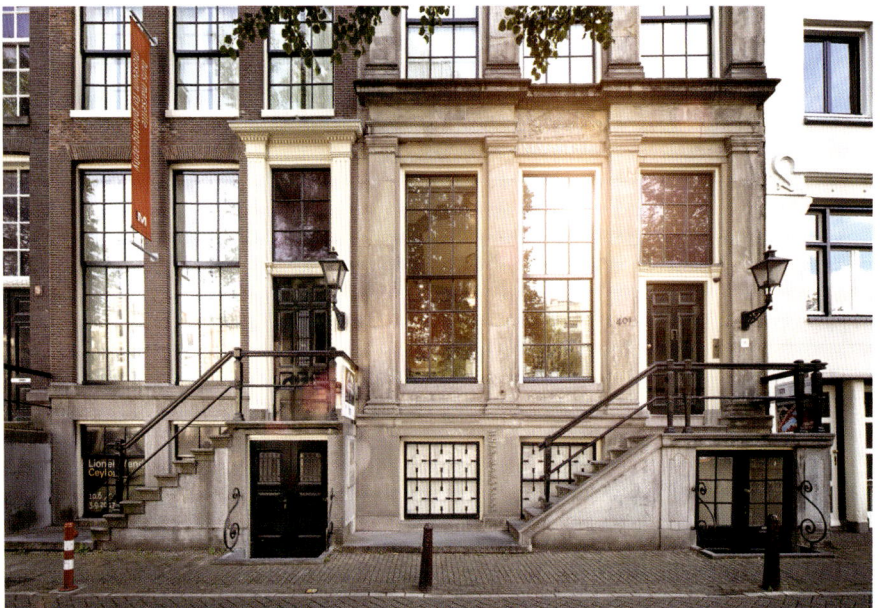

▲ *Entrance to the Huis Marseille Museum.* (Huis Marseille)

also has a varied exhibition programme, changing approximately every season. The museum focuses on photography as a visual language that is relevant artistically as well as reflecting on the period in which it was taken. Avant-garde experimentation is one of the areas frequently covered within the museum.

Guided tours of the current exhibitions can be arranged, likewise a tour of the colourful history of the two canal houses occupied by Huis Marseille. Previous owners have included a flamboyant merchant, an Indonesian writer, an early feminist and a fugitive living in a secret annex. Many of the original details of these seventeenth-century buildings are intact such as dramatic ceiling paintings, stucco work and a Louis XIV period room.

**Nearby attractions:** Het Grachtenhuis, Rembrandt's Amsterdam, Vondelpark.

### Huis Met de Kabouters
Ceintuurbaan 251, 1074 CZ Amsterdam

A quirky nineteenth-century building, which has some distinctive sculptures. Huis Met de Kabouters means House with the Hobgoblins. These large, painted Gothic Revival-style gargoyles appear to be throwing a ball from one to another among the roof cornices. According to legend, no one is ever

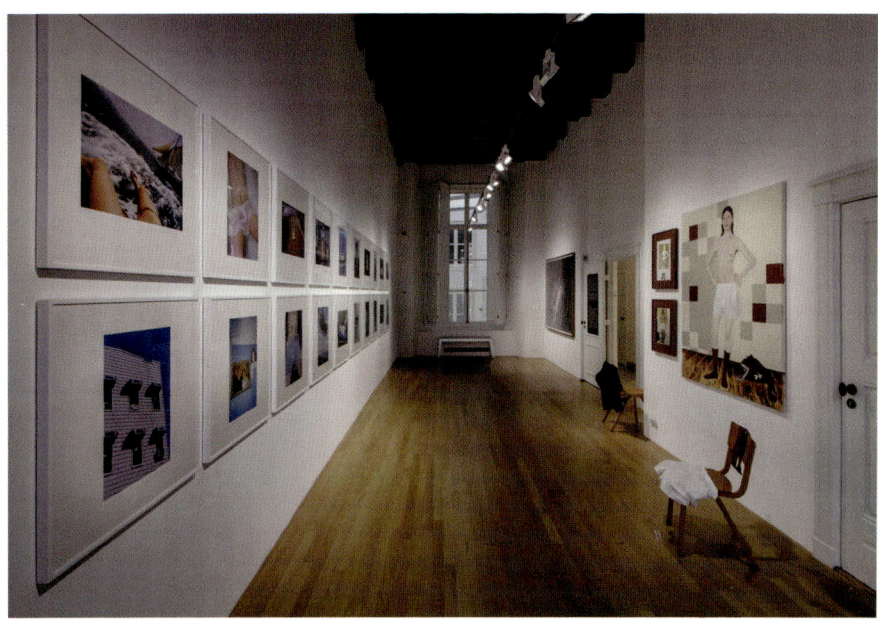

▲ *Exhibition at Huis Marseille.* (Huis Marseille)

quite sure as to which hobgoblin has the ball, as they throw it in secret. The architect was A.C. Boerma, who worked for Amsterdam City Council and designed many Gothic-style buildings around Amsterdam, although none are as distinctive as this one. It can only be viewed from outside.

**Nearby attraction:** Rijksmuseum.

## Kattenkabinet
Herrengracht 497,
1017 BT Amsterdam
**www.kattenkabinet.nl**

One of the most idiosyncratic art displays anywhere – everything relates to cats. If you are a cat lover, you will certainly love this museum. Dedicated to the role of the cat in art and culture through the centuries, it offers a fascinating look at the mischievous, the headstrong and the dignified feline. Located in a pretty canal house, the narrow staircases lead into room after room filled with cat pictures, posters, artworks, statues and items relating to cats.

It was founded in honour of a ginger cat known as John Pierpoint Morgan (1966–1983), the headstrong companion of

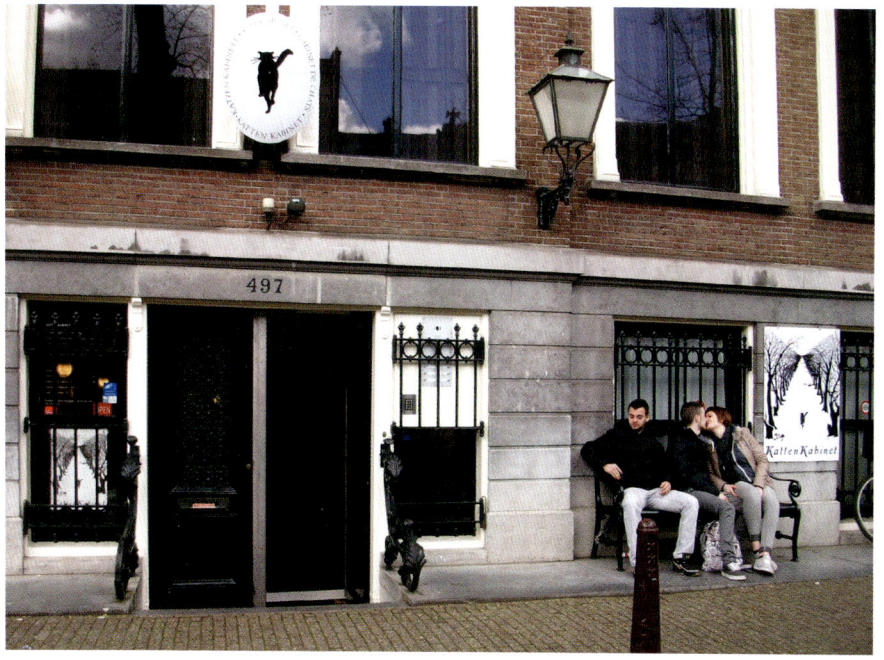

▲ *Entrance to the Kattenkabinet.*

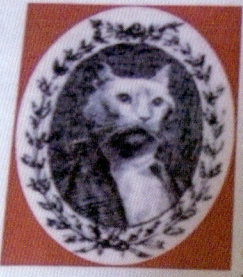

The Cat Cabinet was founded in commemoration of the red and frisky Tom Cat John Pierpont Morgan, the life-long companion and buddy of the museum's founder, Bob Meijer. Every five years, J.P Morgan would receive a special present related to himself. In honor of his first "lustrum", he was given a self portrait by Ansèl Sanberg. On his tenth birthday his gift was a bronze statue of himself. Unfortunately, this statue was stolen just before the Cat Cabinet opened its doors. To commemorate Morgan's 15th birthday, a plan was conceived to compile a booklet of cat limericks dedicated to Morgan. A "Hanige kat uit Toulouse" was soon published.

On that same birthday, J.P Morgan would get a second gift. Aart Clerxkz realized that the portrait of Washington on the American dollar bill could easily be replaced by Morgan's portrait . For this special occasion of Morgan's 15th birthday party, a single edition of dollar bills was.

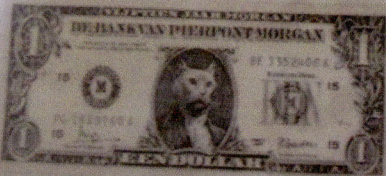

The words "In God we trust " were replaced by "We trust no dogs".

▲ *We Trust No Dogs.* (Karis Youngman)

Bob Maijer, founder of the Kattenkabinet. Bob had given his cat a special present every five years, including compiling a book of cat limericks entitled 'A Cocky Cat from Toulouse and Other Cats' and an iconic American dollar bill replacing George Washington with John Pierpoint Morgan and the words 'We Trust No Dog'. The original painting is now on display within the museum.

Among the paintings on display are works by Sal Meijer, Henriëtte Ronner-Krip, Ed van der Elsken, Nicolas Tarkhoff, Han van Meegeren and Édouard-Marcel Sandoz. Other works on display include lithographs such as Rudyard Kipling's The Cat that Walked by Himself, posters by Joseph Colemann made in 1900

and a playbill entitled Catoscope by Wolfgang Hulk. There are many unusual curiosities too such as a 1980 Grizabella costume from the musical *Cats*, a bottle of Dubonnet with a cat on the label and a chair with the model of a cat on top. Naturally, there are usually one or two cats prowling the museum, and ready to pose for any admiring artist or photographer.

**Nearby attractions:** FOAM, Hermitage Amsterdam, Museum van Loon, Outsider Art.

### KochxBos Gallery
Eerste Anjellersdwarsstraat 36
1015 NR Amsterdam
**www.kochxbox.com**

An independent pop-surrealist art gallery in Amsterdam with a constantly changing collection of art. It's fun, different, and decorative, designed as a platform where contemporary artists can explore trending topics, explore visual perception and offer views on what is meant to be human. Claire Partington's ceramics portray historical figures giving opinions on current situations. Ray Cesar uses computers to create works full of eroticism. Among the artists, illustrators, graphic designers and photographers who regularly exhibit work at KochxBos are Ciou, Sarah Maple, Martina Johanna, Dadara and Bethany de Forest.

**Nearby attractions:** Amsterdam Tulip Museum, Anne Frank House.

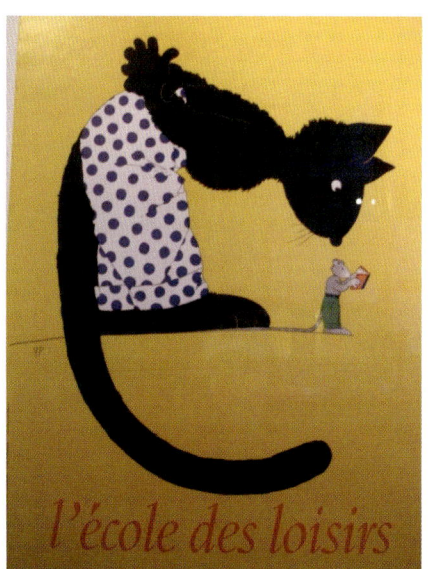

▲ *L'ecole des loisirs.* (Karis Youngman)

## Koninklijk Paleis

Damsquare,
Amsterdam
**www.paleisamsterdam.nl/en**

Located in the heart of Amsterdam, the Koninklijk Paleis (Royal Palace) is King Willem-Alexander's official reception palace where he undertakes receptions, gala dinners and award ceremonies, and is a venue for state visits. Built in the seventeenth century as Amsterdam's town hall, it was designed to reflect the city's power and prestige. It is the largest and most impressive building from the Dutch Golden Age. The building became a royal palace during the reign of King Louis Napoleon and later of the Dutch Royal House. Much of the palace is open to visitors, particularly the Citizens' Hall and the marble galleries containing sculptures and paintings by artists including Ferdinand Bol and Govert Flinck. The main theme within the paintings is to portray Amsterdam as the centre of the universe, powerful and strong. Also worth seeing is the collection of eighteenth-century French Empire furniture, clocks and chandeliers. Each year, there is a special exhibition focusing on the history of the palace, while in the autumn the Royal Award for Modern Painting is presented

▼ *Koninklijk Paleis – the royal place of Amsterdam at night.*

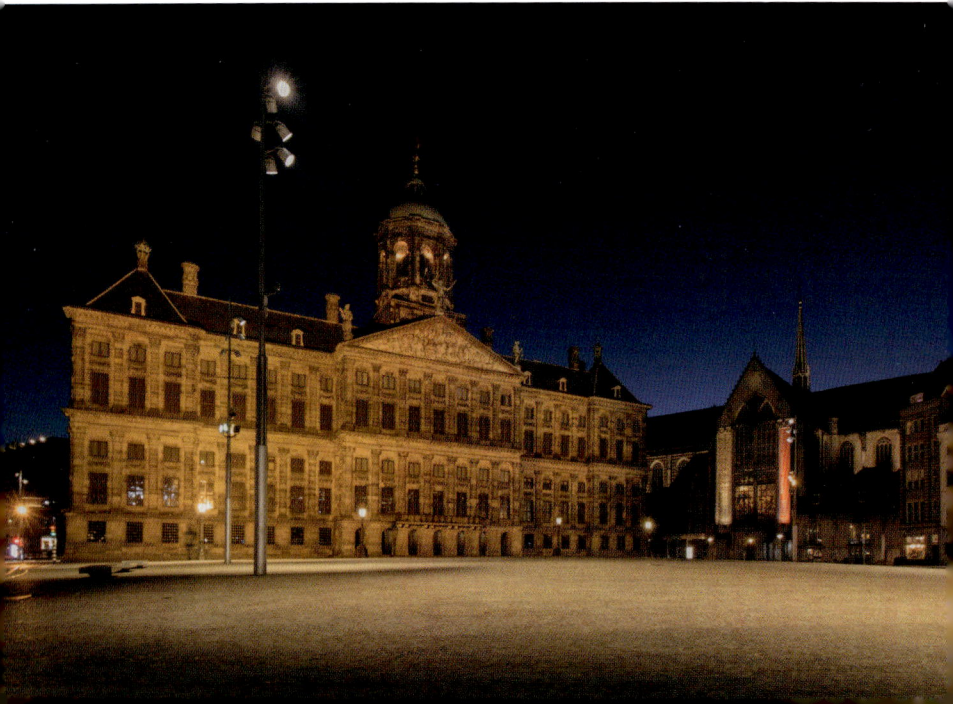

by the king as part of an exhibition of winning artworks, and artworks by other young painters who have taken part in the competition. It is possible to book a guided tour of the palace and its exhibitions.

**Nearby attractions:** Amsterdam Illusions, Civic Guard Museum, Nieuwe Kerk.

## Museum of the Canals (Het Grachtenhuis)

Herengracht 386,
1016 CJ Amsterdam
**www.grachten.museum/en**

A fascinating museum exploring the development of the seventeenth-century city via the creation of Amsterdam's canal ring, which now possesses UNESCO World Heritage status. There are numerous interactive displays, and illuminated silhouette-style images. The museum is located within a typical seventeenth-century period canal-side house, and was designed by Philip Vingboons, the son of David Vingboons, an Antwerp painter. Philip originally intended to become a painter himself, and created a number of drawings and paintings for Jacob van Campen, who designed the Royal Palace in Amsterdam.

For artists, one of the most notable aspects of this museum is the Andriessen Room. This is the oldest part of the building and contains large-scale murals created by Jurriaan Andriessen,

a decorative painter of mythological landscapes who also designed painted wallpapers, many of which can be seen in the Rijksmuseum. Probably originally intended for a different room within the house, the murals were cropped to meet space requirements. The ceiling contains a painting by a modern painter, Pascal Amblard, recreating a work by Andriessen using similar colours, yet with modern touches such as non-white angels.

Elsewhere in the museum are examples of other Dutch artists such as the eighteenth-century still life painter Johannes Christianus Roedig. The majority of his work can only be seen at the Hermitage in St Petersburg, but the Museum of the Canals does possess two examples of his flower scenes.

Elsewhere in the building are decorative designs deliberately created to give an illusion of symmetry often using false doors. The period rooms have all been restored using original techniques.

Guided tours are available but must be pre-booked. Such tours aim to provide greater in-depth knowledge of the people who lived here, the functions of the period rooms and the work of Philip Vingboons. Special exhibitions are often available, highlighting aspects such as animals in eighteenth-century art and how they are portrayed within paintings on display.

**Nearby Attractions:** Amsterdam Pipe Museum, Huis Marseille, Rembrandt's Amsterdam.

## Museum ons'Lieve Heer op Solder (Our Lord in the Attic)

Oudezijds Voorburgwal 38
1012 GD Amsterdam
**www.opsolder.nl**

This is an unusual museum offering a glimpse into what life was like within a traditional, narrow canal house. The stairs are steep and narrow, leading to fascinating, historically furnished living rooms, kitchens and bedrooms. Ultimately visitors reach the attic, where an entire Catholic church can be found. The story behind this project dates back to 1663 when Dutch people were forbidden to celebrate mass, although in practice the authorities tended to ignore any such attendance. In order to celebrate freely, the owners of the house, Catholic merchant Jan Hartman and his family, set up their own church within their home. Today, the house and church is a museum, telling the story of life within a seventeenth-century canal house, of tolerance, freedom of religion and issues of conscience.

The church is decorated in the Baroque fashion, with a combination of architecture, sculpture and painting creating the illusion that it is larger than it really is. The altar painting is interchangeable, allowing it to be changed according to the religious calendar. Three of the original paintings still exist – The Baptism of Christ by Jacob de Wit, The Resurrection of Christ and The Descent of the Holy

Spirit. A fourth painting has since been added to the collection, The Crucifixion, painted by Johannes Voorhout in 1676. Three of the four paintings are now displayed in a room just behind the altar. Other paintings on display include works by Pieter Coecke van Aelst (1535) showing The Descent from the Cross as well as sculptures of the apostles Peter and Paul.

**Nearby attraction:** Beurs van Berlage.

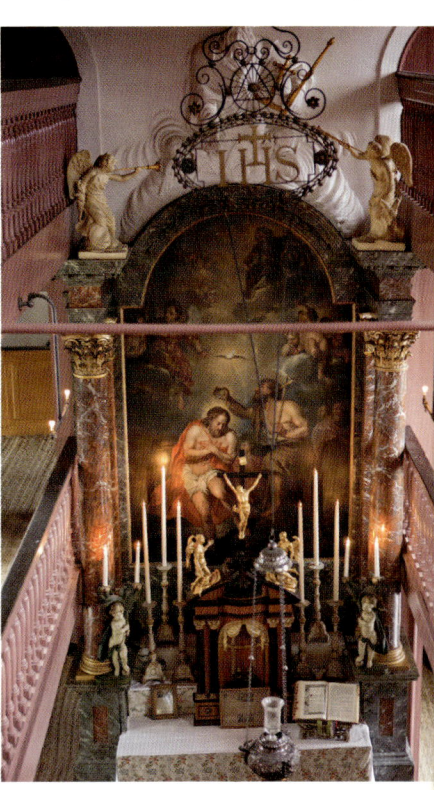

▲ Art on display in the Museum ons'Lieve Heer op Solder.

## Museum van Loon

Keizersgracht 672
1017 ET Amsterdam
**www.museumvanloon.nl/museum/huis**

A spectacular seventeenth-century house, this was the home of the painter Ferdinand Bol, a pupil of Rembrandt. The interior has remained relatively unchanged and is furnished opulently in period style. All the rooms are adorned with a vast array of paintings, particularly portraits and group scenes, and intricate vivid period wallpaper, while the kitchen is covered in blue and white decorated tiles. The owners of the museum are the van Loon family, who co-founded the Dutch East India Company in 1602. The house, garden and art collection has been open to the public since 1973, giving a glimpse of what life was like for Dutch merchants in the seventeenth century. Exhibitions are often held on the premises, such as exhibitions relating to contemporary artist Mick La Rock and portraits by Adolf Pirsch in the Netherlands.

**Nearby attractions:** Kattenkabinet, FOAM, Rijksmuseum.

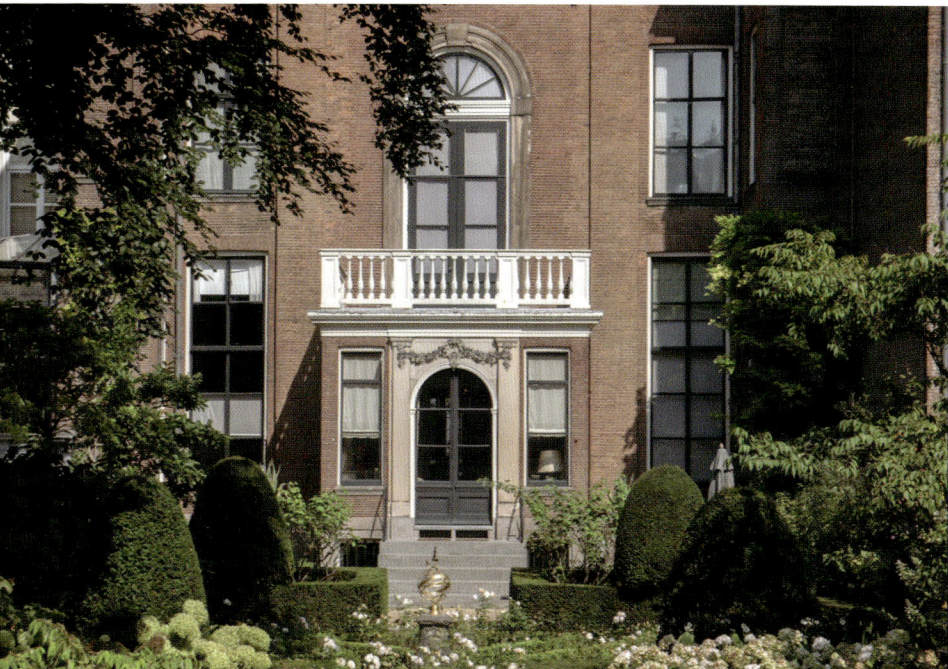

▲ *The pretty garden and exterior of the Museum van Loon.*

## National Maritime Museum

Kattenburgerplein 1,
1018 KK Amsterdam
**www.hetscheepvaartmuseum.com**

Located in the northern Oosterdok area of the city, within ten minutes' walk of Amsterdam Centraal, the National Maritime Museum is adjacent to the estuary of the River Amstel. On hot days, people have been known to go swimming from the jetty outside the museum.

The National Maritime Museum is housed in a beautiful white stone building on the quayside. Originally designed as a storehouse for the Amsterdam Admiralty, this imposing building known as Lands Zeemagazijn (the Arsenal) dates from 1658. The sheer size of the building reflects the power of Amsterdam in the seventeenth century, and the sheer amount of trade that passed through the port. Quite apart from vast stores of maritime equipment, food and cannon, more than 40,000 litres of rain water were stored in just some of its cellars before being dispatched as drinking water on board ships travelling all over the world. The Arsenal remained in use by the Dutch Navy until the 1970s, when the decision was taken to turn it into a home for artefacts from the collection owned by

▼ *The National Maritime Museum, Amsterdam.*

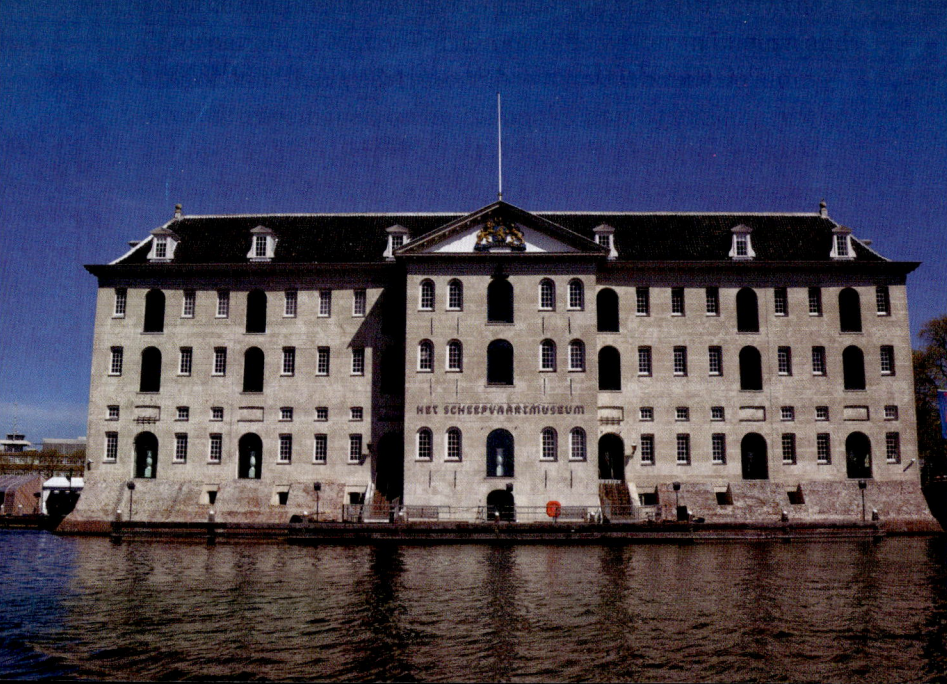

the National Maritime Museum. After renovation work, the Arsenal opened as the new National Maritime Museum in 1973. Further refurbishment took place in 2007–11, with care taken to maintain the ambiance of a seventeenth-century storehouse.

On display are a superb collection of paintings and seascapes reflecting the Netherlands' maritime heritage. Displays focusing on the Republic at Sea tell the story of how the Netherlands became the dominant maritime nation in Western Europe during the seventeenth and eighteenth centuries. On view are more than fifty large-scale seascapes, paintings depicting naval engagements as well as portraits telling battle stories. There are highly decorative maps showing trading routes, drawings and paintings with scenes within the ports in what became the Dutch colonies in Asia. Among the highlights of this section of the museum is the very large painting depicting the Battle of Gibraltar during the Eighty Years' War and portraits of naval officers and their families. Among the portraits is one of Admiral Cornelis Tromp by Ferdinand Bol, which also includes a portrait of a man believed to have been Tromp's slave. Other works of art owned by the National Maritime Museum include paintings and sketches by the leading marine artists of the seventeenth century, a father and son team known as Willem van de Velde de Oude (the Elder) and Willem van de Velde de Jonge (the Younger), who specialised primarily in pen drawings and oil paintings. There are also two enormous tapestries designed by Willem van de Velde de Oude.

Many other artefacts on display include artistic elements worth exploring. The dramatic Royal Barge, for example, is richly decorated with life-size models of Neptune and his seahorses covered in gold leaf, along with many smaller images of marine life and marine plants.

The museum has a changing programme of exhibitions. This has included a retrospective of the work of the Van de Velde duo.

**Nearby attractions:** Nemo Science Museum, Hermitage Amsterdam, Rembrandt House Museum.

### NEMO Science Museum
Oosterdok 2,
1011 VX Amsterdam
**www.nemosciencemuseum.nl**

Although its origins date back to 1923, NEMO Science Museum now occupies a specially designed building created by Renzo Piano in 1997. The striking design incorporates elements of the stern of a great ship rising up over the waves. It is a large museum with five floors of displays, exhibitions and workshops. Much of the museum is very interactive, focusing on different aspects of science such as DNA, the human mind, metals, buildings, light and sound, machines

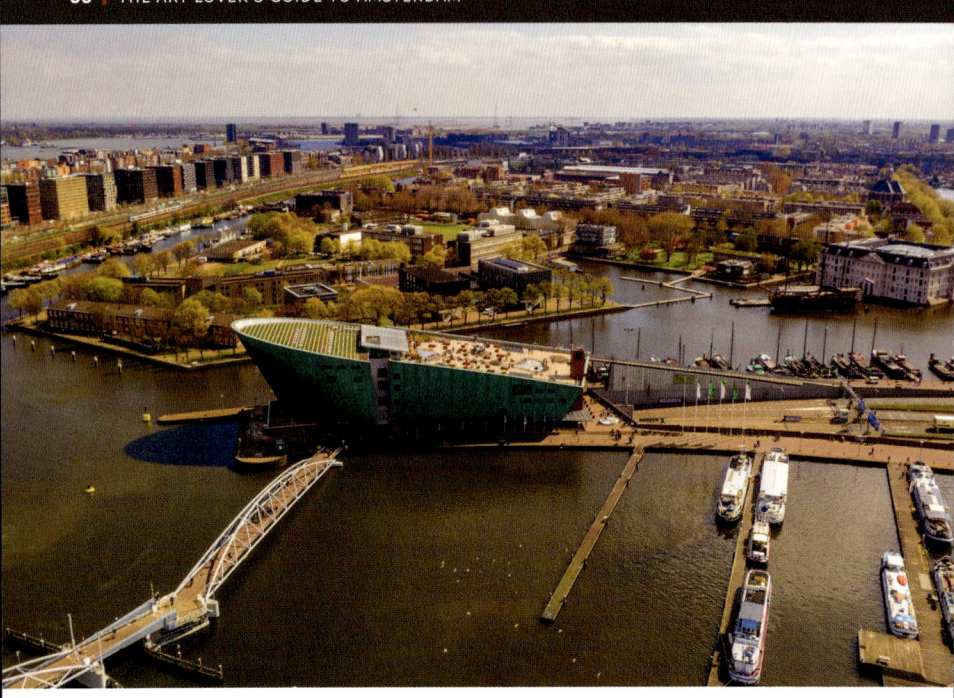

▲ *Aerial view of the NEMO Science Museum.*

and the water cycle. The section entitled Museum of the Age of Enlightenment highlights the collection created by an eighteenth-century Dutchman, Pieter Teyler van der Hulst, who believed in the importance of art and science. He amassed a large quantity of drawings, books, fossils, minerals and scientific instruments, many of which can now be viewed at NEMO Science Museum.

Sculpture forms a focal point within the Humania exhibition at NEMO. This is an exhibition highlighting similarities and differences, how brains work and the cells that make up the human body. Dominating the exhibition is the massive 8.5m sculpture known as A

Handstand produced by Dutch artist Florentijn Hofman. It depicts a human figure standing on its hands while wearing a black skeleton suit. The sculpture aims to encourage viewers to question our position in the world, and whether there is or is not someone inside the suit. Visitors are encouraged to replicate the sculpture's design by doing a handstand nearby and seeing the museum from a different perspective.

**Nearby attractions:** The National Maritime Museum, Rembrandt House Museum, Hermitage Museum, Amsterdam Museum.

## Nieuwe Kerk
De Dam,
1012 NL Amsterdam
**www.nieuwekerk.nl**

A fifteenth-century church sited adjacent to the Royal Palace in Amsterdam. One of its most spectacular pieces of artworks is a Commemoration Window designed by Toon Verhoef as a reminder of the liberation of the Netherlands in 1945. It regularly hosts exhibitions related to art and applied arts, photography and culture, attracting in excess of 250,000 visitors annually. Typical exhibitions have included the World Press Photo Exhibition and Maison Amsterdam portraying the city as a fashion capital. The church hosts royal ceremonies and other official events.

**Nearby attractions:** Amsterdam Illusions, Civic Guard Museum, Koninklijk Paleis.

## Nieumarkt
1011 GK Amsterdam

Dominating the Nieumarkt square is the De Waag (Weigh House) building, which is the oldest non-religious building in the city. At one point the site was a major entry point into the city known

▼ *Nieumarkt Square and the De Waag house.*

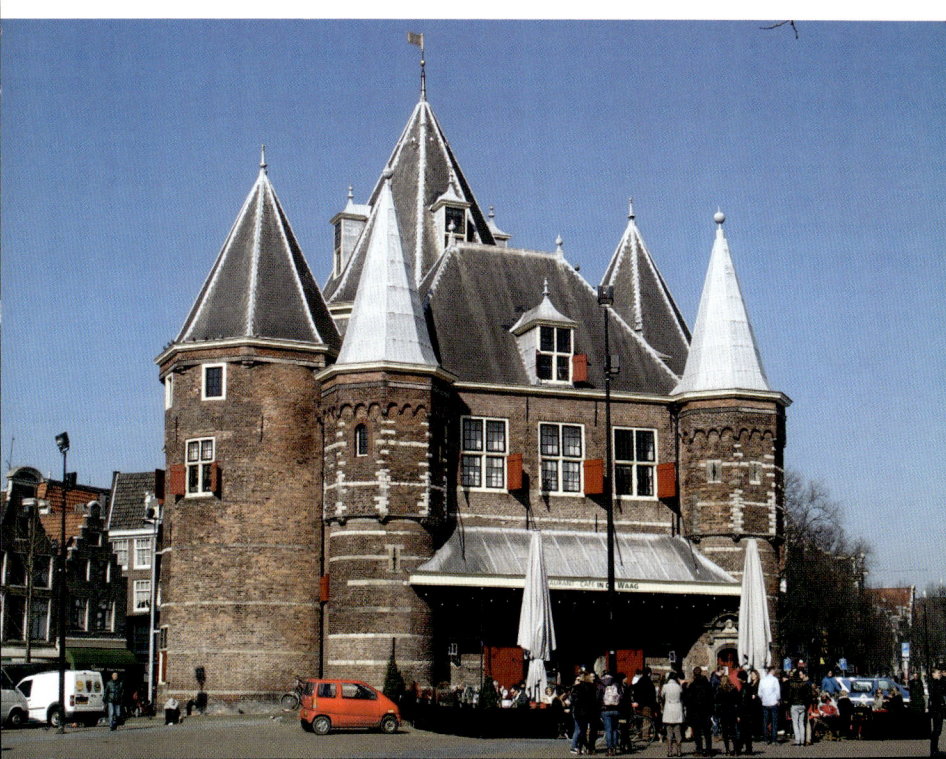

as St Anthony's Gate, before taking on other roles such as a Guild House and a place where surgeons carried out dissections. De Waag's main claim to artistic fame is the fact that it was here that Rembrandt painted the world famous painting The Anatomy Lesson of Dr Nicolaes Tulp, showing such a dissection in process. Although the upper levels of the building are not open to the public, the lower levels house a very popular restaurant.

The Nieumarkt is renowned for its nightlife and hospitality venues. Markets continue to be held within the square each day, and during the summer there is a popular antiques market.

**Nearby attractions:** Rembrandt House Museum, Hermitage Museum, Amsterdam Museum.

### Ravestijn Gallery
Westerdok 824
1013 BV Amsterdam
**www.theravestijngallery.com**

Founded in 2012 by Jasper Brode and Narda Van 't Veer, the Ravestijn Gallery has become one of the leading photographic galleries in the Netherlands. The gallery aims to focus on 'inquisitive and provocative approaches to contemporary photography', with an international perspective. It houses a continually changing programme of exhibitions, focusing on the work of contemporary

photographers such as Michel Lamoller, Blommers & Schumm, Ruth van Beek, Anja Niemi and Patrick Waterhouse. These may be solo exhibitions or group shows linked by a theme.

**Nearby attraction:** Museum Het Schip.

### Rembrandt's Amsterdam
Weteringschans 2, 1017 SG Amsterdam
**www.rembrandtsamsterdam.com**

This is an immersive experience designed to bring Rembrandt's last studio to life. Using projections and special effects, visitors step back 350 years to the seventeenth century and enter a reconstruction of Rembrandt's

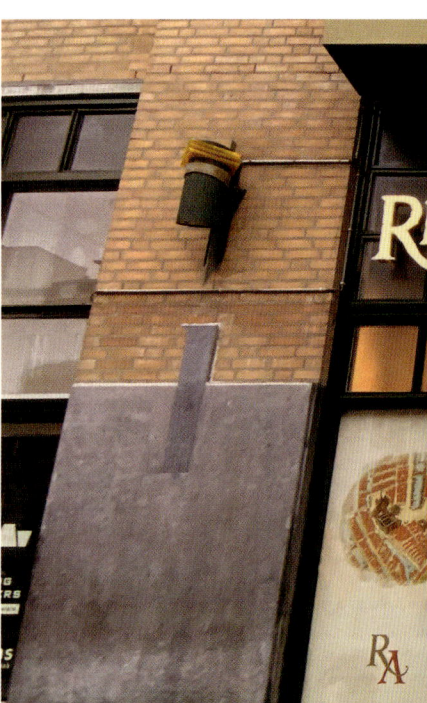

final studio where he created oil paintings such as Simeon in the Temple, Self Portrait with Beret and a portrait of Titus van Rijn. It focuses on the last years of Rembrandt's life, after he had been declared bankrupt and was only able to continue painting because his mistress Hendrickje and son Titus became his employers. During this time, the family moved into a house on the Rozengracht, near the Westerkerk. It is the story of their lives on the Rozengracht that is told in this immersive video art experience.

Apart from visiting the studio, visitors meet Rembrandt, Hendrickje and their children, Titus and Cornelia. In addition, visitors are given a map of seventeenth-

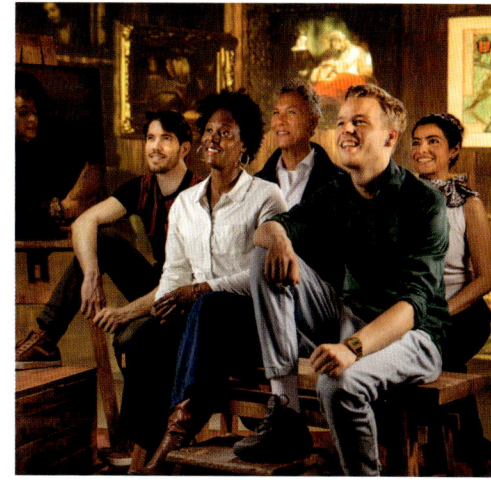

▲ *Discovering the world of Rembrandt.*

▼ *Rembrandt's Amsterdam.* (Rembrandt's Amsterdam)

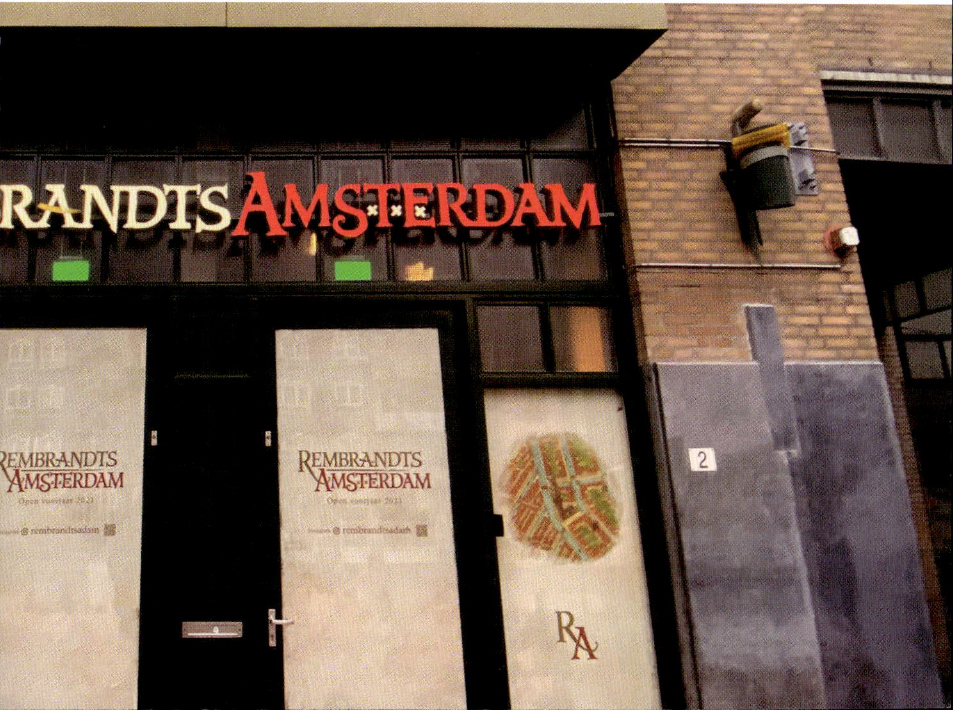

century Amsterdam highlighting locations linked to Rembrandt such as where he painted The Night Watch and the Rembrandt huis. After leaving Rembrandt's Amsterdam, visitors can use the map to visit the various locations. Tickets have to be pre-booked.

**Nearby Attractions:** Rijksmuseum, Vondelpark.

## Rembrandtplein

1017 CT Amsterdam
Named in honour of Rembrandt van Rijn, creator of works such as The Night Watch, the Rembrandtplein is a large open square in the centre of Amsterdam. A statue of Rembrandt dominates. Rembrandtplein was originally a butter and dairy market, but is now a busy entertainment area. The Royal Palace and Dam Square are nearby. The statue of Rembrandt originally stood at the side of the square, and was moved to its current spot in 1876 when the square was renamed as Rembrandtplein. Louis Royer, a nineteenth-century Flemish sculptor working in the classical style, created the sculpture of Rembrandt during a period in which he was undertaking public commissions relating to leading Dutch personalities from history. Royer was the leading sculptor of the period, and was often described as the 'Canova of the Netherlands'.

## Sex Museum Temple of Venus

Damrak 18,
1012 LH Amsterdam
**www.sexmuseumamsterdam.nl**

Definitely unique, this is a museum devoted to everything related to sex – and that includes art of every possible kind from paintings to photography, clothing, ceramics and figures. Every room has a different name such as Mata Hari, Marquis de Sade, Marquise de Pompadour and Rudolf Valentino. The building itself is an historic seventeenth-century row house in which the two back houses are connected via an impressive staircase. The museum contains Europe's largest collection of erotic art. From massive nude statues to glass-fronted display cases containing fragile ceramics, there are items sourced from all over the world. Many are set out in themed areas, leaving little to the imagination. The artefacts cover the entire period of human history from ancient times to the 1960s, there are rare exquisitely decorated objects from the Far East, as well as items that are very pornographic in content.

**Nearby attraction:** Art'otel.

## St Nicolas Kerk

Prins Hendrikkade 73
Amsterdam
**www.nicolaas-parochie.nl**

Located beside the Amsterdam Centraal railway station is a very beautiful

Roman Catholic church, filled with stained glass and rose windows. Designed in an unusual combination of neo-baroque and neo-renaissance, St Nicolas Kerk has an impressive dome. There are sculptures on display such as a statue of St Nicholas by Bart van Hove in 1886, as well as bas relief showing Christ and the four Evangelists, which was sculpted in the Van den Bossche en Crevels workshop during 1886. There are several large murals with religious themes.

**Nearby Attractions:** Amsterdam Centraal, Art'otel, STRAAT Museum.

## Torch Gallery

Lauriergracht 94,
1016 RN Amsterdam
www.torchgallery.com

One of the oldest contemporary art galleries in Amsterdam, it has been trading since 1984. Torch was established by Adriaan van der Have as a gallery focusing on the work of Dutch and international contemporary artists, especially those working in expressionism, photography and veejay art. Now owned by Adriaan's son, Mo, the gallery displays works by veteran contemporary artists as well as up and coming young artists keen to push the boundaries of their various mediums. Both solo and group exhibitions are held here. Erik de Bree, Tinkebell,

Nadav Kander and Annie Sprinkle are among the artists who have exhibited at Torch.

**Nearby attraction:** Huis Marseille.

## Tulip Museum

Prinsengracht 116
1015 Amsterdam
www.amsterdamtulipmuseum.com

A small museum devoted to the tulip, unofficially the flower most associated with Amsterdam. It tells the story of the arrival of the tulip in the Netherlands, tulipmania and how the tulip industry has developed over the years. The displays contain a wide array of objects including botanical illustrations, paintings, packaging and films relating to the tulip.

**Nearby Attractions:** Electric Ladyland, Huis Marseille.

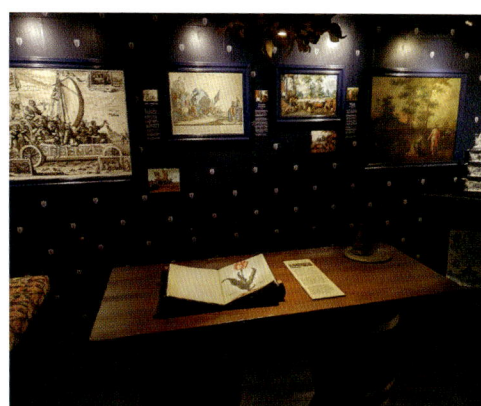

▲ *Art on display in the Tulip Museum.* (Tulip Museum)

## WM Gallery

Elandsgracht 35 Amsterdam, 1016TN
**www.gallerywm.com**

Devoted to photography, it aims to showcase 'true photographer's photography', to be thought-provoking and creative. There is a changing programme of exhibitions, which can involve all kinds of subjects from vintage prints and archival images through to contemporary fine art, staged photography and digitally enhanced imagery. Typical exhibitions have included ones exploring the 'soul of service stations' and Homo Turisticus. Some exhibitions are devoted to one artist, while others are groups and collaborations.

**Nearby attraction:** Huis Marseille.

## Willet-Holthuysen House

Herengracht 605
1001 AC Amsterdam
**www.amsterdammuseum.nl**

Part of Amsterdam Museum, the Willet-Holthuysen House is located in a traditional tall canal-side house and houses a collection of fine and applied art acquired over the years by Abraham Willet and his wife Louisa Holthuysen at the latter part of the nineteenth century. All the rooms are decorated in a period style, although some of the rooms such as the Kitchen and the Garden Room have been restored to their eighteenth-century style. Artwork can be seen displayed on walls, as well as large painted ceilings. Among the artwork are decorative paintings by Jacob de Wit as well as flower paintings by Adriana Johanna Haanen. The museum is administered by the Amsterdam Museum. There are special exhibitions of work by contemporary artists such as Maaike Schoorel. Guided tours are available around this museum, or you can explore it independently.

**Nearby attractions:** the Herengracht canal, Civic Guards Gallery.

## De Plantage

H'Art Museum
Nieuwe Keizersgracht 1,
1011 RL Amsterdam
**www.hartmuseum.nl/en**

Located in the seventeenth-century Amstelhof on the banks of the River Amstel, the Hermitage Amsterdam began life as a branch of the famous Hermitage Museum in St Petersburg, reflecting the historical links between the Netherlands and Russia. The building had been a retirement home for women ever since its construction in 1682, and eventually opened to men as well in the nineteenth century. Little remains of that original interior as it has undergone major alterations to accommodate large galleries and display space. Exhibitions originally

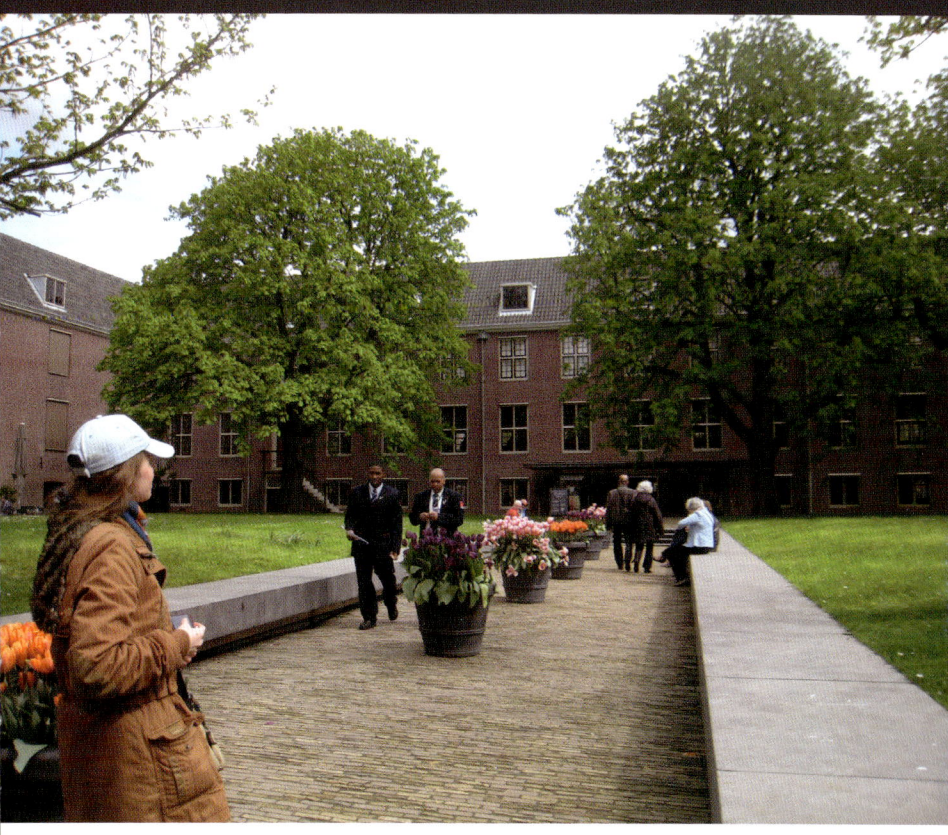

▲ *H'Art Museum.* (Angela Youngman)

included works of art loaned from the Hermitage in St Petersburg. Links between the two museums ended abruptly in March 2022 following the Russian invasion of Ukraine.

This created an immediate problem for the museum, which had to rethink and reorganise its entire programme and business concept, along with its long-term future. It has now become a museum in which famous works of art and stories worldwide are brought together to form unique exhibitions working in conjunction with the British Museum (London), Centre Pompidou (Paris), and Smithsonian Art Museum (Washington DC). Typical exhibitions have focused on specific paintings such as Vermeer's The Milkmaid and Julius Caesar, his life and times.

H'Art also houses the Museum of the Mind, featuring special exhibitions relating to mental health and health care, stories and themes relating to the mind. Outsider Art holds various short exhibitions featuring all types of contemporary art created by artists, many of whom have an intellectual or mental disability.

The museum also has exhibitions relating to the history of the Amstelhof as well as a seventeenth-century group portraits exhibition comprising a series of thirty giant portraits owned by the Amsterdam Museum and the Rijksmuseum. These include Rembrandt's famous painting The Anatomy Lesson of Dr Deijman and portraits of Govert Flinck and Nicolaes Pickenoy.

H'Art aims to be a cultural oasis with its own indoor garden and café combining art exhibitions, art education, concerts, lectures and movie nights.

**Nearby attractions:** Hermitage Amsterdam, Kattenkabinet, Outsider Art, FOAM, Rembrandt House Museum.

### Jewish Historical Museum and JHM Children's Museum
Nieuwe Amstelstraat 1,
1011 PL Amsterdam
**www.jck.nl**

The Jewish Museum is located within four synagogue museums within the Jewish Cultural Quarter of Amsterdam. It tells the story of past and present Dutch Jewish life and culture. On display are

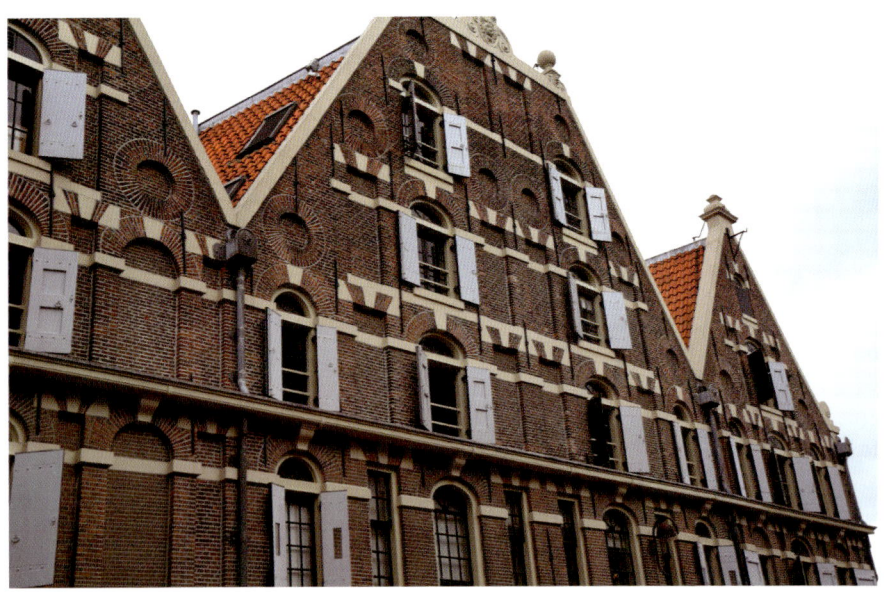

▲ *The Jewish Historical Museum in Amsterdam.*

a vast array of artefacts ranging from paintings to films, jewellery to graphic art and religious items. The Portuguese Synagogue contains a collection of 900 ceremonial items including prints and photos. Among the many items are photographs showing Jewish workers at work in the diamond industry, family portraits and personal albums. In addition to the permanent collections, there are always two temporary exhibitions. These have included Children of Al-Andalus, portraits of Andalusian–Moroccan Muslims and Jews featuring photos, film and stories of Moroccan descendants of Jews and Muslims from Al-Andalus. Guided tours of the museum and area such as walks around Jewish Amsterdam can be booked.

**Nearby attractions:** Amsterdam Museum, Rembrandt House Museum.

## Outsider Art / Museum Van de Geest

H'Art Museum
Nieuwe Keizersgracht 1,
1011 RL Amsterdam
**https://museumvandegeest.nl/english-information**

This is the only Dutch museum that focuses on artworks made by Dutch and international Outsider Artwork. Unconventional in style, few of these artists have been formally trained and many have disabilities. It forces visitors to explore art in a new way. Set up in 2016, the museum is housed in the Hermitage Amsterdam and is backed by the Dolhuys Foundation. It provides opportunities for people in society who have not previously been represented within the cultural landscape to discover their voices.

This type of art gained attention after the First World War when psychiatrist Hans Prinzhorn published a book entitled *Bildnerei der Geisteskranken* containing artworks that had been created by people being cared for in psychiatric institutions. Salvador Dali and Karel Appel were among the artists inspired by this book, while the Museum of Modern Art in New York described such self-taught art as being one of the three 'great movements of modern art' alongside surrealism and abstraction.

Nearest attractions: Hermitage Museum, Amsterdam Museum, Jewish Museum.

## Rembrandt's House (Museum Rembrandthuis)

Jodenbreestraat 4,
1011 NK Amsterdam
**www.rembrandthuis.nl**

A unique building, it offers a glimpse into the world of Rembrandt van Rijn. It is the only building that still survives from the seventeenth century in which Rembrandt actually lived. He had his home and studio here between 1639 and 1658, until he encountered financial problems due to his extravagant

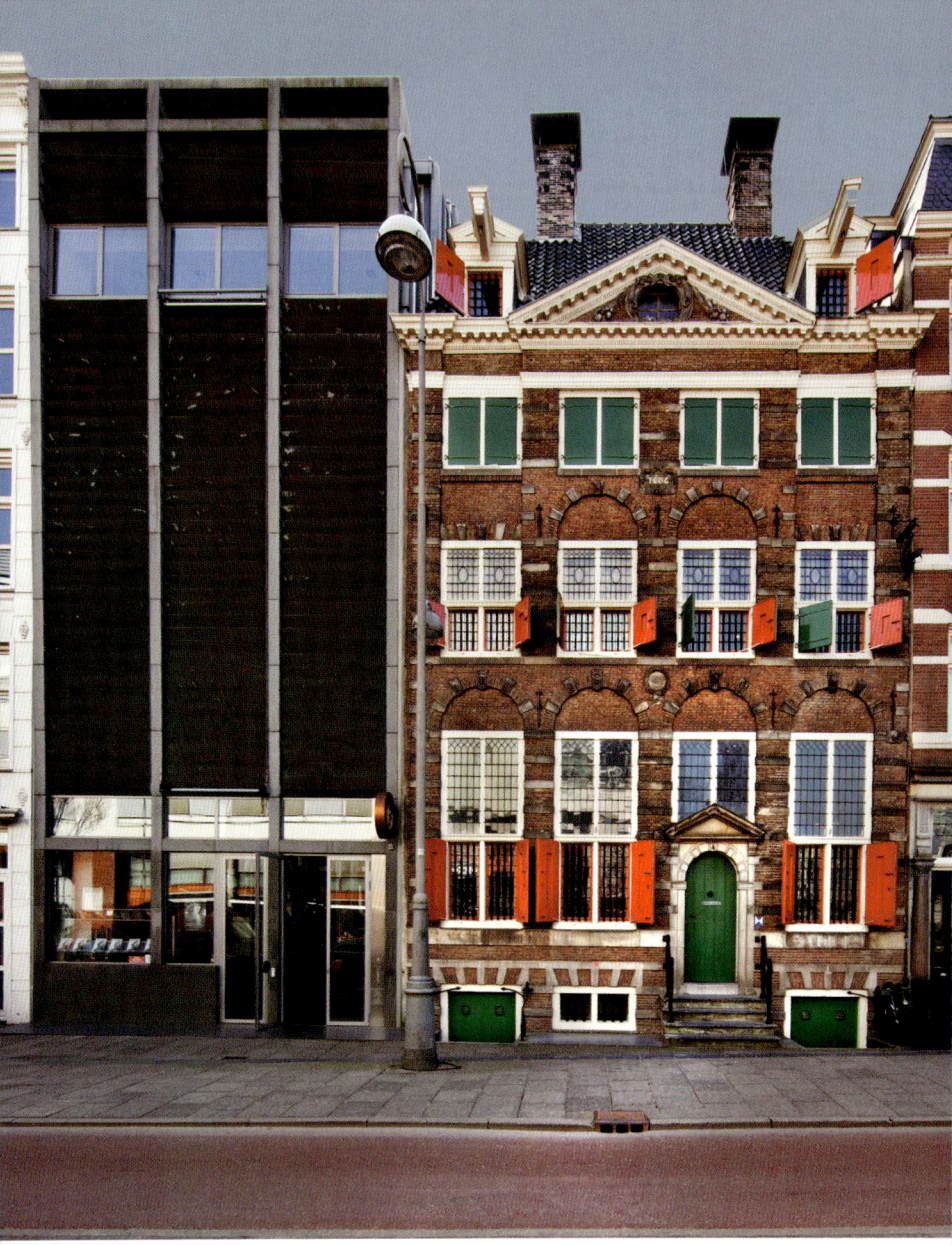

▲ *The exterior of the Museum Rembrandthuis.* (Museum Rembrandthuis)

lifestyle and was forced to move to a more modest house in the Rozengracht together with his mistress and children. Among the famous works created here were The Night Watch, The Hundred Guilder Print, The Three Trees and the Three Crosses. It was a very prosperous area, attracting other artists such as Nicolaes Pickenoy and Pieter Codde, while Nicolaes van Bambeeck lived in a house directly opposite that of Rembrandt. Other notable residents included burgomasters like Gillis Valckenier and Joan Huydecoper van Maarsseveen.

By the end of the nineteenth century, the house had become severely dilapidated, and its history relatively unknown until research revealed the link with Rembrandt.

Rembrandt's House has been a museum since 1911. It contains an almost complete collection of etchings created by Rembrandt, many of which show scenes within his studio. These etchings are regularly on view to the public via a changing programme of exhibitions within the modern museum wing attached to his original house. Other exhibitions include works by Rembrandt's contemporaries and students, and replicas of his paintings and works by modern, contemporary artists who have been inspired by his work.

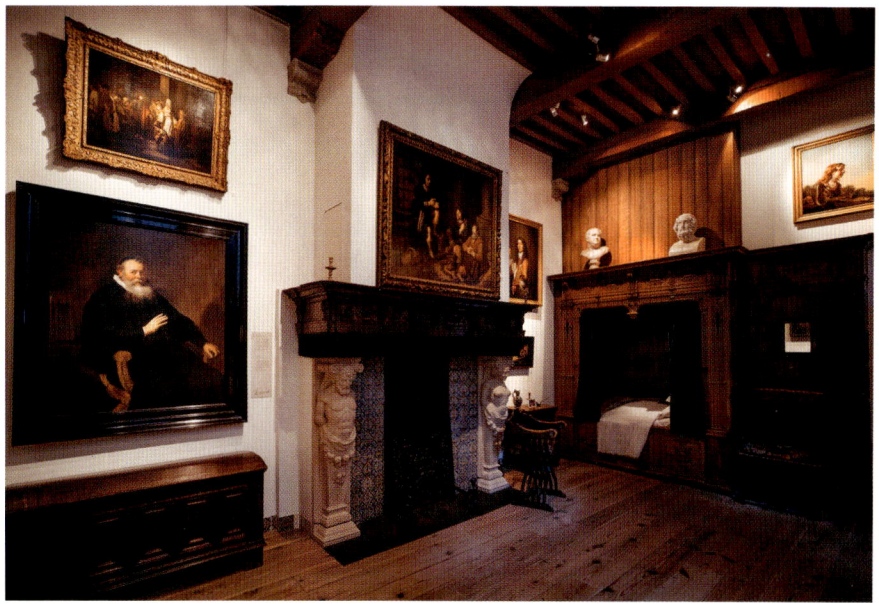

▲ *Interior of Rembrandt's House.* (Museum Het Rembrandthuis)

An inventory dating from the seventeenth century has enabled curators to refurbish and furnish a section of the house as it was when Rembrandt lived here. Visitors are able to explore Rembrandt's studio, old kitchen and the living room. The recreations aim to enable visitors to get to know the man behind the paintings, as a collector, entrepreneur, Amsterdammer and teacher. It is the only place where visitors can truly experience Rembrandt's life and work within a place in which he lived and worked.

**Nearby attractions:** Jewish Museum, Amsterdam Museum.

### Verzetsmuseum (Dutch Resistance Museum)
Plantage Kerklaan 61,
1018 CX Amsterdam
**www.verzetsmuseum.org**

If your country was invaded, what would you do? Would you resist or not? This is the intriguing question posed to all visitors at the Dutch Resistance Museum. Located in the Plantage area of Amsterdam, this is the area once home to thousands of Dutch Jews. The building itself was originally a Jewish cultural centre and synagogue.

Known simply as Verzetsmuseum to local people, the museum tells the story of Dutch resistance to German occupation between May 1940 and May 1945. It takes visitors through all stages of the occupation, and the dilemmas and choices faced by all members of the population. Resistance took many forms, from helping people like Anne Frank in hiding to attacks on military vehicles and transportation, running illegal presses and forging papers. On display are a host of period photographs as well as films, posters and other printed material. As you pass through the exhibition areas, including reconstructed streets, the décor and images steadily become darker, and grimmer. The range of images on display emphasise the horror of the Holocaust. A separate section of the display focuses on the activities of people within the former colonies in the Dutch East Indies, which were taken over by the Japanese. Apart from the main exhibition, the Resistance Museum has a programme of changing displays focusing on different aspects of resistance.

**Nearby attractions:** Jewish Museum, Rembrandt's House.

## Nieuw West

### De Appel
Schipluidenlaan 12, Amsterdam
1062 HE Amsterdam
**www.new.deappel.nl**

De Appel is a contemporary arts venue, hosting a changing programme of exhibitions and education initiatives focusing on alternative art styles and new forms of presentation dealing with international modern art. Among the exhibitions that have been held here are student and artist collaborations highlighting Stories of Belonging and a solo exhibition by Lydia Ourahmane. De Appel is also a research centre, artistic archive and art library. It is regarded as one of the most important arts exhibition spaces within the city.

**Nearby attractions:** Rembrandtpark, Vondelpark.

### Street Art Museum

Immanuel Kanthof 1,
1064 VR
Amsterdam
**www.streetartmuseumamsterdam.com**

A community-based eco museum using street art as a tool for dialogue with the local community in Nieuw West Amsterdam, as well as providing access to more than 300 examples of street art. These range from small pieces to monumental murals. They include colourful abstracts, a hidden sketchbook and pencil located on the pavement, people, faces, geometric designs, a tree growing up the corner of a building, decorated bollards, flying birds, a train carriage, dominoes and a mural inspired by Vermeer. All are located within a 4km route around the Nieuw West area, just to the north of Schiphol airport. Many of the pieces are in hidden locations such as an underground garage and were

created by members of the Street Art Museum. Private guided walks lasting around two hours can be arranged for small groups. Alternatively, visitors can download a free GPS guided tour from the website.

## Noord

### ABN Amro Bank N.V.

Gustav Mahlerlaan 10,
1082 PP Amsterdam
**www.art-heritageabnamro.nl/
kunstcollectie/home-kunstcollectie**

ABN AMRO is the third largest bank in the Netherlands, and has its headquarters in Amsterdam. More than forty years ago ABM AMRO began developing an art collection, focusing primarily on Dutch post-war visual art. Much of it, particularly the historic collection containing works such as a portrait of a child in profile by Rembrandt and a portrait of John Williams Hope by Angelica Kauffmann, is not open to the public as it is displayed on walls within various office buildings.

In 2021, the ABN AMRO Kunstruimte Gallery was opened in order to create a venue where it could share samples of its collection with the public via a programme of constantly changing exhibitions, as well as providing a platform for new developments in art. This enables recent acquisitions of work by young, rising artists to be hung next to masterpieces from ABN AMRO's existing

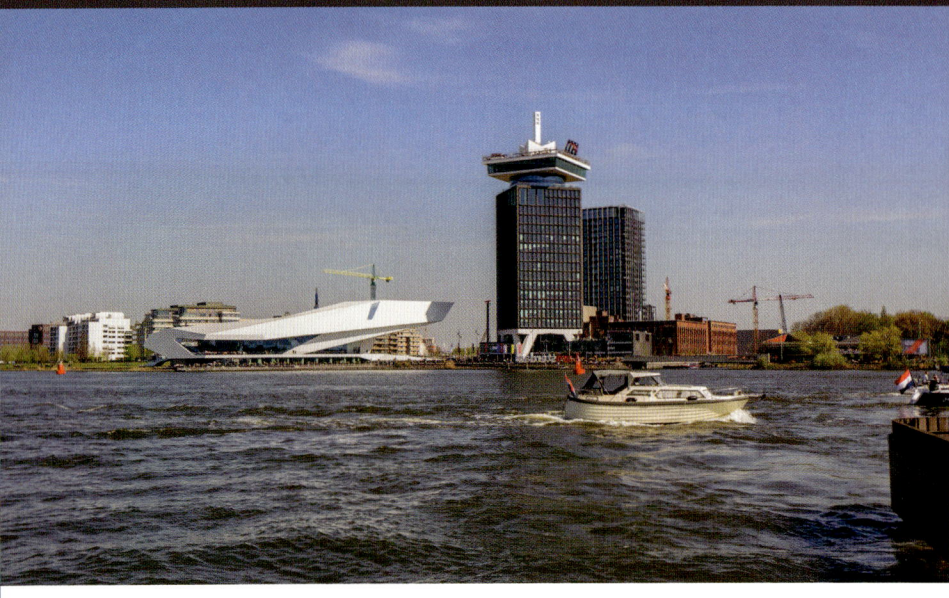

▲ *The Eye Film Museum in Amsterdam.*

collection. Typical works include Sol Lewitt's Loopy Doopy showing mingled blue loops against a red background, Marlene Dumas's painting of Magdalena, a Vertigo Verde sculpture by Hans van den Ban and Constant's artwork showing The Painter in his Studio.

**Nearby attraction:** Upside Down Amsterdam.

### Eye Film Museum

IJpromenade 1 Museum Quarter,
1013 KT Amsterdam
**www.eyefilm.nl**

Explore a huge collection of graphic art, film posters along with Dutch and foreign films within a dramatic, white sculpted waterside building and culture centre. Eye Film focuses on films and objects that make a statement in some way about Dutch film culture. There is a permanent exhibition focusing on cinematic equipment and the world of the moving image. Among the objects on display are a mutoscope showing Charlie Chaplin's film *The Waiter*, a magic lantern and modern compact cameras. Interactive displays enable visitors to explore techniques such as flipbooks and green screen, appear in a movie scene and try a thumb camera. Visitors can explore optical illusions, film illusion techniques and explore strange machines like a praxinoscope and the phenakistoscope. Elsewhere are monitors showing set photos from films including Francis Ford Coppola's *Apocalypse Now* and Stanley Kubrick's *Eyes Wide Shut*. All the scenes and photographs come from the Eye collection of 95,000 images from film sets. Eye's collection centre contains a vast array of magic lantern slides, photographs, posters, acetate films, digital data and film apparatus.

One of the most popular areas of Eye is the unique film poster gallery including advertising work from the early days of film as well as popular films and art house films. It highlights the way in which graphic art has developed over the past century and includes examples sourced worldwide. The poster selection changes on a regular basis. Eye Classics offers an opportunity to watch classic films on the big screen, with different ones screened each week.

The second gallery space has a more varied programme dealing with experimental cinema and the concept of cinema as the 'seventh art'. Previous exhibitions have included video exhibitions and visual artists such as Anthony McCall.

Founded in 1948, the Eye Film Institute began life as the Dutch Historical Film Archive. It was renamed the Netherlands Film Museum upon acquiring the archives of the Filmtheater de Uitkijk. In 2009 the Netherlands Film Museum merged with Holland Film, the Filmbank and the Netherlands Institute for Film Education and was renamed the Eye Film Institute Netherlands.

The Eye Film Institute contains a massive collection of analogue, digitised and non-digital media including 82,000 posters, 700,000 photographs, 1,500 items of pre-cinema and film equipment, and 4,500 magic lantern slides. The oldest film in the collection dates back to 1896.

**Nearby attractions:** Amsterdam Centraal Station, Art'otel, STRAAT Museum.

## Museum Perron Oost
Cruquiusweg 11
1019 AT Amsterdam
**www.museumperronoost.nl**

Occupying just 6 square metres of space, this is one of the smallest museums in the world. In 1993, artist Joep Van Lieshout turned the former cattle market area and railway tracks into a miniature park. It includes this museum in the former supervisor's house. The entire exhibition can be seen through the windows! It tells the stories of local residents via visual art. Radio Perron Oost forms part of the museum, broadcasting online interviews with former residents of the port area.

## Nxt Museum
Asterweg 22,
1031 HP Amsterdam
**www.nxtmuseum.com**

Dedicated to new media art, it hosts large scale, multi-sensory installations designed to challenge and question. There is a changing programme of exhibitions covering a wide range of topics such as 'Shifting Proximities' linking artists, technologists, scientists and musicians. This resulted in artworks combining academic research with creative ideas involving artists like Roelof Knol and Heleen Blanken. The museum is housed in a bespoke building designed specifically for the purpose of displaying multi-sensory installations.

**Nearby attractions:** Eye Film Institute, STRAAT Museum.

## Platanenweg
1091 KS Amsterdam

This is an area notable for its street art located on apartment buildings surrounding the Platanenweg in Amsterdam. Ten large murals sited on the sides of apartment buildings were installed as part of a street art festival in 2019, renovating the area designed to showcase the area as an environment in which everyone felt at home. The official theme was 'If These Walls Could Speak'.

The murals are:

Light Emerging from Darkness by Dan Kitchener (UK)

Floating Woman in Dove Grey with Pigeons by Studio Giftig (Netherlands)

Girl with a Heart Sitting in a Tree by Julieta XLF (Spain)

Giant Bird by DOPIE (Netherlands)

Giant Arms Carrying Belongings by Case Maclaim (Germany)

Giant Crosses by Kash & Chuck (Netherlands)

A Little Wizard by Hera of Herackut (Germany)

Elements of Faces by Sjem Bakkus &IVES.one (Netherlands)

Head & Shoulders of Man by Smug One (Australia)

In Case of Lost Childhood Break Glass by Leon Keer (Netherlands).

## Straat
NDSM-Plein 1,
1033 WC Amsterdam
**www.straatmuseum.com**

Opened in 2020, STRAAT is a museum/ art gallery devoted to street art from all over the world. It is located in the former NDSM shipyard just across the river IJ from Amsterdam Centraal station. A free GVB Amsterdam ferry link that takes approximately fifteen minutes provides quick access from behind Amsterdam Centraal Station.

The moment you step off the ferry, you are greeted with the sight of a massive giant mural of Anne Frank (Let Me Be Myself) painted by Brazilian street artist Eduardo Kobra. NDSM-Plein has become well known for its constantly changing graffiti art, with new pieces appearing on the sheds and shipping containers around the area.

STRAAT is sited within a former warehouse on the NDSM Wharf and has been described as a 'total outdoor playground for graffiti and street art in Amsterdam'. Part of its remit is to address the question as to whether street art can be truly street art if it is exhibited inside. In order to maintain authenticity, artworks were created on site, and artists asked to provide perspectives about the creation process.

The galleries utilise a street style layout, enabling visitors to explore the artworks via streets and road junctions. On display are more than 150 artworks created by more than 130 artists. The artworks are grouped into five main themes:

Personal – street art as a reflection of the artist's world

Aesthetical – creating perfect design

Grounded – the connection of street art with its surroundings

Conscious – using street art to raise awareness of issues.

Emotional – exploring emotions

An indoor panorama deck plus café allows visitors to gain an overall view of the galleries from above. Audio tours and private guided tours can be booked for an extra fee, likewise street art and graffiti workshops.

Among the artists displaying work at STRAAT are, Snik, Dvate, Dourone, Skount, TWOONE and Alex Senna.

**Nearby attractions:** Amsterdam Centraal, Eye Film Museum.

## Oost

Museum Tot Zover
Kruislaan 124
1097 GA Amsterdam
**www.totzover.nl**

An unusual museum located within a cemetery and housed in the former director's residence. Also known as the Funeral Museum, it explores art, photography, death and the afterlife. The museum is believed to be unique, illuminating death in all its aspects. Since opening in 2007, it has hosted major exhibitions such as Funeral Train, Afterlife and the Pixelated Revolution. On display are both permanent collections as well as temporary exhibitions. Guided tours can be booked.

**Tropenmuseum**
Linnaeusstraat 2,
1092 CK Amsterdam
**www.tropenmuseum.nl**

The Tropenmuseum began life in 1864 as a colonial museum based in Haarlem, before moving to Amsterdam to occupy a new, richly decorated building in 1926. After 1949, the Tropenmuseum became part of the Tropical Institute in Amsterdam, focusing on cultures different to the Western tradition. Over the years, it has been encouraged to widen its remit and also explore social issues such as hunger and poverty. The museum contains the Dutch National Museum of World Culture, combining collections owned by the Tropenmuseum, Africa Museum, Museum Volkenkunde and the Wereldmuseum.

The main permanent exhibition area is divided into continents. Visitors begin in South America, progress to Africa, and then into Asia and the Antilles. Multimedia, light and sound are used frequently to help bring specific themes or objects alive. Artefacts on display include jewellery, textiles, clothing, ethnographical art, folk art, traditional art and applied arts of all kinds. There is an extensive art collection that includes photographs, drawings, paintings, film and video linked to the portrayal of universal themes such as celebration, mourning, decoration, love and conflict. A theatrical collection includes musical instruments and objects such as masks and puppets. Some of the objects within the museum are extremely complex and intricate in design, like the clove model of a horse pulling a two-wheeled coach complete with coachman. The dedicated Batik Room contains the museum's extensive array of batik materials, with printing in many different styles

including abstracts and pictorial images. Special exhibitions are hosted regularly at the museum, covering topics such as healing practices and world press photography from Africa.

## Westerpark

### Fabrique des Lumières,
Pazzanistraat 37,
1014 BE Amsterdam
**www.fabricque-lumieres.com**

Art comes to life in this incredible immersive digital art centre. Located in a former nineteenth-century gas plant, the 17m-high walls are perfect for this type of project. Exhibitions change each year, and focus on one or two of the most celebrated figures in art history such as Gustav Klimt, Vincent Van Gogh, Claude Monet and Salvador Dali. Within the centre, artworks are brought to life using advanced technology, using 100+ state of the art projectors and accompanying music. The exhibitions are not static and all the projections move constantly and change, transforming from one scene to another and covering walls, ceilings and island blocks within the rooms. You can stand and watch or walk through the pieces, becoming almost part of them.

This is an offshoot of the Fabrique des Lumières centre in Paris, which has proved extremely successful in creating immersive and sensorial artistic experiences.

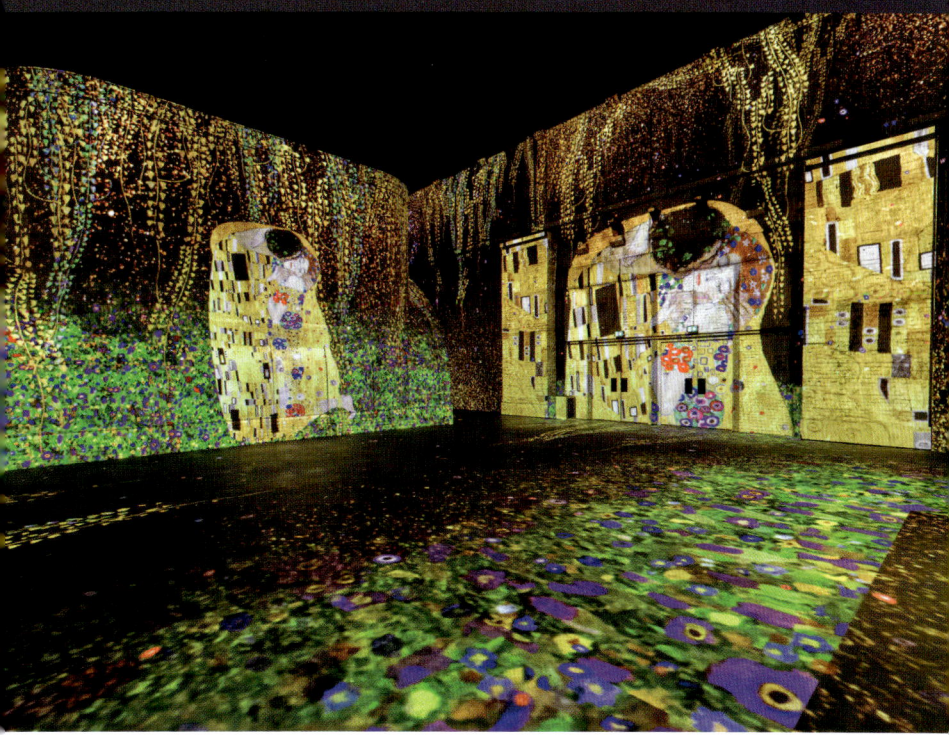

▲ *Immersive, constantly changing art within Fabrique des Lumières.* (Fabrique des Lumières)

Built in 1885 by the Imperial Continental Gas Association, the Westergasfabriek was turned into a cultural space in 1967.

**Nearby attraction:** Museum Het Schip.

### Museum Het Schip (Amsterdam School museum)
Oostzaanstraat 45,
1013 WG Amsterdam
**www.hetschip.nl**

Built in 1919, Het Schip is regarded as one of the premier buildings reflecting the styles of the Amsterdam School, which focused on a combination of decoration and construction that eventually spread throughout the Netherlands. Viewed from the outside, Het Ship resembles a large ocean liner, complete with funnels and curves that give the impression of waves hitting the sides of the ship. A dramatic building, it was created on the orders of the Eigen Haard housing corporation, which still own it and operate it as a housing complex. The building was restored to its full glory in 2018 with the aid of the Getty Foundation.

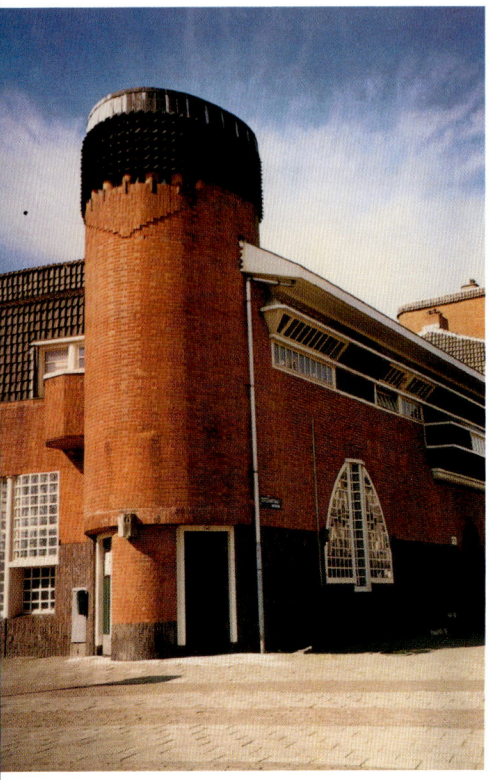

▲ *Post Office Tower within the Museum Het Schip.*
(Museum Het Schip)

The post office at the complex is regarded as an historical monument since it is the only original 1920s-style post office to exist within the Netherlands. Designed by Michel de Klerk, it incorporates a variety of innovative design elements, and has been restored to its original colour scheme. Displays inside the post office highlight its history and includes rare drawings by Michel de Klerk.

Guided tours are available, taking visitors around sections of the housing complex including a visit to the museum

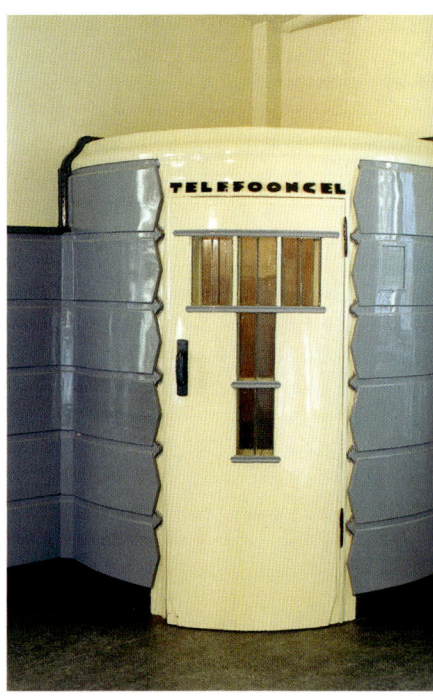

▲ *Unique period telephone booth within the building.* (Museum Het Schip)

The Museum Het Schip is located within a former school building linked to the housing complex. It now houses a permanent exhibition about the work and stylistic ideals of the Amsterdam School, together with an exhibition on housing associations. Temporary exhibitions linked into aspects of housing design, garden cities and members of the Amsterdam School are held here.

flat, the former post office and a reconstructed nineteenth-century slum dwelling. Other daily tours offer access to the shipping house and other distinctive social housing blocks in the area designed by de Klerk and Piet Kramer.

**Nearby attraction:** Fabrique des Lumières.

## Zuid

### Diamant Museum
Paulus Potterstraat 8
1071 CZ Amsterdam
Amsterdam
**www.diamondmuseum.com**

An unusual form of applied arts, the Diamant Museum is not just a museum of jewellery. Exploring it holds many surprises, including an ape skull covered in more than 17,000 diamonds made specifically for the museum, likewise a tennis racket complete with ball.

The museum explores the history of diamonds over the past 400 years. It is the only museum of its kind in Europe. Displays explain how diamonds form and how they are turned into very desirable objects. Many of the items on display are unique in design and artistry.

There are superb collections of crowns, tiaras and other royal jewellery.

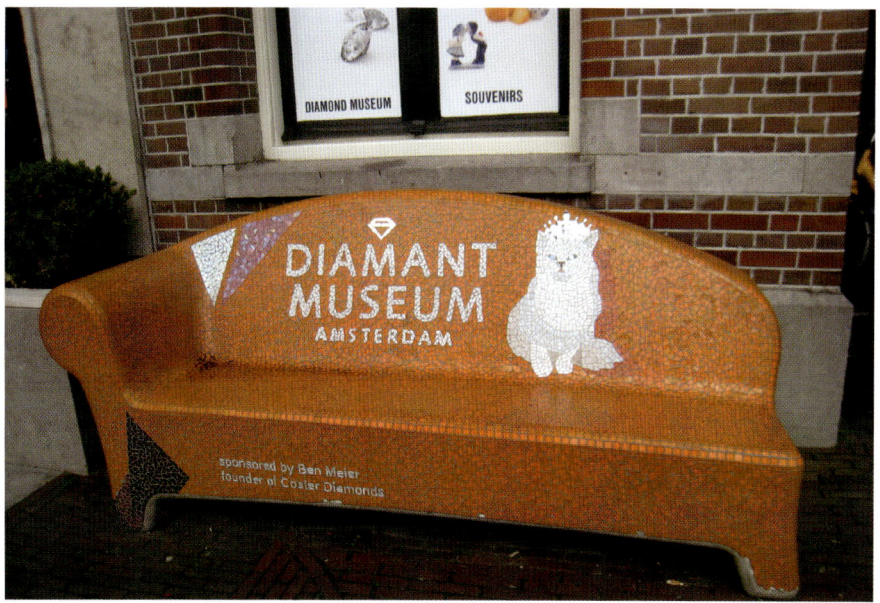

▲ *Mosaic artwork marking the entrance to the Diamant Museum.* (Angela Youngman)

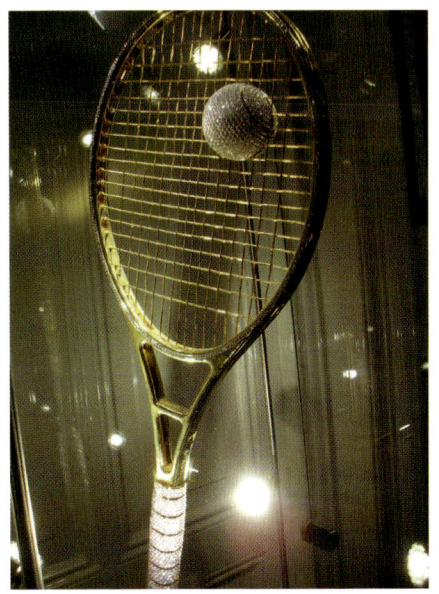

The collection of crowns contains unusual ones such as the Ade Elerin of the King of the Yoruba complete with yellow diamond elephant, and a Chinese bridal crown inspired by the Chao Guan (crown of the Empress), full of symbolic significance such as a phoenix. Other crowns include that of the Queen of Bavaria, set with pearls, diamonds, rubies and emeralds, and the burial crown of Katarina Stenbock of Sweden. The presence of the museum in Amsterdam reflects the fact that

◄ *The Golden Racket, with permission from the Diamant Museum.* (Karis Youngman)

▼ *Tiara (replica silver and zirconia), with permission from the Diamant Museum.* (Angela Youngman)

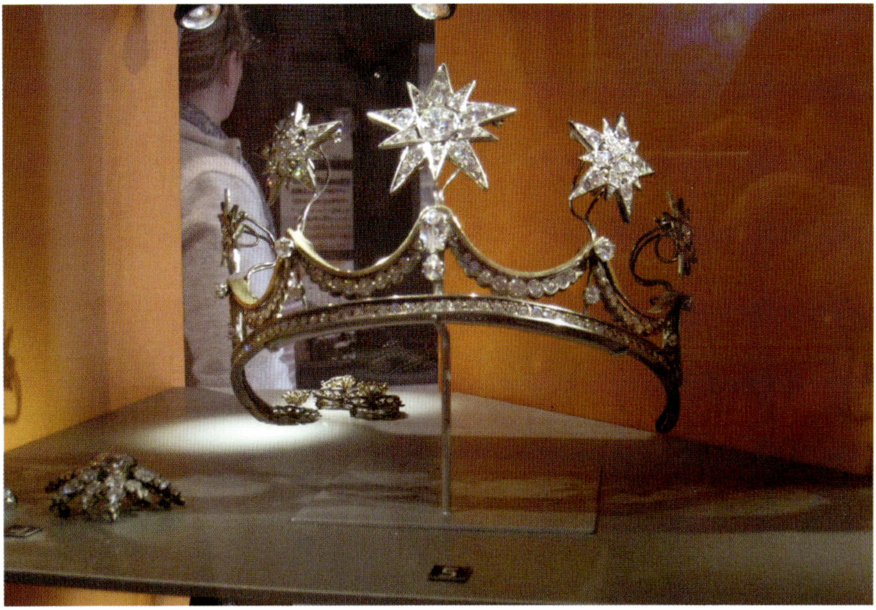

the city is the centre of the worldwide diamond trade. It was set up in 2007 by Royal Coster Diamonds as a way of educating people about the world of diamonds. Located on the Museumplein, it is only a few minutes' walk from the Rijksmuseum.

**Nearby attractions:** Rijksmuseum, Van Gogh Museum, Stedeljik.

## Moco Museum

Villa Alsberg, Honthorstraat 20
1071 DE Amsterdam
**www.mocomuseum.com**

This independent museum focusing on modern, contemporary and street art is beside the Van Gogh Museum. It is housed in a historic townhouse overlooking Museumplein designed by Eduard Cuypers in 1904. Cuypers was the nephew of Pierre Cuypers, designer of the Rijksmuseum and Centraal Station in Amsterdam.

This privately owned museum is the result of an initiative by founders and art collectors Lionel and Kim Logchies. It provides 'one of a kind experiences aimed at a broad audience ... To inspire and enlighten our world through art.' Moco states that it believes in the power of art: 'it connects people, challenges ideologies and inspires the activist within'.

▼ *Moco Museum.*

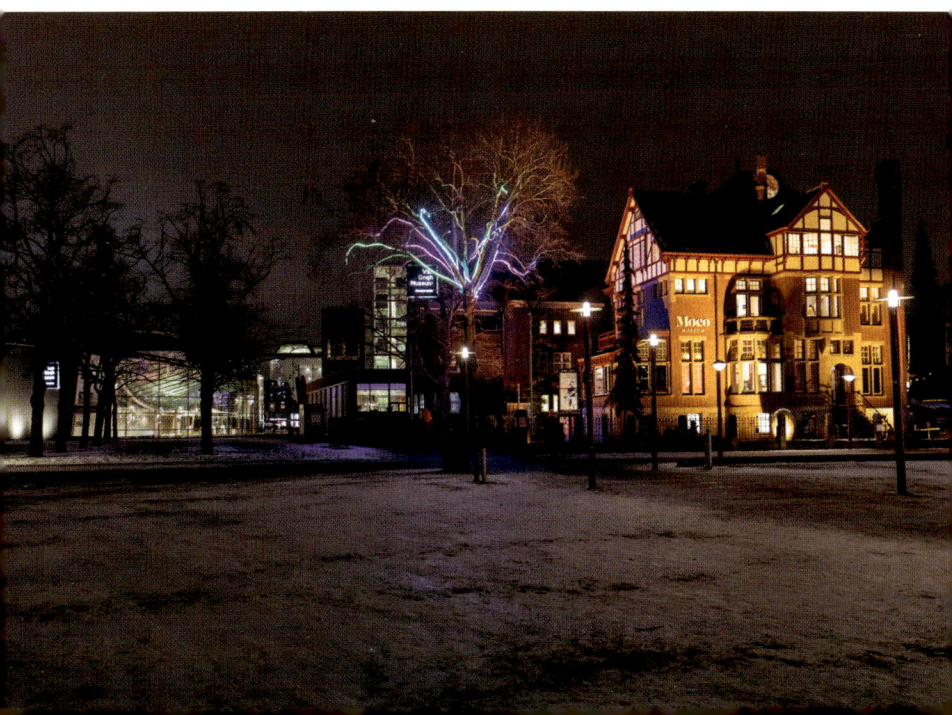

Moco contains a permanent exhibition together with a changing programme of temporary exhibits, which includes works of art loaned by international collectors. The permanent collection includes works by Banksy, Jean-Michel Basquiat, JR, KAWS, Keith Haring, Jeff Koons, Damien Hirst, Tracey Ermin, Yayoi Kusama, Mark Rothko, Andy Warhol and Studio Irma. The Laugh Now exhibition by Banksy includes rare and famous pieces such as Girl with Balloon, Flower Thrower and Beanfield. Moco acts as a platform for rising stars within the world of contemporary art, hosting solo exhibitions by artists such as THE KID and Guillermo Lorca. It aims to cover street art, regarding this art form as being the 'voice of the streets', challenging ideologies, encouraging involvement and connecting people showing the work of artists including Icy & Sot and Stik.

Typical exhibitions have included topics such as digital immersive art and the first dedicated exhibition devoted to the NFT phenomenon with works by Beeple, Andres Reisinger, Mad Dog Jones and FEWOCiOUS. Other exhibitions have featured Pumpkin Art and Night of the Stars dot art by Kusama and a 3D installation by Roy Lichtenstein based on his painting Bedroom at Arles made in the style of Van Gogh's famous artist's room at Arles.

Surrounding the Moco Museum is the Moco Museum Garden. This houses a changing selection of street art and outdoor sculptures such as a huge red bear by Whisby and Fidia's Freaky Mouse.

Apart from exploring the museum and its garden, visitors can also book a joint ticket covering museum entry and a sixty-minute canal cruise with a local guide, starting near the museum.

**Nearby attractions:** Rijksmuseum, Stedelijk Museum, Van Gogh Museum.

**Rijksmuseum,**
Museumstraat 1,
Amsterdam
**www.rijksmuseum.com**

The Rijksmuseum is the premier museum of Amsterdam and throughout the Netherlands, as well as being one of the oldest. This is where you can find some of the most prestigious old masters such as works by Vermeer, Rembrandt and Van Gogh. It is extremely popular and attracts more than 2 million visitors annually.

Queues to enter the Rijksmuseum are common. Depending on the time of day, you may find you have to queue or encounter congestion to see pictures such as Rembrandt's The Night Watch.

Visiting the museum as early as possible during the day will reduce the risk of long queues or congestion. Booking tickets in advance and printing them online will help. You will still have

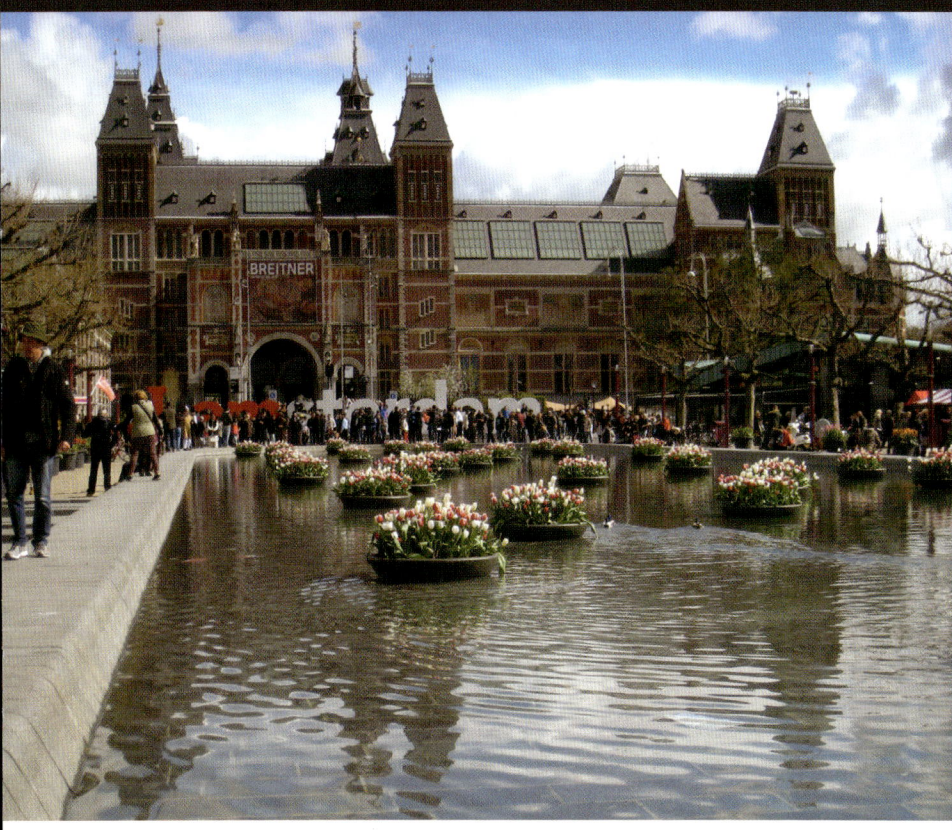

▲ *The Rijksmuseum tells the story of 800 years of Dutch history.* (Angela Youngman)

to wait to enter, but once inside you can go straight into the museum.

## History of the Rijksmuseum

The Rijksmuseum was not originally intended to be located in Amsterdam. In November 1798, the Dutch government decided to develop a national museum similar to the Louvre in Paris. It was regarded as a 'prestige project' designed to develop patriotism as well as a means of storing and displaying important art collections. The resultant National Art Gallery opened on 31 May 1800 at Huis Ten Bosch, The Hague. On display were more than 200 paintings regarded as heritage works sourced from the collections of the Stadtholders and the Dutch East India Company.

In 1806, Napoleon took control of the Netherlands, later incorporating it into the French Empire. He designated Amsterdam as the new capital of the Netherlands. In 1808, the National Art

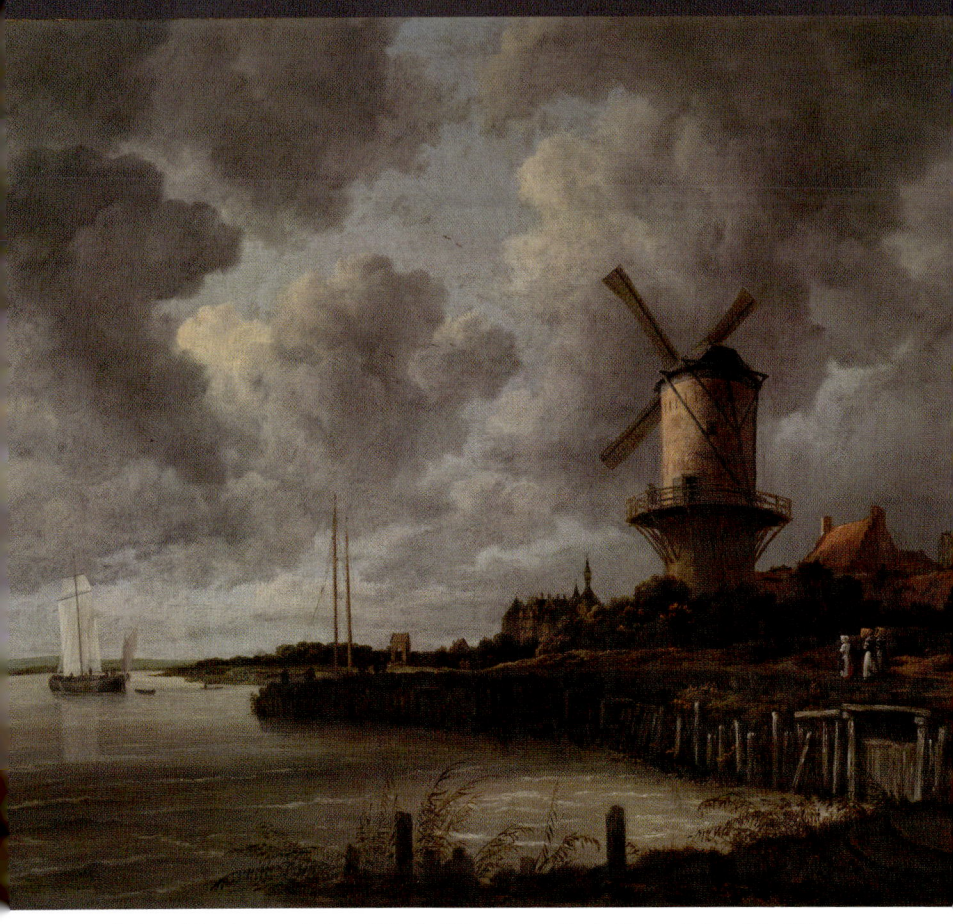

▲ *Typical Dutch landscape painting within the Rijksmuseum. Used with permission of the Rijksmuseum.*
(Rijksmuseum)

Gallery moved to Amsterdam and was placed within the Royal Palace. Paintings owned by the civic authorities such as The Night Watch by Rembrandt were added to the renamed Royal Museum.

In 1813, The Netherlands returned to Dutch rule under King Willem I. The Royal Museum and the National Print Collection (which had formerly been located in The Hague) were relocated from the Royal Palace to the Trippenhuis (a seventeenth-century palace on the Kloveniersburgwal) and renamed the Rijksmuseum. Some items of the Rijksmuseum were moved elsewhere, for example the artefacts dating from classical antiquity were sent to a new Museum of Antiquities in Leiden, while some nineteenth-century artworks were moved to the Paviljoen Welgelegen in Haarlem.

Towards the end of the nineteenth century, it was decided to build a big new national museum building to house the Rijksmuseum and architect Pierre Cuypers was commissioned to design and build it. It was decided to create a building that linked Gothic and Renaissance styles together with elements of national symbolism. Construction started in 1876, and the museum opened in 1885. The new building contained a much wider selection of objects, as previous collections such as those that had been sent to Haarlem and the Cabinet of Curiosities from The Hague were now returned. Other paintings from elsewhere in Amsterdam were added to the museum such as the Jewish Bride by Rembrandt, which was bequeathed to the city. It also made its first acquisition – The Threatened Swan by Jan Asselijn, costing 100 guilders. This painting continues to be one of the top attractions within the Rijksmuseum.

Further expansion to the Rijksmuseum took place in the twentieth century. Several new galleries were added as well as building over two of the original courtyards created by Cuypers. After the Second World War, the layout was amended to move the collections of national history, sculpture and applied Arts to individual galleries. In the 1950s an Asian Art department was added, based on the collection of the Association of the Friends of Asian Art.

During 2003–13, the Rijksmuseum was totally renovated to re-establish Cuypers' original architectural design while at the same time modernising the interior. Paintings, applied arts and history were no longer divided into separate sections, but were brought together to create a chronological story of Dutch Art and history from the medieval period to the end of the twentieth century. The museum has eighty separate display rooms. Apart from the permanent displays, there are also special exhibitions held each year incorporating elements of the Rijksmuseum collections as well as international loans.

Key works within the museum include:

The Night Watch by Rembrandt van Rijn

Kitchen Maid by Vermeer

Woman in Blue Reading a Letter by Vermeer

The Merry Drinker by Frans Hals

The Merry Family by Jan Steen

Self-portrait by Van Gogh

The Threatened Swan by Jan Asselijn

## Museum Layout

This is a vast, four-storey building. Floor plans are available from the information desk. All the galleries are marketed clearly with a number and theme, ensuring they are easy to locate on the floor map.

## The Atrium

The Rijksmuseum is a symmetrical building arranged around two large enclosed courtyards. The museum building is bisected by an arched passageway, which was designed deliberately by Cuyper to connect the old parts of Amsterdam with the new districts being established to the south.

Visitors enter the Rijksmuseum via a passageway into the atrium, a vast area covered by a glass roof. It is the central area of the museum and provides access to all parts of the building. This is the location of the information desk, pay point, museum shop, café and other visitor facilities.

Floor 0 comprises the ground floor housing the atrium and a variety of display rooms along the sides of the building. On display are the Rijksmuseum's special collections including patriotic relics, boxes, cases, glassware, porcelain, gems, locks, keys, historic dresses, goblets and ships

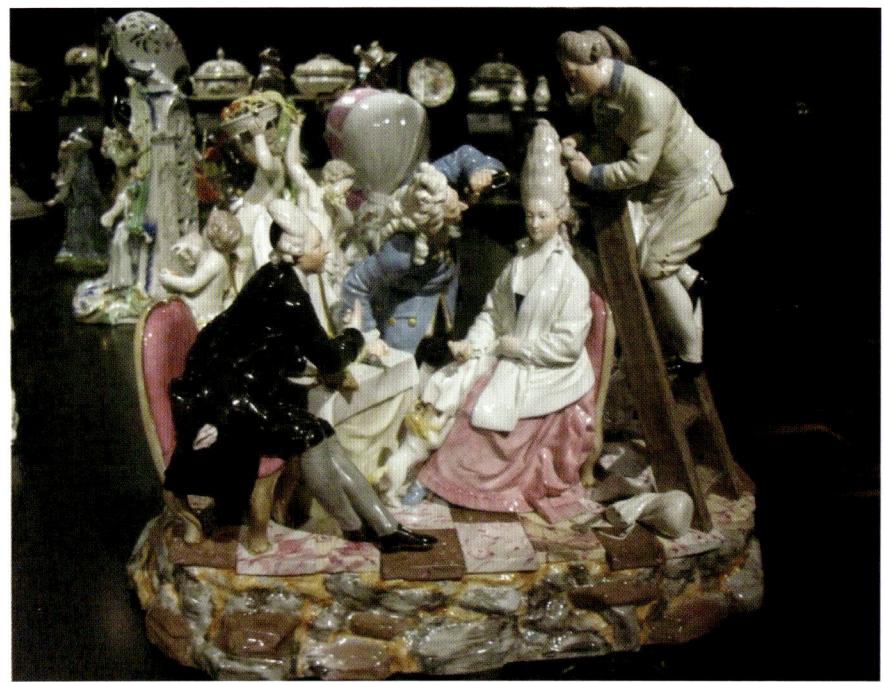

▲ *Porcelain model showing a fashionable lady having her hair done.* (Karis Youngman – used with the permission of the Rijksmuseum)

models. One of the most unusual costumes is a heavily embroidered eighteenth-century dress with a 2m-wide skirt. The magic lantern slides display is extremely extensive, containing lots of individual and group of scenes telling stories and portraying important events. Each one is a work of art in itself.

Paintings on display that focus on the period 1400–1600 include:

Madonna of Humility by Fra Angelico (1440)

Virgin Annunciate by Lorenzo di Niccolo (1412)

The Adoration of the Magi by Geertgen tot Sint Jans (1485)

The Seven Works of Mercy by the Master of Alkmaar (1504)

Worship of the Golden Calf by Lucas Van Leyden (1530)

Mary Magdalene by Jan Van Scorel (1530)

Floor One focuses on the period 1700–1900. Dominating this gallery is the Battle of Waterloo painting created by Jan Willem Pieneman in 1824. This is the largest painting in the Rijksmuseum. It portrays the decisive moment in the battle when the Duke of Wellington is informed that Prussian forces are on their way. The painting shows all the major players in this battle, including

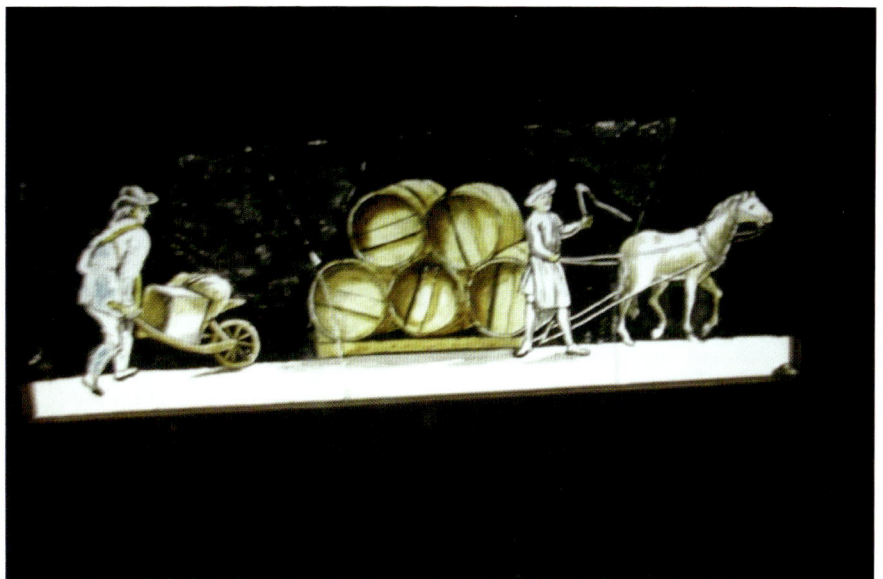

▲ *Magic lantern slide.* (Karis Youngman – used with the permission of the Rijksmuseum)

the Dutch Crown Prince (later William II), who is shown lying wounded on a stretcher in the foreground. Although originally intended as a gift for the Duke of Wellington, King William I of the Netherlands decided to purchase it as a gift for his son, the Crown Prince. Other key items include a seated marble sculpture of Cupid made by Étienne-Maurice Falconet in 1757, and a painting by Adriaan de Lelie entitled The Art Gallery of Jan Gildemeester Jansz (1795). This painting is notable for the way it reflects life in a Dutch house of the period. It actually depicts a scene in Jan Gildemeester's house where he had transformed two rooms into a picture gallery. The walls are densely covered with paintings, and Gildemeester is shown talking to a visitor, discussing one of them. A Rembrandt painting can be glimpsed above the head of Gildemeester.

Elsewhere are three self-portraits and Portrait of Dr Gachet by Van Gogh, La Corniche near Monaco by Claude Monet, The Yellow Riders by George Hendrik Breitner and Fishing Pinks in Breaking Waves by Hendrik Willem Mesdag.

In addition to the period paintings on display, the gallery contains examples of prominent furniture makers including David Roentgen and Abraham Roentgen. There is a recreated fully furnished eighteenth-century canal house reflecting the lifestyle and objects familiar to people living at that time in Amsterdam.

Floor Two covers the period 1600–1700, focusing on the Golden Age of

Dutch Art. There are rooms all around the edges of the floor overlooking the central atrium. The spectacular Great Hall with its inlaid mosaic floors, vaulted ceiling and walls ornamented with massive painted tableaux and stained glass windows is located at one end of the Gallery of Honour.

The Gallery of Honour runs through the centre of Floor Two and leads directly to the Night Watch Gallery. Separate rooms around the sides of Floor Two focus on different artists and periods as well as displays of Delftware and doll's houses. Many of these doll's houses are intricately made, for example the example commissioned by a merchant's wife, Petronella Oortman. It is known that she commissioned numerous carpenters, glass blowers, silversmiths and other craftspeople to make exact miniature replicas of full-size furnishings to place within it. In total, more than 700 items were created.

The Gallery of Honour contains various masterpieces by major seventeenth-century artists. Among the works on display here are:

### The Threatened Swan by Jan Asselijn (1650)

Looking at this picture you can almost feel the texture of the swan's feathers, as well as experiencing its anger when a dog threatens its nest. This painting is often regarded as a political allegory in that the swan represents a Dutch statesman, Johan de Witt, protecting his country.

### The Merry Drinker by Frans Hals (1628–30)

Officially this painting is known as A Militiaman Holding a Berkemeyer. It shows a lively soldier who has already probably had more than one beer, raising his glass in a toast. Animated and lively, he seems to be actually moving, reflecting Frans Hals' skill in using swift, short brushstrokes along with his ability to capture detail.

### The Milk Maid by Johannes Vermeer (1660)

A beautiful painting reflecting his attention to detail, portraying even the holes in the wall. Everything is totally still apart from one movement – the stream of milk being poured into the container.

### Woman in Blue Reading a Letter by Johannes Vermeer (1663)

This is a different style to his earlier painting as it shows only parts of objects such as tables and chairs. Viewers have to work out the remainder as they observe the painting. It also shows his skill in rendering light, since he used pale grey to highlight the woman's skin and light blue for the shadows on the wall.

### The Merry Family by Jan Steen (1668)

This painting shows a family gathering in which everyone is having a great time, but not noticing a little boy sneaking a quick taste of the wine. Jan Steen was well known for his paintings of chaotic, lively households. So popular were these paintings that the term, 'a Jan Steen household' became a frequently used phrase to describe a crazy, chaotic household.

### The Jewish Bride by Rembrandt van Rijn (1665)

A newly wed couple are shown caressing each other. Van Gogh was so impressed by this painting that he is reported to have said that he would give up ten years of his life just to sit watching it for a fortnight, with just a crust of bread to eat.

At the end of the Gallery of Honour, all attention is drawn to just one painting, the massive The Night Watch by Rembrandt, which dominates the room. Painted in 1642, it portrays the Amsterdam militia led by Captain Frans Banning Cocq. Although today it is generally known as The Night Watch, its official title is Militia Company of District II under the Command of Captain Frans Banninck Cocq. It became known as The Night Watch due to the sheer accumulation of dirt over the centuries. So dark was it that viewers believed Rembrandt had painted an evening scene. Only after extensive restoration and cleaning was it discovered that he had portrayed a much more vivid, colourful daytime scene. The painting emphasises Rembrandt's skill in creating light and dark, using light to focus on specific details such as the young girl who was the company mascot, and the captain's hand as he tells the soldiers to move out.

Floor 3 covers the period 1900–2000. This section is dedicated to all aspects of twentieth-century art, including paintings, furniture, photography, films, posters, and even an aeroplane. It aims to represent all aspects of cultural history and cultural movements throughout the century. Displays include paintings by Anton L. Koster and Chris

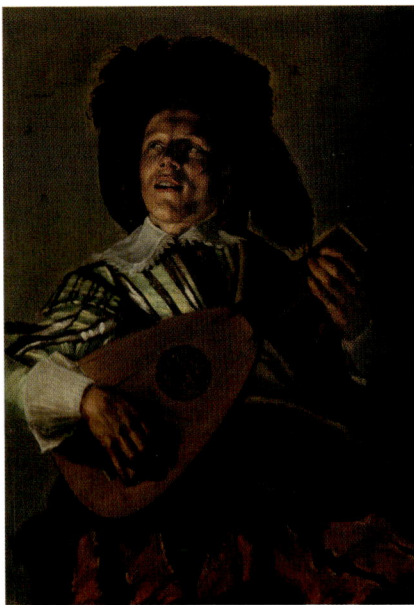

▲ *The Serenade by Leyster on display in the Rijksmuseum. Used with permission of the Rijksmuseum.* (Rijksmuseum)

Lanooy, and furnishings by Dutch designers such as Gerrit Rietveld and Michel de Klerk.

By far the most prominent items are Paul Mondrian's Composition No. 111 with red, yellow and blue and a display of avant-garde art containing works by Karel Appel, and Constant Nieuwenhuys, plus painters from the UK and Germany.

**Nearby attractions:** Diamont Museum, Moco Museum, Stedelijk Museum, Van Gogh Museum, Vondelpark.

### Stedelijk Museum
Museumplein 10,
1071 DJ Amsterdam
**www.stedelijk.nl/en**

Modern art, contemporary art and design since the 1880 are the sole focus of the Stedelijk. Works by Piet Mondrian, Marc Chagall and Karel Appel are among many in the collection, along with those of Van Gogh, Matisse, Jackson Pollock and Andy Warhol. The Museum holds extensive video collections and installations plus Russian avant-garde and Soviet art. In total, the Stedelijk has more than 100,000 objects, with key themes dealing with sculpture, painting, installations, prints, moving image, posters, graphic and industrial design. There are major collections of work relating to De Stijl, Bauhaus, Neo-Impressionism and Pop Art. Among the most famous works owned by the Stedelijk are La Berceuse by Van

Gogh, Odalisque by Matisse, Femme Nue Devant Le Jardin by Picasso and Bellevue 11 by Warhol. There is a changing programme of exhibitions plus various talks and activities on a regular basis. Guided tours and Meet the Masters sessions are held.

**Nearby attractions:** Diamont Museum, Moco Museum, Rijksmuseum, Van Gogh Museum, Vondelpark.

### The Upside Down Amsterdam
Europaboulevard 5, 1079 PC Amsterdam
**www.the-upsidedown.com**

The Upside Down is an unusual interactive combination of museum, nightclub and amusement park creating the largest Instagram museum in Europe. Each room within the building is different, and designed to encourage visitors to create images giving the impression you are standing on the ceiling or kneeling above a throne. Visitors pass through a series of twenty-five rooms such as the Royal Room, the Mondriaan Room, the quirky minimalist, experiential Dutch design room, and the Clubbing room with a dance floor that turns your world upside down. Infinity Under the Sea explores the world below sea level and reflects the fact that without a network of dykes, Amsterdam would truly be under the sea. Mirrors and glowing jellyfish create an immersive undersea experience. There is a shop and café on site. Pre-booking is essential.

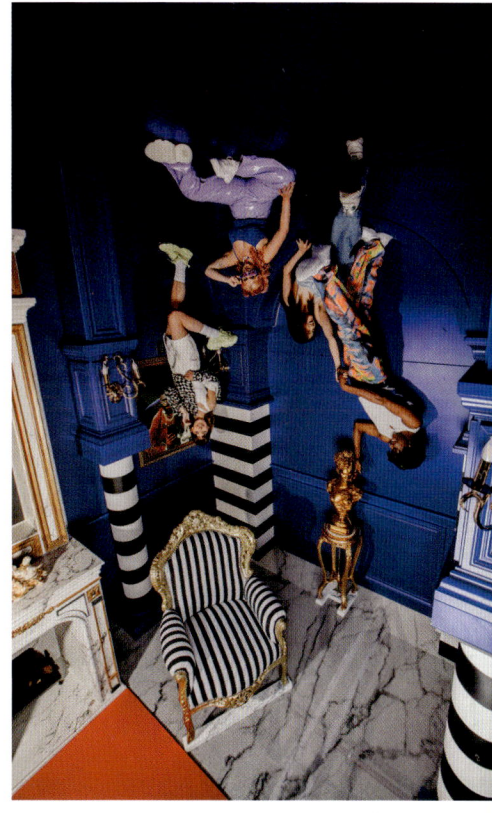

▲ *A room within Upside Down Amsterdam.* (Upside Down Amsterdam)

**Nearby attraction:** Stedelijk Museum.

### Van Gogh Museum
Museumplein 6,
1071 DJ Amsterdam
**www.vangoghmuseum.nl/en**

The Van Gogh Museum holds the largest collection of the artist's work anywhere in the world, enabling visitors to explore his art, paintings and drawings, plus work by artist friends and contemporaries as well as French and Japanese prints. Attracting more than 2 million visitors annually, it is the most visited museum in the Netherlands. Located between the Rijksmuseum and the Stedelijk, the Van Gogh Museum is in Amsterdam's museum quarter with its entrance on Paulus Potterstraat. It is approximately ten minutes' walk from the Rijksmuseum.

The Van Gogh museum is a purpose-built rectangular building designed by Gerrit Rietveld, which opened on 2 June 1973. It was extended in 1999, when an oval wing designed by Kisho Kurokawa was added. The four-storey rectangular building is home to the museum's permanent collection. A museum shop, café, and introductory exhibition about Van Gogh is located on the ground floor. On the first floor, there is a display of his work in chronological order, while on the second floor there are displays relating to painting restoration and temporary exhibition space. The third floor focuses on paintings by Van Gogh's contemporaries, highlighting how they are linked and influenced by him. The three-storey Kurokawa wing is used for temporary exhibitions, and is linked to the main building by a tunnel.

The museum contains 200 paintings, 400 drawings and 700 letters (most of which contain small drawings by Van Gogh). His work is organised chronologically into five periods, each representing a different period of his life: the Netherlands, Paris, Arles, Saint-Remy and Auvers-sur-Oise. The displays include nine self-portraits, some of which are unfinished either because they were practice pieces or he simply didn't want to finish them. Early paintings on display date back to 1882. There are examples from all his varied periods of artwork, including the brilliantly coloured artworks made in Arles such as one of sunflowers through to lesser-known ones including Orchard in Blossom. Among the famous paintings on display in the museum are:

Avenue of Poplars in Autumn, 1884

The Potato Eaters, 1885 (regarded as Van Gogh's first masterpiece due to the way in which he uses light to portray the harsh life of Dutch peasants)

Agostina Segatori Sitting in the Café du Tambourin, 1887

Wheat Field with a Lark, 1887

View from Vincent's Room in Rue Lepic, 1887

The Zouave, 1888

Bedroom in Arles, 1888 (a painting that has inspired generations of artists)

The Yellow House, 1888

Field with Irises near Arles, 1888

The Sower, 1888

Butterflies and Poppies, 1889

Sunflowers, 1889

Orchard in Blossom, 1889

Almond Blossoms, 1890

Wheatfield with Crows, 1890

Irises, 1890

There are examples of his work exploring other artistic styles such as the Courtesan, 1887, which was based on a woodcut of a Japanese painting by Kesai Eisen.

On the second floor of the museum visitors can see his painting materials, and some of the many letters that he wrote to his brother Theo and his many artist friends. These letters frequently included small sketches and drawings showing scenes upon which he was currently working.

The third-floor exhibition area contains many works by his artist contemporaries, especially from within the impressionist and post-impressionist movements. These include paintings by Édouard Manet, Henri de Toulouse-Lautrec, Georges Seurat and John Russell, and sculptures by Auguste Rodin and Jules Dalou.

Among the most important works of art in this area of the museum are:

The Painter of Sunflowers by Paul Gaugin, showing Van Gogh painting sunflowers.

Windmills near Zaandam by Claude Monet, created when he was staying in Zaandam in 1871. Van Gogh is reported to have seen this work in Paris and was impressed by it.

Tulip Fields near The Hague by Claude Monet in 1886. Monet was fascinated by the bright colours of the tulip fields and wrote to a friend commenting that the sight was 'impossible to convey with our poor colours'.

View of Amsterdam by Claude Monet, 1874, a canal-side scene complete with sailing boats at anchor.

She Who Was Once the Helmet-Maker's Beautiful Wife, a cast bronze sculpture designed by Rodin in 1885.

The core of the collection consists of art that was owned by Vincent when he died. Van Gogh sold very little of his art during his lifetime. All these unsold works passed to his brother, Theo. When Theo died six months later, his widow Johanna Van Gogh-Bonger sold some works in order to raise awareness of Van Gogh's work but kept the majority of the collection. In due course, her son, Vincent Willem Van Gogh, inherited the collection in 1925. He loaned it to the Stedelijk Museum in Amsterdam, before transferring it to the Vincent Van Gogh Foundation in 1962.

In 1991, the museum was the target of the largest art theft in the Netherlands when twenty paintings including The Potato Eaters were stolen, although all were recovered from an abandoned car within thirty-five minutes of the theft taking place.

The programme of temporary exhibitions held at the museum is quite extensive. Typical examples have included a 3D installation of Van Gogh's room at Arles; Van Gogh and the olive groves – an exploration of the varied paintings he created using olive groves as a theme; and Maurice Denis Amour – a look at the origins of the Maurice Denis print series and the relationship between collector and artist.

If visiting the museum, book tickets in advance and go as early as possible in the morning. Otherwise you can expect very long queues, especially by the middle of the day when tour groups arrive, and you might not be able to get in.

**Nearby attractions:** Diamant Museum, Moco, Rijksmuseum, Stedelijk, Vondelpark.

### Villa del Arte
Nieuwe Spiegelstraat 34, 1017 DG Amsterdam
**www.villadelarte.com**

Located close to the Rijksmuseum within the historic Spiegelkwartier, the Villa del Arte is a commercial art gallery working with more than forty international artists such as Alea Pinar du Pre, Joan Tarragó and Marti Bofarull. Work on display covers all disciplines

of contemporary photography, painting and sculpture. Villa del Arte also has branches in Barcelona, Spain and Palm Beach, USA.

**Nearby attractions:** Diamant Museum, Moco, Rijksmuseum, Van Gogh Museum.

### Vondelpark
1017 Amsterdam
**www.hetvondelpark.net**

The Vondelpark is an extremely popular public park, loved by locals and tourists alike. It is the largest city park in Amsterdam and is located within a few minutes' walk of the Rijksmuseum. It dates from 1864 when a group of Amsterdam citizens founded a public park. They acquired 8 hectares of land and commissioned landscape architect Jan David Zocher to design a park in the popular English landscape style complete with vistas, ponds, flowers and pathways to create the illusion of natural surroundings. Zocher worked on the project alongside his son, Louis Paul Zocher, both of whom were also responsible for the development of the Keukenhof gardens just outside Amsterdam.

The Vondelpark opened to the public in 1865, initially with the name Nieuwe Park. It became the Vondelpark two years later, when the statue of Dutch poet Joost van den Vondel was installed in the park. The park was subsequently extended between 1875 and 1877 to reach its current size of 47 hectares. The original design has been maintained with only a few changes to make it easier to maintain. The paths are popular with cyclists as well as walkers. The Vondelpark now has the status of a rijksmonument (national monument) and attracts more than 10 million visitors each year.

For many years, the Pavilion Building in the Vondelpark housed the Film Museum, which has now been renamed the Eye Institute and moved to a new site in the north of the city. The Vondelpark is used frequently for open-air art exhibitions, particularly during the summer period. Apart from various cafés within the park, there is also an open-air theatre on site providing a variety of shows throughout the summer. Hidden in the middle of the park under a bridge is the Vondelbunker, designed originally as a nuclear bomb shelter. In the late 1960s, it was transformed into a recording studio (used by Pink Floyd) and various practise rooms. Nowadays, the Vondelbunker plays host to a variety of activities including art exhibitions.

There are three notable sculptures located in the Vondelpark:

A 3m-high bronze monument of the Dutch poet Vondel created in 1867 by Louis Royer. Pierre Cuypers (designer of the Rijksmuseum and Amsterdam Central Station) designed the pedestal on which the statue is placed.

▼ *Statue of Vondel within the Vondelpark.*

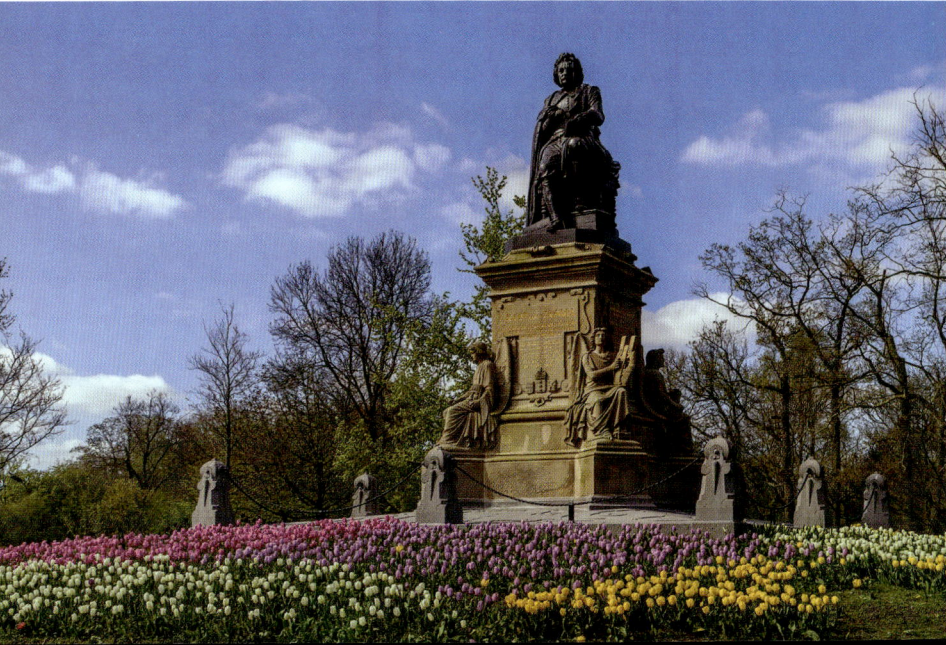

Mama Baranka is a bronze statue representing Caribbean women. It was made in 1985 by Amsterdam sculptor Nelson Carrilho.

An abstract statue known locally as Picasso's Fish Statue was first displayed in the city during an exhibition of artworks commemorating 100 years of the Vondelpark. The statue was actually designed by Picasso as a bird, and is known officially as 'Figure découpée l'Oiseau'. Made in 1965, it was a gift to Amsterdam by Picasso.

**Nearby attractions:** Diamant Museum, Moco, Rembrandt's Amsterdam, Rijksmuseum, Stedelijk Museum ,Van Gogh Museum.

## Zuidas Noord

### AkzoNobel Art Foundation
Christian Neefestraat 2,
1077 WZ Amsterdam
**www.artfoundation.akzonobel.com**

AkzoNobel is a Dutch multinational company, with its headquarters in Amsterdam. The company manufactures paints and performance coatings for use by industry and consumers, with its products sold in more than eighty countries worldwide. Since 1996, AkzoNobel has been collecting art by internationally renowned artists and rising artistic talents and displaying the artworks within its buildings. Artistic innovation and cultural reflection form key elements within the collection. The AkzoNobel Art Foundation was set up to manage and preserve cultural heritage for the future, because the company believes strongly that 'art reflects who we are – as a society, as individuals and as a company'.

In 2016, the AkzoNobel Art Foundation opened a public art space within the atrium of its headquarters building at Christian Neefestraat. The artwork on display changes regularly, with new exhibitions being set up that often involve new acquisitions fresh from the artist's studio as well as special art treasures from the historic collection. Among the artworks within

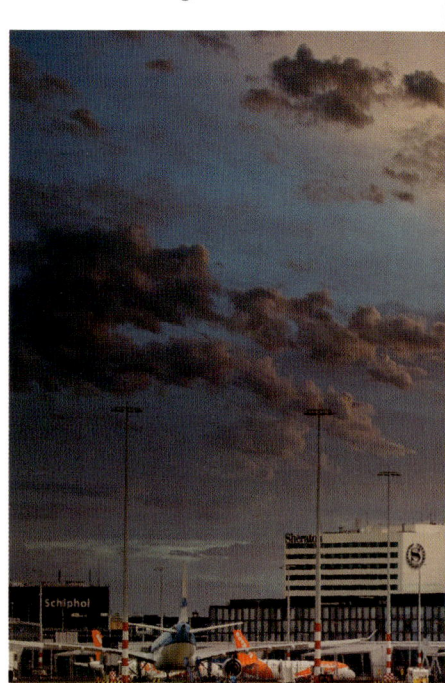

the AkzoNobel collection are earth rubbings by Herman de Vries, Luciano Magno's film Trans Amazonica, Sophie Steengracht's VR experience The Arched Garden and works by Otobong Nkanga and Buhlebezwe Siwani.

## Rijksmuseum Schiphol
Holland Boulevard,
Schiphol
Amsterdam
**www.schiphol.nl/en/at-schiphol/
discover/facilities/rijksmuseum**

Opened in 2002, and refurbished in 2018, the Rijksmuseum Schiphol offers an oasis of culture within a busy airport. Access is free and the museum is open twenty-four hours a day, seven days a week.

Rijksmuseum Schiphol was the first museum to be created within an airport. It is the only auxiliary branch of the Rijksmuseum in existence.

Within Rijksmuseum Schiphol, original masterpieces are displayed in art gallery conditions within a series of solid glass walls, enabling visitors to enjoy close-up views of the art. The museum contains a small rotating sample of famous works of art owned by the Rijksmuseum and can include landscapes, portraits and interiors. All exhibitions held in the Rijksmuseum Schiphol tend to be thematically linked, reflecting different aspects of travel,

▼ *Schiphol airport – home to a branch of the Rijksmuseum.*

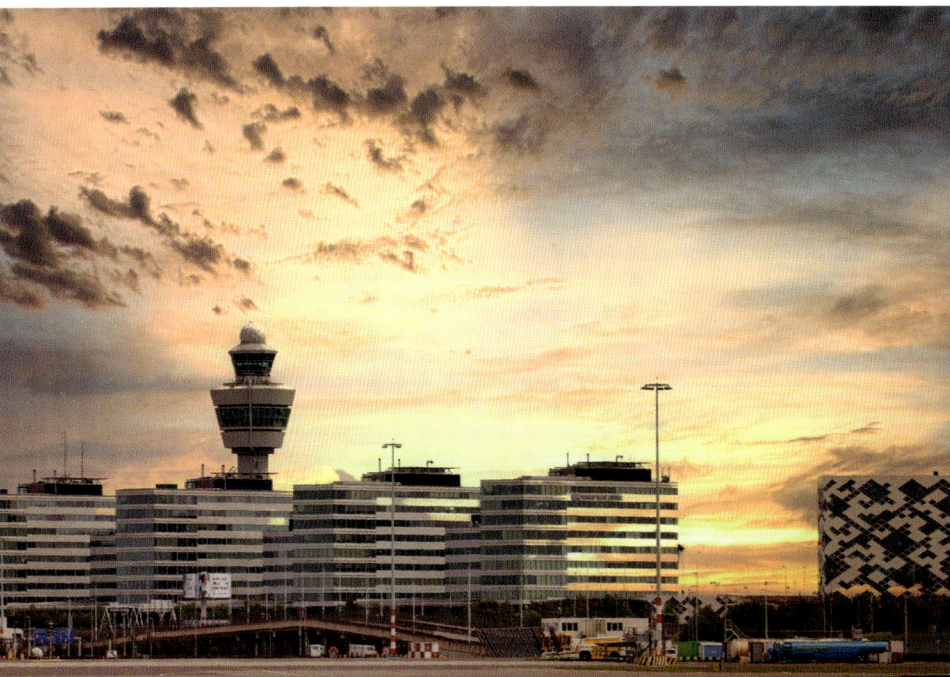

business and the history of Dutch art. Themes have included Brueghel in business, The Art of Flying – bird pieces by Melchior d'Hondecoeter, Holland and Japan – 400 years of trade, Vincent Van Gogh: nature close up and Dutch Cows – symbol of Prosperity. A recent exhibition focused on women in paintings from the seventeenth to the nineteenth centuries, including the work of female artists from the period such as Rachel Ruysch. Displays have included the work of many famous Dutch artists including Jan van Goyen, Willem van de Velde the Younger and Michiel van Mierevelt.

Access to the museum is only possible after passing through passport control. Rijksmuseum Schiphol is located on the first floor of the terminal building within the Holland Boulevard. It is sited between lounges two and three, and between E and F Piers. An adjacent museum shop provides an opportunity to buy souvenirs relating to the Rijksmuseum and other Dutch museums.

# WITHIN EASY REACH OF AMSTERDAM

## Alkmaar

A small city renowned as the centre for Gouda cheese making with numerous events held here every year, particularly the traditional cheese markets where visitors can see cheeses being weighed, bought and sold with many participants wearing traditional costumes. In terms of art and culture, the Stedelijk Museum and Kaas Museum offer the opportunity to study around six centuries of art, particularly an unusual collection of sixteenth-century female artists.

▼ *Historic houses in Alkmaar.*

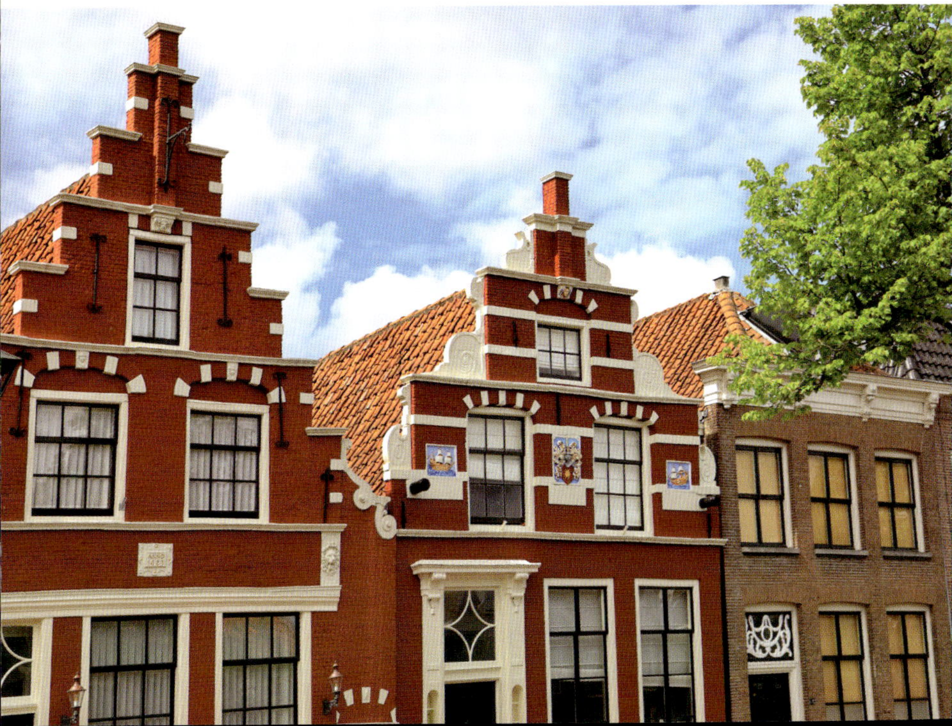

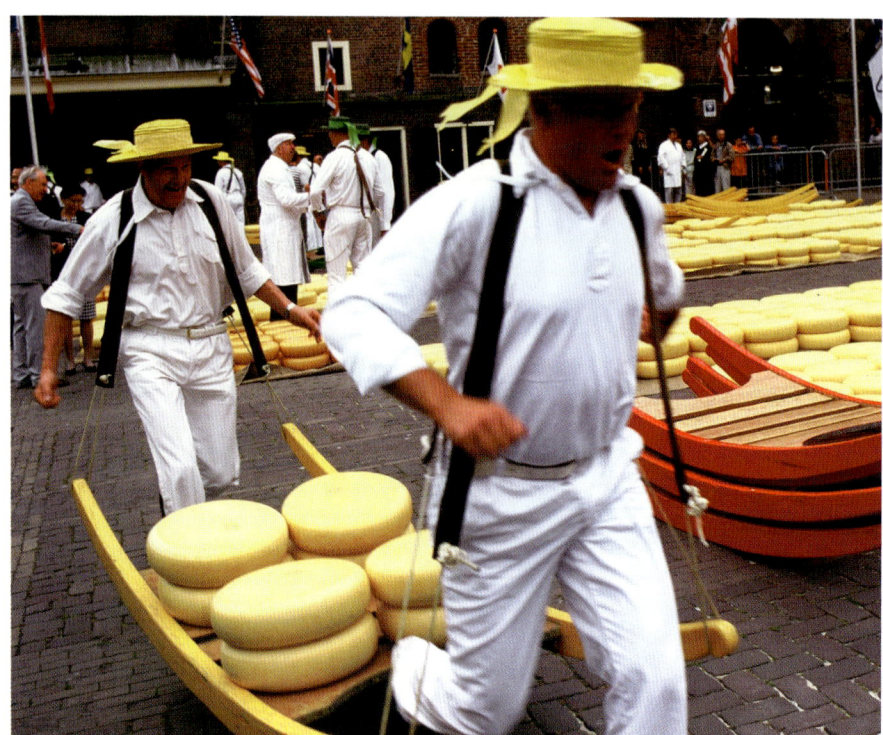

▲ *A cheese market.*

Alkmaar is 24 miles (40km) north of Amsterdam. Access by road is easy via the A10 and A9, and there are frequent trains from Amsterdam Centraal station, with the journey lasting approximately half an hour.

### Stedelijk Museum
Canadaplein1, 1811 KE Alkmaar
**www.museumalkmaar.nl**

The Stedelijk Museum is one of the oldest museums in the Netherlands and possesses extensive collections of art and applied art (crafts, pottery, glassware, silver, furnishings, textiles) especially from the seventeenth-century Dutch Golden Age as well as more contemporary works. On display are masterpieces by artists including Salomon van Ruysdael, best known for his watery landscapes and estuary scenes; Pieter Saenredam, a pioneer of paintings showing church interiors and architectural designs; and Caesar van Everdingen, who focused more on portraits and history paintings. Another influential section of the museum deals with the Bergen School, a movement in Dutch painting between 1915 and 1925 characterised by expressionist, cubist style and the use of dark colours. It was centred around a group of artists living in the village of Bergen in North Holland. Works on display include examples by Arnout Colnot, Gerrit Willem van Blaaderen, Dirk Filarski and Charley Toorop. Temporary art exhibitions focusing on a particular artist or art theme are held frequently at the Stedelijk.

### The Dutch Cheese Museum
Waagplein2, Alkmaar
**www.kaasmuseum.nl**

Founded in 1983, the Dutch Cheese Museum is located within the historic Waag building, overlooking the cheese market. It contains a vast array of items relating to the history and development of the cheese industry in Alkmaar. Among the items on display are a number of portraits of Dutch women dating back to the sixteenth century, as well as film and photographic images.

## Amstelveen

Amstelveen is just outside the centre of Amsterdam. It contains historical villages such as Bovenkerk and Nes aan de Amstel as well as new housing developments serving Amsterdam. Amstelveen is home to two art museums, and a statue of Rembrandt can be seen overlooking the River Amstel near the Amstelpark. The 20km journey from Amsterdam to Amstelveen takes around twenty minutes by car. Alternatively, it is well served by frequent bus and tram routes.

### CoBrA Museum of Modern Art
Sandbergplein 1
1181 ZX Amstelveen
**www.cobra-museum.nl**

The CoBrA Museum of Modern Art focuses on art and ideas related to the CoBrA art movement, including modern versions of CoBrA style linking it to contemporary artists, modern art movements and current affairs. The CoBrA Movement was active within Europe between 1948 and 1951 and dealt with avant-garde art in which participants utilised spontaneity and experimentation to create new types of expressionist paintings inspired by children's art style.

The majority of the CoBrA artists came from Amsterdam, Brussels and Copenhagen. Many of these works can be seen at the Cobra Museum of Modern Art. It contains a number of key works by artists working within the CoBrA Movement such as Karel Appel, Constant, Lucebert and Comelle. All these works had originally been collected by Karel P. Van Stuijvenberg and eventually donated to the museum, forming its core collection. One of the key items on display is The Fountain by Karel Appel. Standing 5m high, it contains four water outlets incorporating a bird representing freedom and a fist heralding strength. Another iconic display is the haiku-based inner garden devised by Shinkichi Tajiri, adopting a Japanese Zen style in which plates of steel reflect earth, water and sky.

There is a changing programme of exhibitions covering a variety of related topics such as Korda: Cuba; Moroccan art since 1956; and Humanity's End as a New Beginning involving watercolours painted by Japanese–American artist Yuriko Fujita Yamaguchi in which age-old myths are used to create images of what the end of the world might be like while it creates something new.

**Museum JAN**
Dorpsstraat 50,
1182 JE Amstelveen,
Near Amsterdam
**www.museumjan.nl**

Established in 1991 by Jan van der Togt, a collector of Modern Art. He was also a very successful businessman, the founder of the Tomado company renowned for its functional shelving and storage products. Some of the Tomado products such as the Tomado rack containing coloured metal shelves are now part of numerous museum design collections. Jan van der Togt had always enjoyed art and design, commissioning sculptor Ossip Zadkine to sculpt a large relief for his factory at Etten-Laur. After selling his factories in 1971, van der Togt concentrated on developing his interest in modern art by collecting artwork, sculptures, painting and contemporary glass.

Deciding to make his collection accessible to the public, van der Togt created a museum foundation and set up the Museum Jan. Among the works one is a bronze sculpture by Zadkine. Other artists with works in the museum include Jan Verschoor, glasswork by Stanislav Libenský and Vaclav Cigler, abstract impressionist works by Sam Francis and surrealist paintings by Hans Kanters. One of the museum's specialities is a collection of studio art glass, an art movement allowing glass artists to create autonomous work away from the glass factories that resulted in works by artists including Sybren Valkema, Andries Copier and Bert Frijns. The main focus is on modern sculptural glass from the twentieth and twenty-first centuries. In addition to the cast and cut glass works, other glass techniques such as blown glass are featured. The museum hosts numerous special exhibitions covering a wide range of contemporary painting, sculpture, photography and fashion.

## Brabant

Brabant is a region in the southern part of the Netherlands bordering Belgium. Van Gogh was born in Brabant and its scenery was a major influence on his work. Den Bosch ('s-Hertogenbosch) is the regional capital.
**www.visitbrabant.com/en**

### Van Gogh cycle route

Explore the world of Vincent Van Gogh by cycle and see the places he knew as a child, and where he was initially inspired to paint. It was in Brabant that he created his first masterpiece, The Potato Eaters, and also the location of many of his sketches. Information columns along the way explain his links with each location. The routes are marked by Van Gogh cycle signs at all crossroads.

The route is divided into shorter circular tours:

Van Gogh Etten-Leur South (18 miles/29km). This is the area where the Van Gogh family lived between 1875 to 1882.

Van Gogh Nunen (30 miles/49km). The route takes you past the location where The Potato Eaters was painted as well as De Vogelenzang windmill (a Van Gogh monument), the places where he lived and worked.

Van Gogh Tilburg (29 miles/48km). Tilburg is where Van Gogh took his first drawing lessons and includes the countryside he would have known so well.

Van Gogh cycle route Breda (20 miles/33km). Van Gogh is known to have visited Breda and its area while a youth at school, or when visiting family. The area is typical of the scenery that provided him with so much inspiration.

Van Gogh Zundert Northeast (34 miles/56km). This route covers six Van Gogh monuments in Zundert.

Van Gogh Helvoirt (13 miles/21km). Located in the Van Gogh National Park, it includes the parsonage in which his family lived in 1871–75 and where Van Gogh visited his family on numerous occasions, as well as Den Bosch where original Van Gogh works are on display in the Noordbrabants Museum.

## Den Bosch/'s-Hertogenbosch

A small city to the south of Amsterdam, it is officially known as 's-Hertogenbosch', but colloquially as Den Bosch. Part of North Brabant, it is best known as the birthplace of Hieronymus Bosch (1450–1516). Bosch is one of the most famous of the painters of the period and especially renowned for his highly imaginative, strange, almost nightmarish paintings

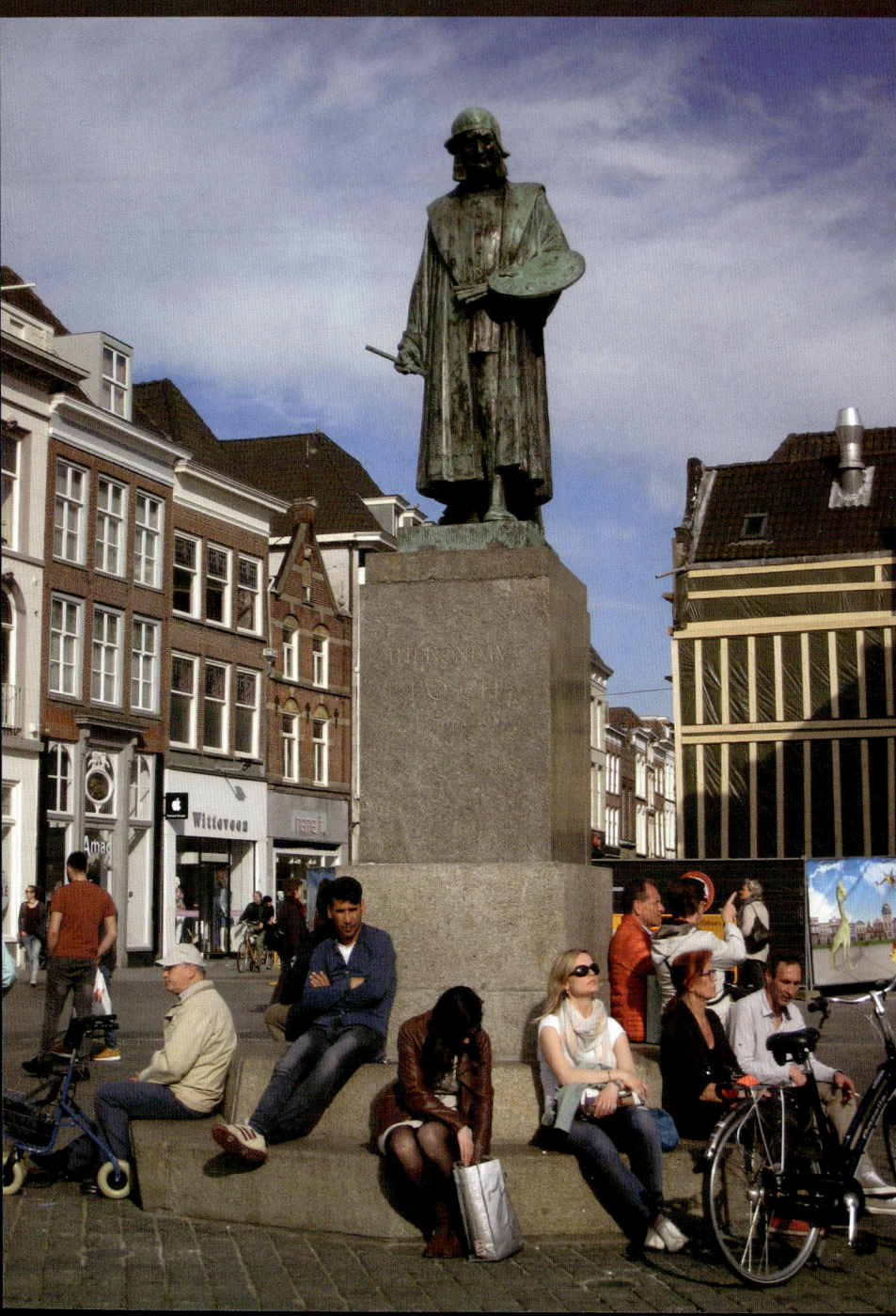

of hell. Among his works is the triptych known as The Garden of Earthly Delights with scenes ranging from the Garden of Eden to the Last Judgement, complete with fantastical animals such as unicorns. Other works by Bosch include numerous religious paintings such as the Temptation of St Anthony and The Creation of the World.

A statue of Hieronymus Bosch can be seen in the marketplace, directly opposite the house in which he lived.

It takes just over an hour to drive the 54 miles (87km) via the A2 between Amsterdam and Den Bosch, or just under an hour by train from Amsterdam Centraal.

### Jheronimus Bosch art centre
Jeroen Boschplein 2,
5211ML Den Bosch
**www.jheronimusbosch-artcenter.nl**

Dedicated to the life and work of Hieronymus (Jheronimus) Bosch, it contains replicas of many of his works. Guided tours can be arranged that explore the works of art, his lifestyle and the hidden visual language within his paintings. The building is a former church and panoramic views of the city can be enjoyed from the tower.

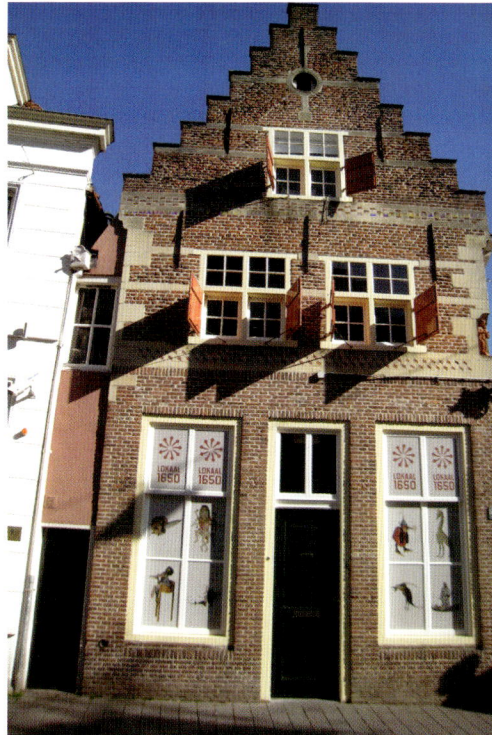

▲ *The exterior of the Jheronimus Bosch art centre.*
(Angela Youngman)

### Noordbrabants Museum
Verwersstraat 41,
5211HT Den Bosch
**www.hetnoordbrabantsmuseum.nl/en**

This museum focuses on the art and culture of the Brabant region. It contains numerous paintings by Van Gogh, as well as works by Pieter Brueghel, Theodoor van Thulden, Jan Sluijters and Ambrosius Bosschaert.

◀ *Statue of Hieronymus Bosch.* (Angela Youngman)

It has a particularly large collection of paintings, prints and drawings from the sixteenth to the nineteenth centuries, including flower paintings by Cornelis van Spaendonck, plus contemporary art by artists including Jolanda van Gennip, Thomas Trum and Mark Manders. There are displays of applied arts in the form of textiles, silver and craft work. The museum holds a changing programme of exhibitions such as Van Gogh in Brabant and Discovering Modernity focusing on the work of Picasso, Dali, Klee and Mondrian. One of its most stunning exhibitions was a special one in 2016 to celebrate the anniversary of Hieronymus Bosch in which a collection of his works was gathered up from all over the world for the first time. The city itself does not possess any works by Bosch, only replicas.

**Design Museum Den Bosch**
De Mortel 4,
5211 HV Den Bosch
**www.designmuseum.nl**

Originally known as the Stedelijk Museum 's-Hertogenbosch, it changed its name to Design Museum Den Bosch in 2019. The museum aims to highlight the influence of design in daily life. It holds a changing programme of exhibitions dealing with themes such as radical Italian design between 1960 and 1980, Californian design, Goth as a subculture across two centuries of cultural history dealing with ways of designing darkness, and the future of the human body.

## Den Haag (The Hague)

A coastal city complete with its own beaches, The Hague is the third largest city in the country, located to the south of Amsterdam. Architecturally, it is a very modern city with skyscrapers, but also a large number of mainly seventeenth- and eighteenth-century buildings located in the older part of the city. Unlike other Dutch cities characterised by canals and narrow streets, The Hague has long and wider boulevard-style streets. Museums such as the Mauritshuis contain extensive collections of Dutch masterpieces, as well as a considerable number of modern, contemporary pieces of art. The Escher Museum is devoted to the work of Dutch graphics artist M. C. Escher. Among the artists who have lived in Den Haag are Van Gogh, Jan Steen, Jan Van Goyen and Paulus Potter. The city was also the setting for an artistic grouping known as the Hague School during the nineteenth century.

The 39-mile (64km) journey by car from Amsterdam to The Hague takes approximately an hour via the A4. The train from Amsterdam Centraal takes around fifty minutes.

## Buitenmuseum
Dunne Bierkade 17
Den Haag
**www.buitenmuseum.com**

An outdoor museum containing the homes of Dutch master painters Jan van Goyen, Paulus Potter and other artists. Van Goyen lived at Dunne Bierkade 16a, and it is where he painted hundreds of paintings. Fellow painter Jan Steen painted the van Goyen family in this house. Dunne Bierkade 17 was the home of animal painter Paulus Potter and it is where he painted 'the Bull', his most famous work. Inside the house, there are stunning ceiling paintings created by Stortenbeker, who worked for the royal palace. During the nineteenth century, a family of Jewish artists known as the brothers Verveer lived in Dunne Bierkade 18. Other nineteenth-century painters living here included Bartholomeus van Hove and Johannes Bosboom, while van Gogh was seen frequently in the area. He initially lived and worked in a nearby courtyard as an art dealer. Reprinted examples of Van Gogh's art related to the neighbourhood form the central part of an exhibition within van Goyen's house.

## De Panorama Mesdag
Zeestraat 65,
2518AA The Hague
**www.panorma-mesdag.nl/en**

Painted by Hendrik Willem Mesdag, his wife and students, this is a unique 'circular' painting of Scheveningen during the nineteenth century. It is believed to be the biggest painting of its type in Europe. The panorama measures 120m long, 14m high and nearly 40m in diameter. The design gives the impression that the viewer is standing high on top of a tower, looking out over Scheveningen, especially the beach as it appeared in 1880. In creating the panorama, Mesdag worked from photographs, and sketches of varying scenes around Scheveningen.

## Design Museum Dedel
Prinsegracht 15,
2512 EW The Hague
**www.designmuseumdedel.nl/en**

Located in a beautiful seventeenth-century house, the Design Museum focuses on artwork relating to the advertising, graphic arts and design sectors over the past 150 years. Among the themes covered within the permanent exhibitions are topics such as the Russian avant-garde, art deco and the Seventies. Artworks include everything from posters and postcards to wallpaper, stamps, TV commercials and storage cans. It comprises one of the largest collections in Europe. There is a changing programme of exhibitions, which might focus on a theme or an individual such as Jan Sluyters. The house itself contains interesting artistic features such as staircase stucco work by Italian craftsmen. It is one of the few

Dutch interiors that still contains much of the original wallpaper, some dating back to 1799, revealing a variety of designs and historical styles.

### Escher in het Paleis Museum
Lange Voorhout 74,
2514 EH Den Haag
www.escherinhetpaleis.nl

Maurits Cornelis Escher (1898–1972) is regarded as one of the most influential graphic artists worldwide due to the way in which he used perspective, space and reality. This museum contains a large proportion of his work, including the distinctive lithographs Belvedere and the Hand with Reflecting Sphere, showing the interior of a room within the sphere, while his work Convex and Concave explores differing perspectives. There are also documentaries on his life and work, and interviews with Escher, which can be watched.

The building in which the museum is located is itself a work of art. It was once the home of Dutch royalty, owned by Queen Emma, the Queen Mother in the early part of the twentieth century, and was later the home of other members of the Royal Family. It is owned by The Hague municipality on the basis that it can only be used for cultural activities. The interior staircase is itself an optical illusion as it gives the impression of rising to the second floor, but actually ends on the first. Temporary exhibitions are often held here, such as displays relating to Auguste Rodin and Venetian glass.

### Fotomuseum Den Haag
Stadhouderslaan 43
2517 HV Den Haag
www.fotomuseumdenhaag

Located next to the Kunstmuseum, the Fotomuseum Den Haag was one of the first Dutch museums to focus on photography. It concentrates on the provision of a changing programme of exhibitions and over the years it has hosted displays of the work of photographers including Emmy Andriesse, Sally Mann, Erwin Olaf, Robin du Puy and Peter Fink. The museum aims to 'give people a space for quiet reflection, where they can discover the layers, meanings and context of photography'.

### Galerie Pulchri
Lange Voorhout 15
2514 EA Den Haag
www.pulchri.nl

Founded in 1847, the Pulchri Studio is an artists' association and gallery. It hosts around sixty different exhibitions per year. The subject matter can be wide ranging, for example exhibitions relating to Riëlle Beekmans showing amusing statues of dogs in a garden and an exhibition by Lynda Deutz exploring the invisible reality where individuals do not seem to exist.

**KM21**
Stadhouderslaan 43,
2517 HV Den Haag
**www.km21.nl**

Formerly known as the GEM Museum of contemporary art, KM21 undertakes a changing programme of exhibitions showcasing Dutch and international artists, emerging talents as well as established artists. Typical exhibitions have included works by Oscar Murillo, Tala Madani, Kati Heck, Folkert de Jong, Shirin Neshat and Mickey Yang.

**Huis van het Boek**
Prinsessegracht 30-31,
2514 AP Den Hague
**www.huisvanhetboek-nl**

This is the oldest book museum in the world, exploring all aspects of books across the centuries. The collections on display include superb examples of decorated medieval manuscripts and other illustrated books. Central to the collections on display are works collected by Baron Westreenen van Tiellandt and his nephew, Johan Meerman, during the eighteenth and nineteenth centuries. The museum reflects their wide interests, not just in books, but also in objects from ancient cultures such as Egypt, Rome and Greece. There are many pieces from van Tiellandt's collection on display as well as family portraits and souvenirs from his travels. The museum has continued to develop the book collection, focusing on the period from 1850 to the present day. There are permanent displays of books highlighting form and design, as well as an exhibition of ex libris, the printed proprietary marks used in books, of which it holds the largest collection in the Netherlands.

**Kasteel Duivenvoorde**
Laan van Duivenvoorde 4,
2252 AK Voorschoten
**www.kasteelduivenvoorde.nl**

Located close to Den Haag, the castle houses an extensive art collection with works by Dutch masters including Adriaen Steengracht, Gerrit Alberts, Jan van Ravesteyn, Jacob Cuyp, Heinrich Siebert, Jan van Goyen and many more. There are extensive collections of furniture, drawings, sculpture, ceramics, Delft blue pottery, Chinese porcelain and costumes on display.

The castle is quite unusual as it has remained a family possession for eight centuries, which has meant that collections have remained intact. One of the key areas are the fourteen historic interiors dating between the seventeenth and nineteenth centuries that are permanently on display, showing interiors that have remained unchanged over the years. Wallpaper and even a mother-of-pearl ceiling are still in good condition and there is a children's ceiling design with

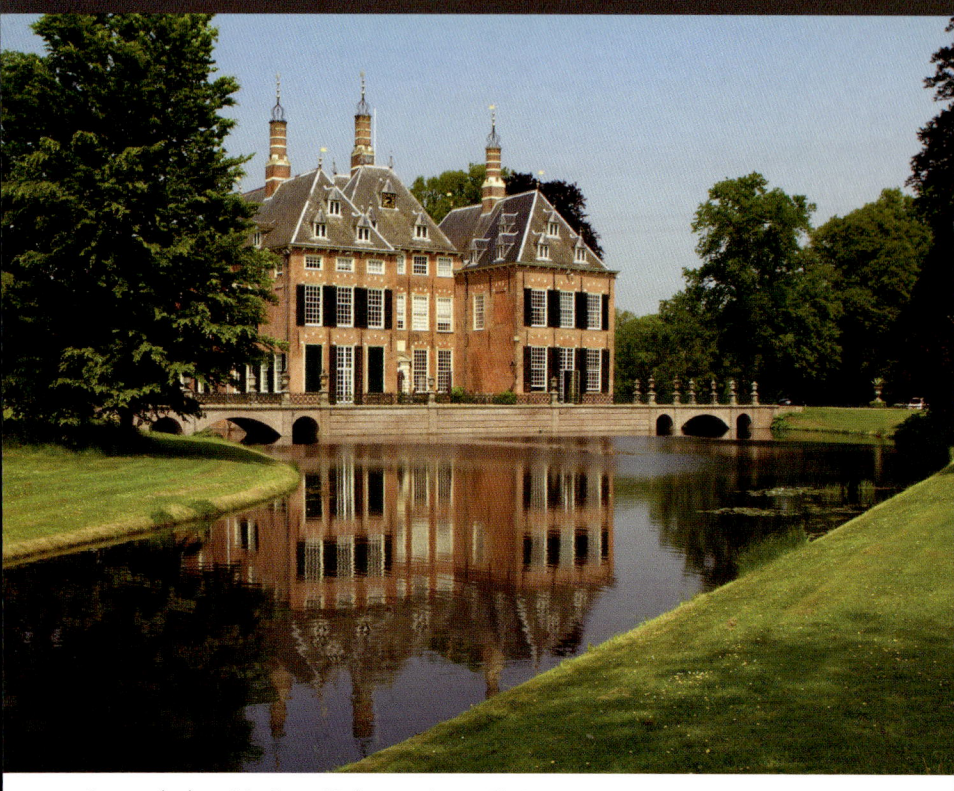

▲ *Panoramic view of the Kasteel Duivenvoorde near The Hague.*

animal motifs. The castle is a short distance outside The Hague, between Voorschoten and Leidschendam.

### Kunstmuseum Den Haag
Stadhouderslaan 41,
2517 HV Den Haag
**www.kunstmuseum.nl**

For admirers of the work of Piet Mondrian, the Kunstmuseum is definitely the place to visit. It possesses 300 of his works, one of the largest collections worldwide. The display on Mondrian enables visitors to study the way his art developed into abstract art, and see how he was influenced by painters including Monet, Picasso and Kandinsky.

Apart from the Mondrian collection, the Kunstmuseum contains more than 160,000 works covering fine art, applied art, Chinese glass and fashion. There are major collections relating to the Hague School, impressionism, art nouveau, Dutch Delftware, expressionism and silver from Indonesia.

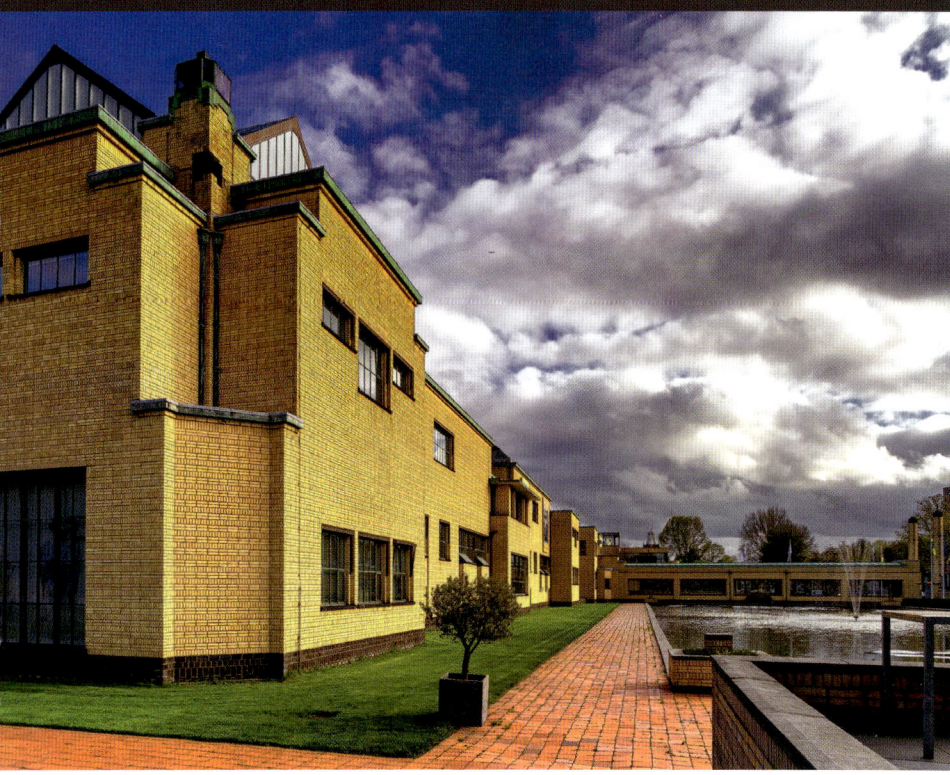

▲ *The Kunstmuseum Den Hague.*

There is a changing programme of exhibitions, which have included Alphonse Mucha, Grayson Perry and Paula Rego. The museum is located within a spectacular art deco building, complete with decorative brickwork and tiling.

## Louwman Museum
Leidsestraatweg 57,
2594 BB The Hague
**www.louwmannmuseum.nl/en**

The Louwman Museum contains a unique private collection of 275 cars and artwork created by Dutch car importer Evert Louwman. It covers the period from the development of the car since 1886, when the first vehicle was built, to the present day. All types of cars are on display, including early examples, vintage cars, classic cars, racing cars and luxury limousines. Some are extremely unusual, such as the Brooke Swan Car with bodywork representing a swan gliding through water, complete with lotus flower design in gold leaf, and electric bulbs within the swan's eyes allowing it to glow in the dark. There is also a smaller version 'Cygnet the Baby Swan Car' made for the Maharaja of Nabha, which has two cygnets (one large, one small) at the front.

In addition to the superb vehicle collection, the museum possesses the largest collection of automotive art including paintings, sculptures and posters in the world. The artwork is displayed in a specially designed room. On the ground floor of the museum is a square containing 1920s house fronts, mostly from buildings in The Hague.

### Mesdag Collection
Laan van Meerdervoort 7-F,
The Hague
**www.demesdagcollectie.nl**

The Mesdag Collection contains the work of nineteenth-century artist Hendrik Willem Mesdag and his wife Sientje as well as the work of numerous French and Dutch artists. Mesdag was so enthused by the artworks he possessed that he built a museum specifically to allow them to be seen by everyone. During his lifetime, he used to personally guide people around the museum, talking about the various paintings. The museum offers an opportunity to discover the work and life of Hendrik and Sientje as well as their art collection, which includes works from painters from the Hague

School and the Barbizon movement. Among the artists represented here are Corot, Daubigny, Millet, Willem Maris, Johannes Bosboom, Anton Mauve and Lawrence Alma-Tadema. Also on display is Mesdag's collection of Japanese decorative art containing sculptures, vases, porcelain, samurai and daggers decorated with relief decorations and a collection of Colenbrander ceramics.

### Mauritshuis
Plein 29,
2501 CM The Hague
**www.mauritshuis.nl/en**

Located within the historical city centre, the Mauritshuis is adjacent to the Binnerhof, the Dutch parliament buildings. The collection of artworks on display is outstanding, including iconic works such as Johannes Vermeer's Girl with a Pearl Earring, and Rembrandt's The Anatomy Lesson of Dr Nicolaes Tulp. Other well-known artists represented here include Steen, Hals, van Dyke and Rubens. There are around 800 paintings, plus a large collection of miniatures and sculptures focusing on Dutch and Flemish paintings from 1400 to 1800. It has a superb collection of works by Steen depicting Dutch daily life in the seventeenth century, plus works of art by Dutch female painters working during the Golden Age of Dutch painting. Architecturally, the building dates from the seventeenth century

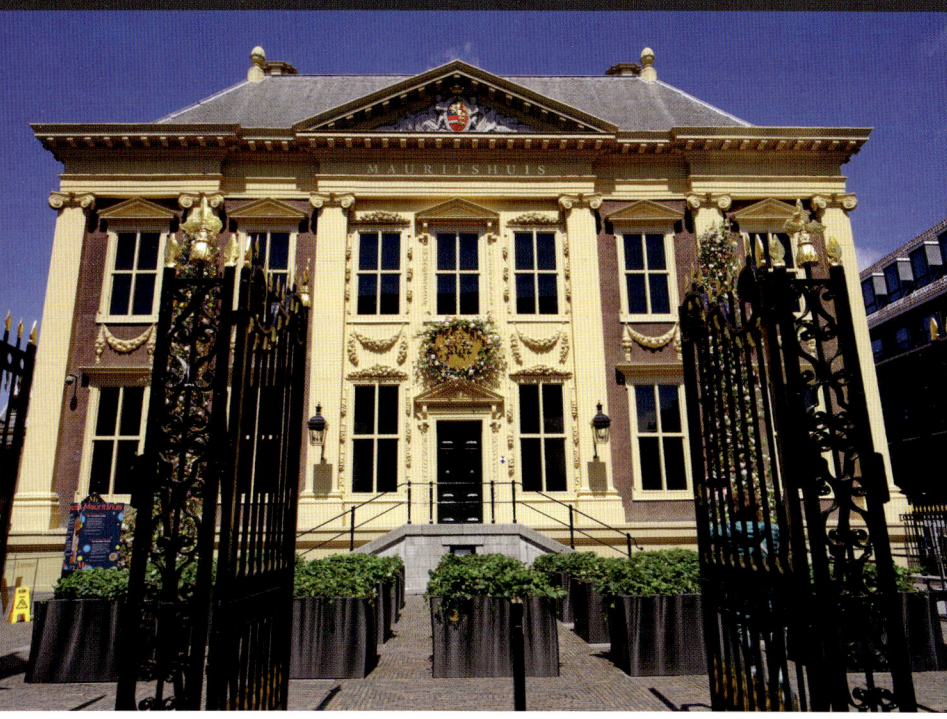

▲ *The Mauritshuis Museum in The Hague.*

and was constructed in the Dutch classical style.

### Museum Bredius
Lange Vijverberg 14,
2513 AC Den Haag
**www.museumbredius.nl**

Located in an eighteenth-century mansion, the Museum Bredius contains the private collection of art historian Dr Abrahm Bredius (1855–1946). During his lifetime, he acquired a collection of more than 200 paintings, plus drawings, silverware and porcelain.

Among the highlights of the many works on display are paintings by Rembrandt, Meindert Hobbema, Steen, and van der Neer.

### Museum Sophiahof
Sophialaan 10,
2514 JR The Hague

The building is a national monument and displays focus on the story of Dutch colonial history in the East, including the stories of eyewitnesses and their descendants. Paintings and drawings provide visual depictions of Dutch colonial history.

### Prince William V Gallery

Buitenhof 33,
2513 AH Den Haag
**www.mauritshuis.nl/nu-te-doen/vaste-collection**

Often described as the hidden gem of The Hague, this gallery was built by Prince William V of Orange-Nassau to allow the public to see his impressive collection of paintings. When the museum opened in 1774, it was the first in the Netherlands to allow public access. More than 150 old masters are hung on silk covered walls. The room is extremely lavish and opulent, creating a very regal appearance. Among the paintings on display are works by Rubens, Jan Steen, Gerard van Honthorst and Paulus Potter. The collection is a modern reconstruction of the original gallery, as many of the original paintings

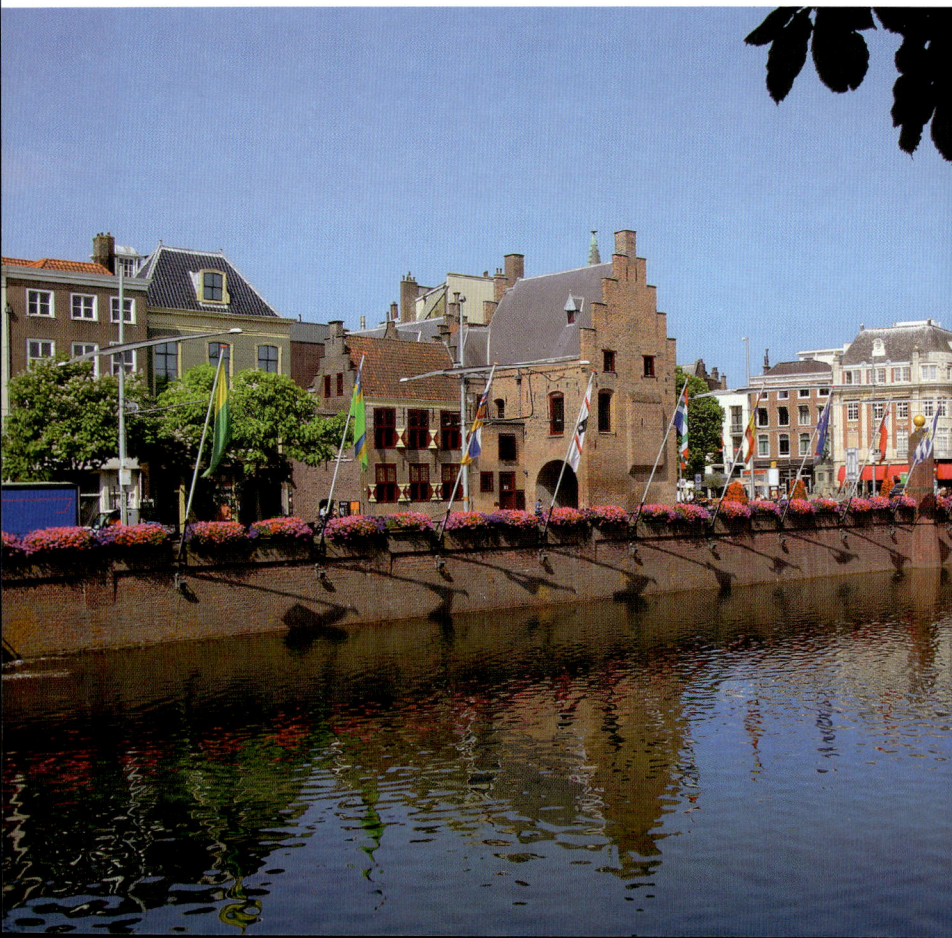

were dispersed during wartime. The gallery is now in the care of the Mauritshuis, which owns the remainder of Prince William's collection. Access to the Prince William V Gallery is via a special staircase linking the building with the Mauritshuis.

▼ *View towards the Prisoners' Gate and the Prince William V Gallery.*

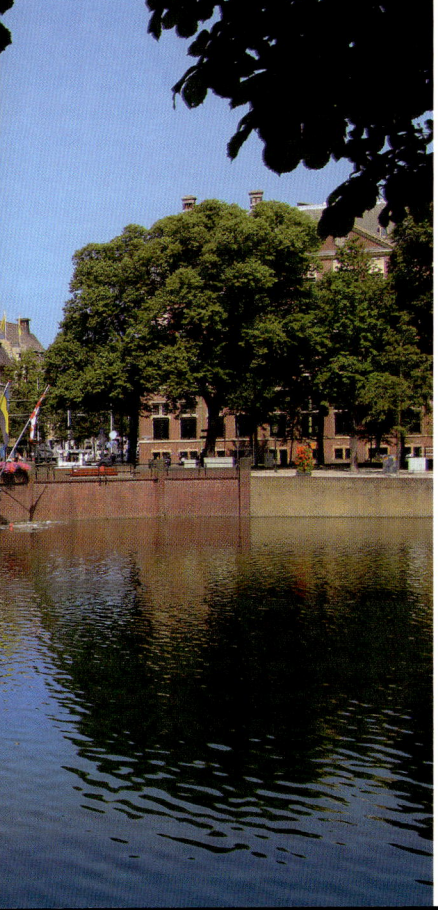

## The Hague's Historic Museum
Korte Vijverberg7,
2513 AB Den Haag
**www.haagshistorischmuseum.nl/en**

The building has always played a major role in the city, since it was here that the archers of the Guild of St Sebastian gathered. Among the objects on display are numerous paintings from the Dutch Golden Age, twentieth-century graphic art and posters, architectural drawings, civic guard paintings, group portraits of civic dignitaries and numerous city views. Some of the cityscapes date back to 1553.

## Delft

Best known as the home of the characteristic blue and white Delftware pottery, it was also the birthplace of the Dutch master painter Johannes Vermeer. Other famous painters active in Delft included Jan Steen, Pieter de Hooch, Paulus Potter and Carel Fabritius. William of Orange, also known as William the Silent, led the war for independence from the Spanish Empire and in 1584 he was assassinated within the Prinsenhof – a building that is now a museum and art gallery.

Delft is located close to the Dutch coast, around 40 miles (67km) south of Amsterdam. It is accessible by train or by road, with journey times typically less than an hour.

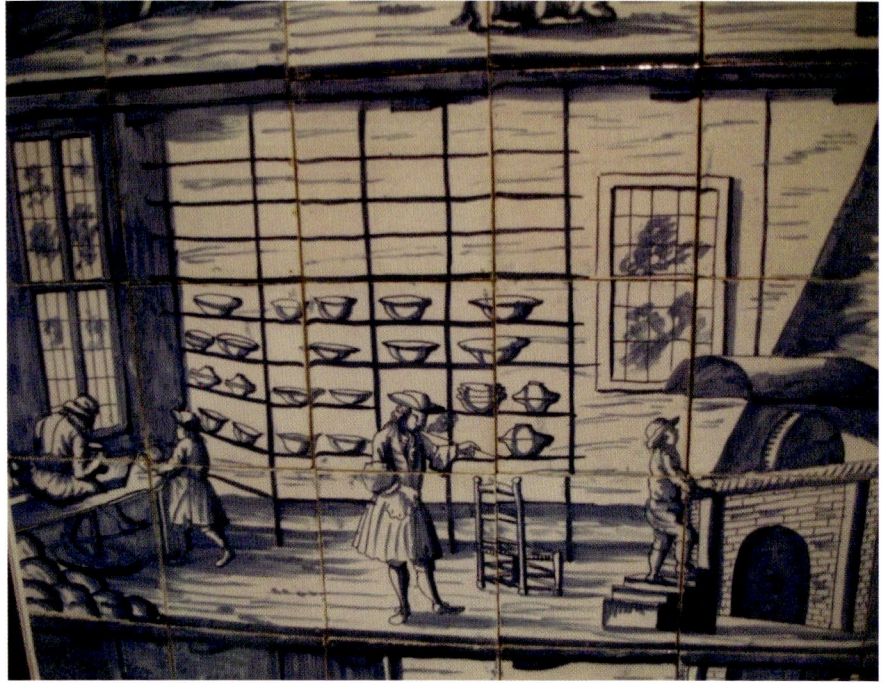

▲ *Typical seventeenth-century blue and white Delftware.* (Karis Youngman)

## Museum Paul Tetar van Elven
Koornmarkt 67,
2611 EC Delft
**www.museumpkaultetarvanelven.nl**

Paul Tetar van Elven was a nineteenth-century artist and drawing teacher at the local polytechnic school. He collected art, antiques, Delft pottery and Oriental porcelain, weapons and costumes. In his will, he stipulated that his home and all its contents should become a museum enabling visitors to enjoy the artworks he had collected

over the years. The interior of the house has remained relatively unchanged, so visitors experience what life was like in a late nineteenth-century Dutch house. The rooms are lavishly furnished, just as van Elven left it. On the walls are many family portraits that he created.

## Royal Delft
Rotterdamsweg 196, 2628AR Delft
**www.royaldelft.com**

The characteristic blue and white Delft pottery is instantly recognisable

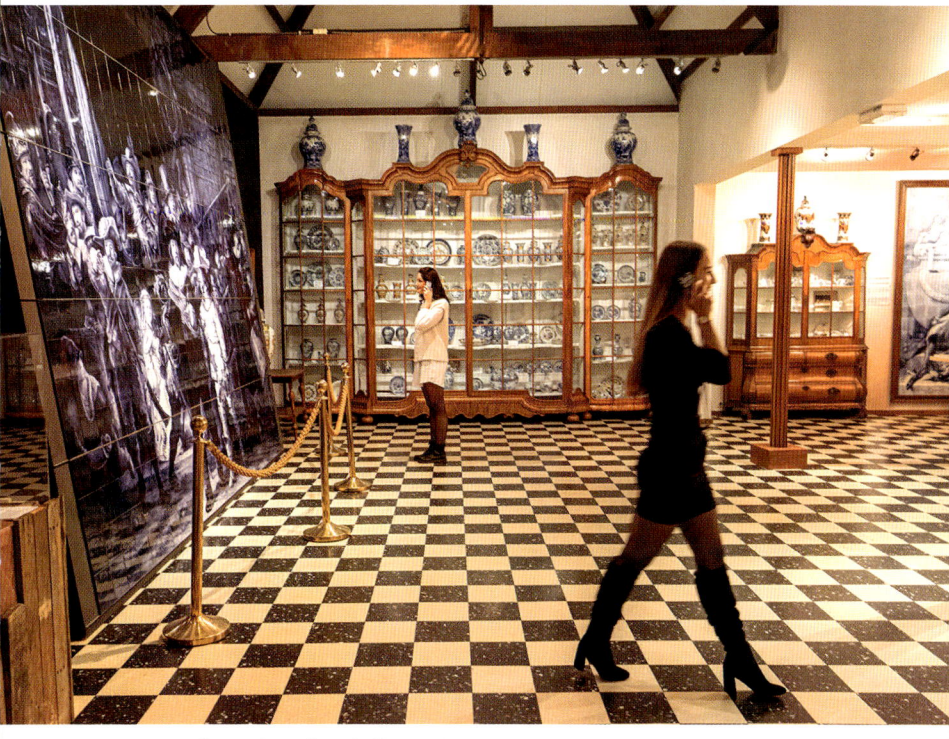

▲ *Royal Delftware on display, from gigantic tile murals to small plates.* (Royal Delft)

worldwide. The museum enables visitors to see how this art form has developed since its creation in the seventeenth century. Explore the cultural heritage resulting from the development of Delft blue, as well as watching a master painter at work, painting by hand on the pottery just as it has been done for centuries.

The museum contains the King Willem II Delftware collection, enabling visitors and students to explore the varied shapes and decorative techniques that have been used. Other displays highlight the story of Thooft & Co. in the late nineteenth century, who revitalised Delftware, as well as the work of contemporary artists including Jan Snoeck, Borek Sipek and Dick Bruna with his much-loved children's character Miffy. Temporary exhibitions on related subjects are held frequently, such as a display exploring the links between Delft Blue and the art of tattooing that highlighted the way in which images were applied by hand using a needle or paintbrush.

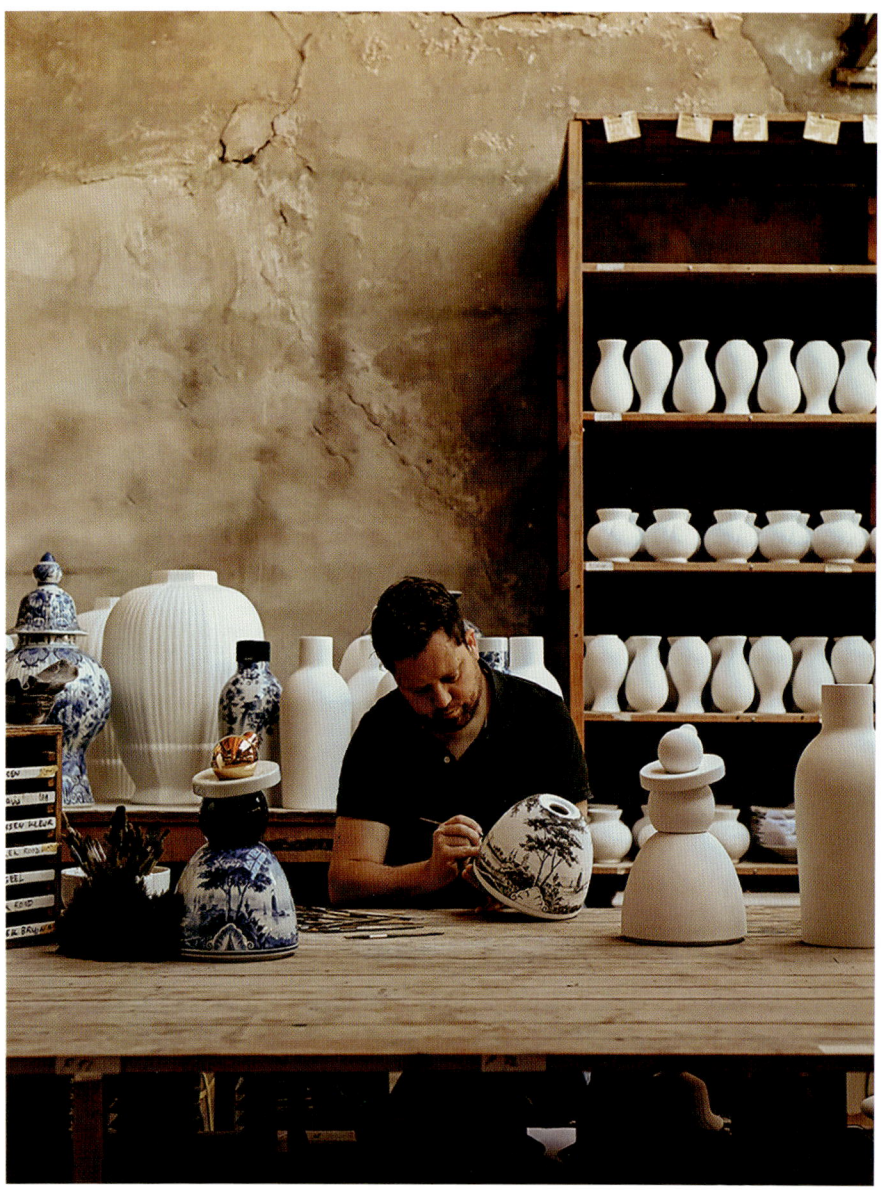

▲ *Hand painting Royal Delftware.* (Royal Delft)

### Museum Prinsenhof Delft
Sint Agathaplein1, 2611HR Delft
**www.prinsenhof-delft.nl**

The Museum Prinsenhof tells the story of William of Orange, who was responsible for the creation of the Dutch Republic following its war of independence with Spain. There are many sixteenth- and seventeenth-century paintings, together with silverware, seventeenth-century textiles and Delftware. The Delft Masters is a permanent exhibition focusing on the leading painters and artists in each genre. Among the masterpieces on display is a self-portrait of Michiel van Mierevelt as he transfers his studio to his grandson.

There are works by Pieter de Hooch and seascapes by Heerman Witmont showing scenes of ships amid stormy scenes. In addition, there is a changing programme of temporary exhibitions, which have included art nouveau and a display purely on Pieter de Hooch.

### Vermeer Centum Delft
Voldersgracht 21, 2611 EV Delft
**www.vermeerdelft.nl**

Renowned for his beautiful Dutch interiors, Johannes Vermeer lived

▼ *Exterior of the Vermeer Centre in Delft.* (Vermeer Centre)

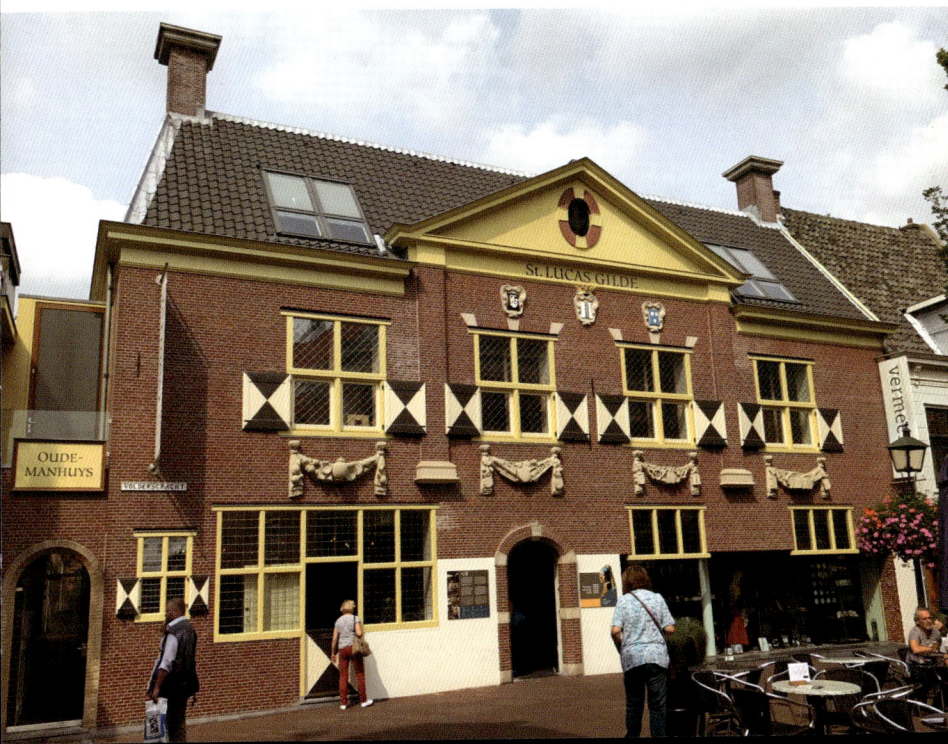

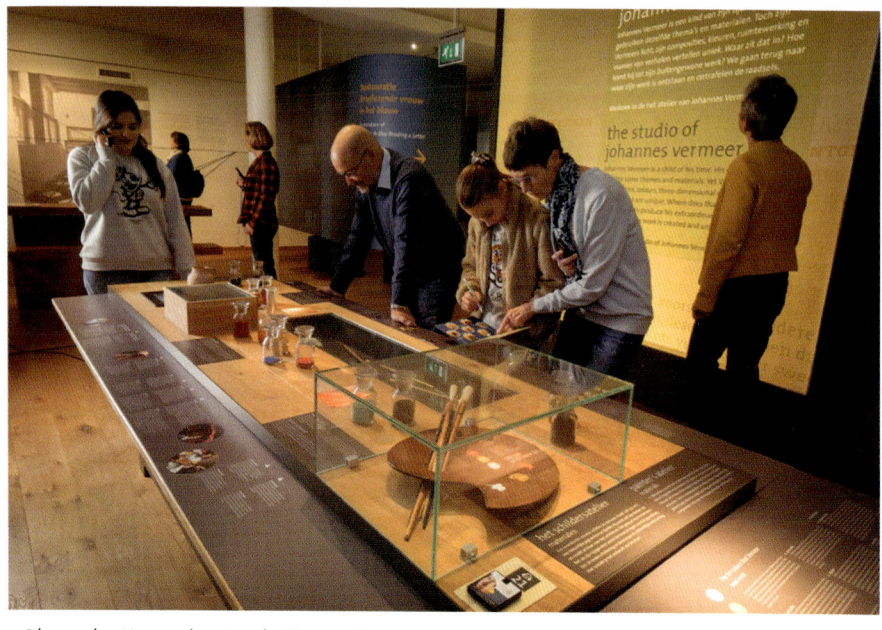

▲ *Discovering Vermeer's art at the Vermeer Centre.* (Vermeer Centum)

and worked in the city of Delft. The Vermeer Centre provides a great introduction to the life and times of this seventeenth-century painter. Although the centre does not own any of the original paintings, it has created an invaluable resource for anyone who wants to explore Vermeer's work. It includes a study of his works, with high-quality reproductions hung in chronological order showing how his style developed throughout his career. Other exhibits include a studio where visitors can explore colour, his experiments with the camera obscura, hidden views and perspective, along with love symbols that can be seen in the paintings. There are many original seventeenth-century artefacts on display, including items that are typical of those seen in his paintings such as pots and candlesticks. Guided tours of Delft and the Vermeer Centre can be booked.

## Haarlem

Known as the most Flemish city of the north, Haarlem is a city of narrow streets, historic buildings and squares. Fire destroyed much of the city in 1576, resulting in a massive rebuilding process led by the city architect, Lieven de Key. His work is regarded as extremely important in Dutch architectural history and every building, doorway or even gable created by de Key or one of his followers is designated as a 'rijksmonument'. The most important artist associated with Haarlem is Frans Hals the Elder. A Dutch Golden Age painter, he played an influential role in the development of seventeenth-century group portraiture.

Haalem is 11 miles (17km) to the west of Amsterdam using the A5 and A200 roads. There are frequent trains from Amsterdam Centraal station, with the journey taking around fifteen minutes.

## Frans Hals Museum

Groot Heiligland 62, 2011 ES Haarlem and Grote Markt 16, 2011 RD Haarlem
**www.franshalsmuseum.nl**

Portraits, especially group portraits, were highly popular during the Dutch Golden Age of painting, as people wanted to show off their wealth and status. Frans Hals became one of the most sought after masters of the genre. The Guild of St Luke, Haarlem, registered him as a master painter in 1610. One of his most famous early paintings is the Banquet of Officers of the Civic Guard of St George at Haarlem (1616), utilising loose brushwork skills unlike any other painter of the

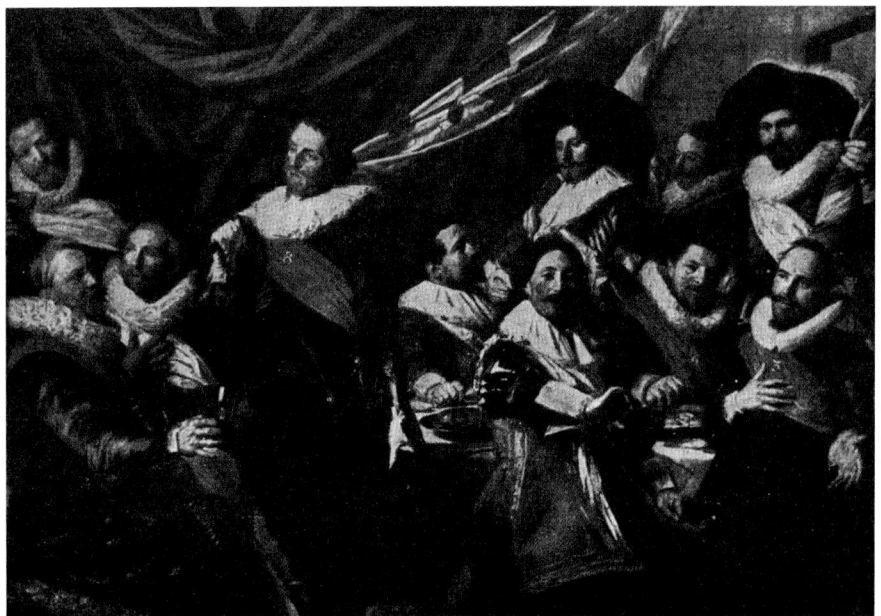

▲ *Scene from a Frans Hals painting showing the officers of the St George Civic Guard, Haarlem.*

period. A second portrait of the same scene was undertaken in 1627 displaying his skills in creating dramatic effects. Other well-known paintings by him are The Merry Toper of 1627, showing a man clutching a beer mug, and Malle Babbe, showing an elderly woman laughing with an owl perched on her shoulder. The museum contains the largest collection of the artist's work worldwide, including the Civic Guard paintings.

Haarlem began collecting art more than 400 years ago and displaying it within the city hall, known as the Grote Markt. Over the years, the museum has spread across two sites, the Grote Markt and the Groot Heiligland. One ticket covers both sites and they are within walking distance of each other. Apart from the Frans Hals collection, the museum contains works of art dating from the sixteenth and seventeenth centuries, such as works by Jacob Jordaens, a collection of furnished eighteenth-century doll's houses, antique furniture and objects, plus extensive collections of Haarlem impressionist art. There is a changing programme of contemporary art and photography exhibitions.

### Teylers Museum
Spaarne 16, 2011 CH Haarlem
**www.teylersmuseum.nl**

Teylers Museum is one of the oldest in the Netherlands, dating from 1784. It is the result of a bequest from Pieter Teyler, a wealthy Haarlem resident, and initially it occupied just the Oval Room. Visitors entered via marble corridor to view artworks and scientific inventions. Napoleon, Tsar Alexander

▼ *Teylers Museum, Haarlem.*

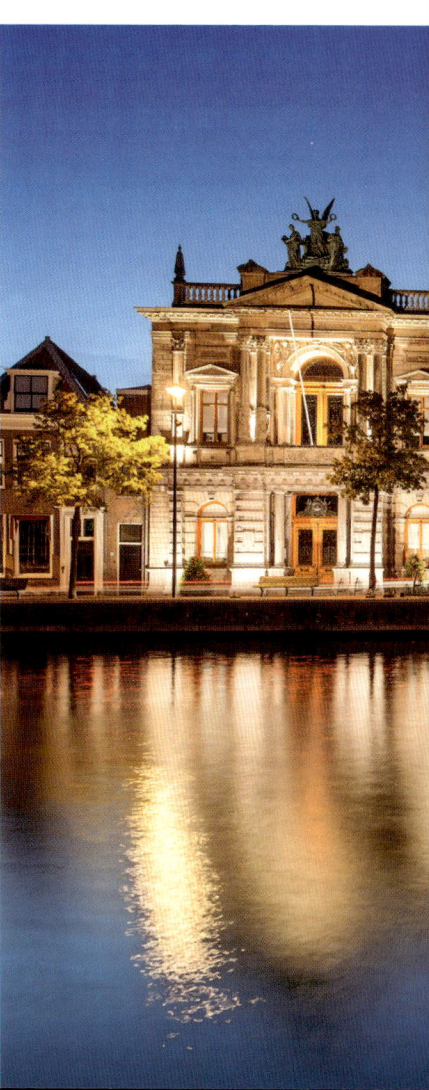

and Albert Einstein are among the many people who have visited over the centuries. The museum now occupies a complex of four linked houses extensively restored to their original colours and design. Visitors can explore all parts of the museum, including Teyler's original house. The Oval Room is the only authentic eighteenth-century museum interior in the world. Other exhibits include art and prints by various artists such as Rembrandt, Michelangelo, Raphael and Goltzius, plus fossils, coins and historic

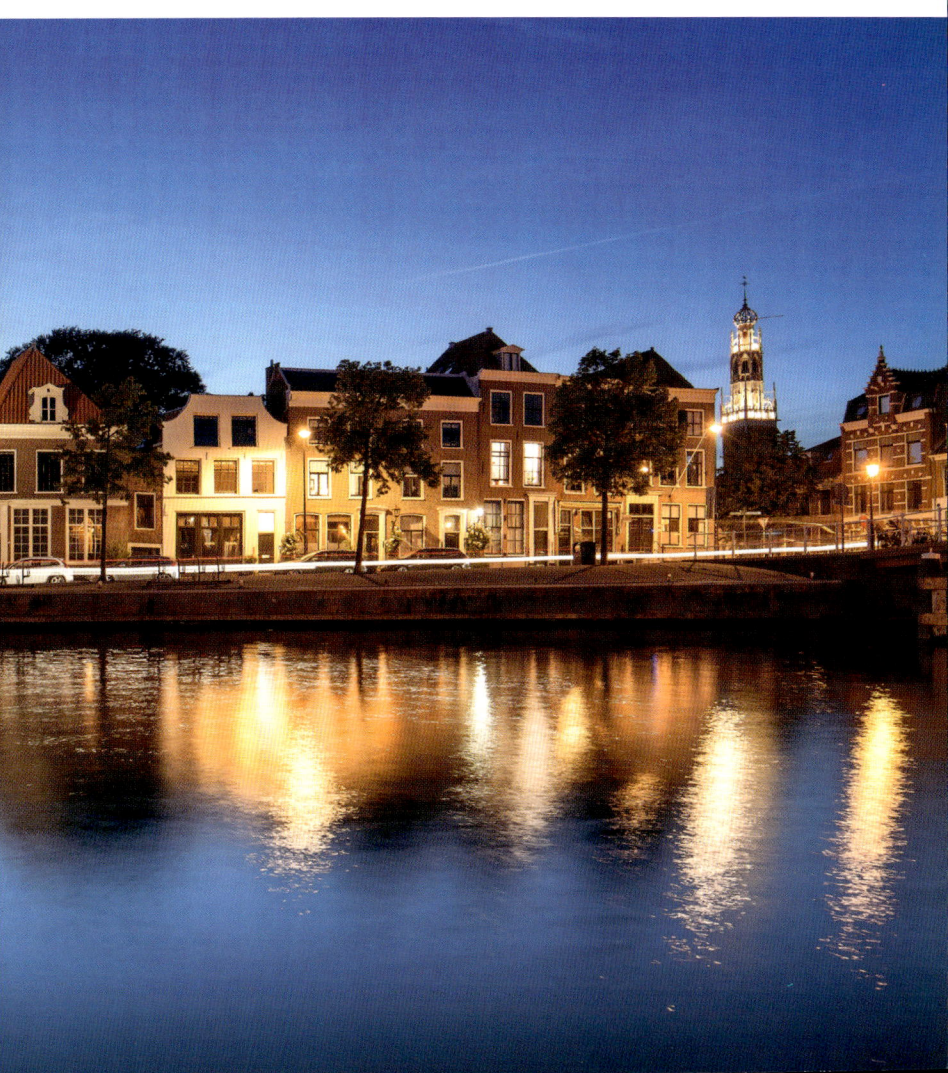

scientific machines reflecting Teyler's interest in Enlightenment ideas. Check out the unique collection of incredible bird illustrations, including the legendary Birds of America dating from 1827.

### Draaiorgelmuseum/Stichting Het Kunkels Orgel
Kuppersweg 3,
2031 EA Haarlem
**www.draaiorgelmuseum.org**

A unique part of Dutch culture, ornately decorated street organs have provided popular entertainment for decades. The Draaiorgelmuseum in Haarlem is one of the few places in the country containing a range of historical barrel organs. The oldest on display dates back to 1900.

## Laren

A small town within the Het Gooi region, Laren is situated east of Amsterdam and forms part of the Amsterdam metropolitan area. The town's architecture is traditionally Dutch with historic brick buildings surmounted by gables. It was a haven for artists during the nineteenth and twentieth centuries. The iconic artist Maurits Cornelis Escher lived here.

Laren is approximately 19 miles (31km) from Amsterdam, a journey of about thirty minutes by car. Public transport takes around forty-five minutes, with inter-city trains providing a link between Amsterdam Centraal and Hilversum followed by a short bus ride.

### Singer Laren
Oude Drift1, 1251 BÍ Laren Hilversum
**www.singerlaren.nl**

A small museum with a theatre and sculpture garden, Singer Laren contains a very diverse collection of international visual art covering 1880 to 1950. An American couple, Anna and William Singer, lived in the villa at Laren and were members of a local artists' colony. They collected an impressive range of art. Following the death of William Henry, his widow created the Singer Memorial Foundation.

The museum contains the Singer collection of paintings and sculpture, including expressionist and cubist works as well as pointillism and geometric abstraction. There are works by French Barbizon School painters, traditional impressionist painters from the area around Hilversum and American artists. More than 3,000 artworks are contained within the museum. Artists represented include Bart van der Leck, Jan Sluijters, Leo Gestel, Chris Beekman and Jan Toorop. The sculpture garden houses works by contemporary Dutch artists, focusing on the relationship between nature and culture.

# Leiden

Leiden possesses a rich artistic heritage dating from the Dutch Golden Age. Apart from Rembrandt, it was home to many other artists including landscape painter Jan van Goyen; marine painter Jan Porcellis; David Bailly, a specialist in portraits and still life paintings; and Jan Davidsz de Heem, who has been described as one of the greatest painters of still life and vanitas symbolic paintings.

Much of the historic architecture remains, and Leiden is second only to Amsterdam for the size of its seventeenth-century town centre. One hundred buildings are decorated with large poetry murals, a project that began in 1992.

Located 45 miles south of Amsterdam via the A4, it takes approximately forty minutes by train from Amsterdam Centraal.

## Leiden American Pilgrim Museum
Beschuitsteeg 9,
2312 JT Leiden

Located within a medieval house, the Leiden American Pilgrim Museum deals with the story of the Pilgrim Fathers as people from Leiden were among the settlers who sailed on the *Mayflower*'s historic voyage to America. On display are period furnishings, examples of highly decorated grey and blue German Westerwald stoneware. There is a major collection of sixteenth- and seventeenth-century maps and engravings by artists including Gerard Mercator and Adriaen van Ostade.

## Museum de Lakenhal
Oude Singel 32
2312 RA LEIDEN
**www.lakenhal.nl**

A museum devoted to fine arts, crafts and Leiden city history. Art on display includes works by Rembrandt such as the Pedlar Selling Glasses (1624) and his contemporaries, and The Last Judgement by Lucas Van Leyden (1526). Other artists include Willem Thibault, Pieter Xavery, Jan van Goyen and Theo van Doesburg. David Bailly's Vanitas Still Life with Portrait of a

▼ *Façade of the Lakenhal museum of history and fine art with a statue of Rembrandt in front.*

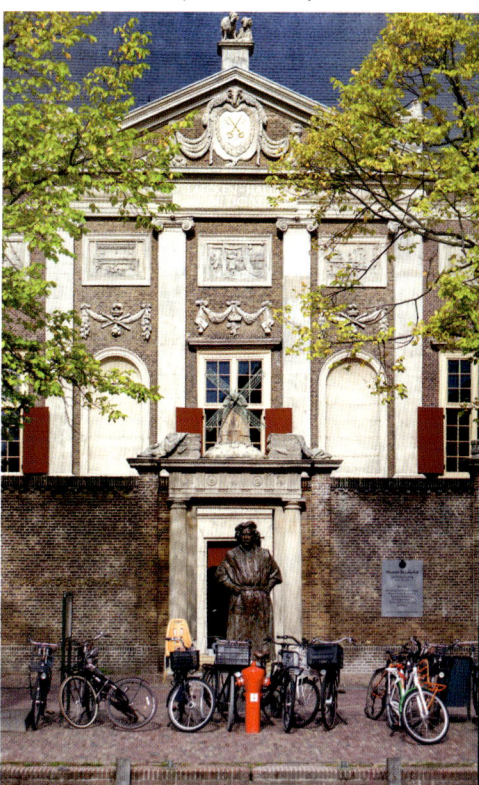

Young Painter is a study in the genre of the cherished objects and the transience of life. There are collections of stained glass and textiles. Themed displays include Leiden as the birthplace of Dutch painting, and the Plantations of Cloth Merchant Daniel van Eijs.

### Museum Volkenkunde
Steenstraat 1,
2312 BS Leiden
**www.volkenkunde.nl**

This ethnology museum contains a globally important collection of objects and art from non-Western cultures, including Indonesian statues and a folding screen decorated with a harbour scene highlighting Japanese culture and showing Deshima, the Dutch trading post in Nagasaki, as portrayed by Kawahara Keiga (1786–1860). There are objects from China, glittering jewellery and temple bells from Indonesia, African artefacts plus a changing exhibition programme that has featured Aztecs, Australian art and First Americans.

### Rembrandt Route
**www.visitleiden.nl**

Born in Leiden, Rembrandt spent the first twenty-five years of his life there. The Rembrandt Route highlights places linked to him. It starts at the Rembrandt Bridge and

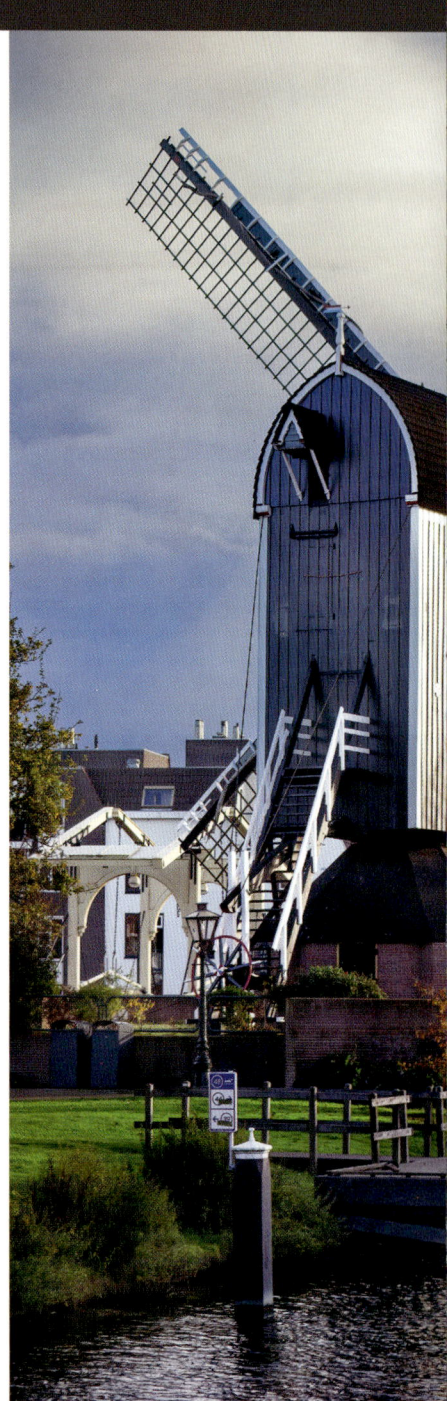

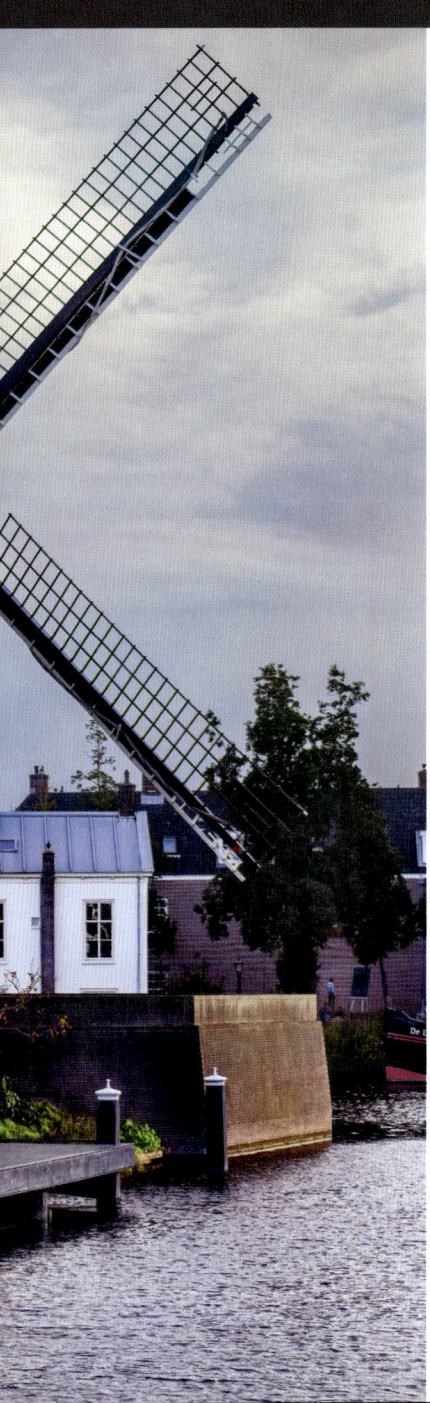

*◀ Landscape near the birthplace of Rembrandt Van Rijn, Leiden.*

Park, close to Weddesteeg where he was born. A statue and gable stone now marks his birthplace. The route continues through the Pietrskwartier neighbourhood to the Pieterskerk, then to the Latin School where he was educated. Rembrandt was briefly enrolled at Leiden University, before starting an apprenticeship in Jacob van Swanenburg's workshop. A gable stone now marks the spot. As a young man, Rembrandt had his own studio at Kort Galgewater, near the Stadstimmerwerf, and paintings created by his student Gerrit Dou are in the Museum de Lakenhal.

This self-guided walking tour around Leiden can be purchased from the Leiden Tourist Information Office, and contains information about the locations.

### Rijksmuseum van Oudenhenden
Rapenburg 28
2311 EW Leiden
**www.rmo.nl**

The National Museum of Antiquities contains permanent displays relating to the Egyptians, Greeks, Romans, Etruscans, Near East and The Netherlands. Egyptian mummies and sarcophagi are one of the biggest displays. Additional exhibitions are held frequently, such as one about Emperor

Domitian highlighting murals, mosaics, jewellery, glassware and ceramics, busts and statues. A light show set against a replica Egyptian Temple brings history alive.

### The Siebold House
Rapenburg 19,
2311 GE Leiden
**www.sieboldhuis.org/en**

The museum contains thousands of unique cultural and artistic treasures from Japan, which were collected by Philipp Franz von Siebold, a nineteenth-century physician. The displays include Japanese prints, lacquerware, ceramics, maps, textiles and artworks of animals and other objects, plus temporary exhibits such as Sōsaku hanga print art.

### Young Rembrandt Studio
Langebrug 89,
2311 TJ Leiden
**www.visitleiden.nl/en/highlights/
young-rembrandt**

A small museum covering the first twenty-five years of Rembrandt's life, highlighting the people who influenced him and encouraged him to develop his artistic skills. Visitors are able to discover the type of materials and paints that he used, and exactly how he used them. It includes a large video presentation.

## Lisse

Located south west of Amsterdam, Lisse is the home of the Keukenhof Tulip Garden, a spectacular springtime sight containing millions of spring flowering bulbs. This is the main tulip-growing area within the Netherlands. Walking and cycling routes are available. By car the journey takes thirty minutes. There are frequent buses, plus trains from Amsterdam Centraal.

### Keukenhof Tulip Garden,
Stationsweg 166A
2161 AM Lisse
**www.keukenhof.nl**

The Keukenhof Tulip Garden shows how the Dutch use colour and design with their biggest industry – the production of garden bulbs. Anyone visiting the Keukenhof Gardens is reminded of how artists have been inspired by the landscape. Artwork is interspersed among the flowers. The Keukenhof Gardens are only open during the spring period, from March to mid-May. The bulbs are planted in layers so as to ensure a continual display.

The horticultural links of the Keukenhof date to the fifteenth century. The estate now comprises Keukenhof Castle with adjacent gardens, and the separate Keukenhof Garden.

The Keukenhof Gardens date from 1949, when bulb growers and exporters decided to use the Keukenhof to exhibit

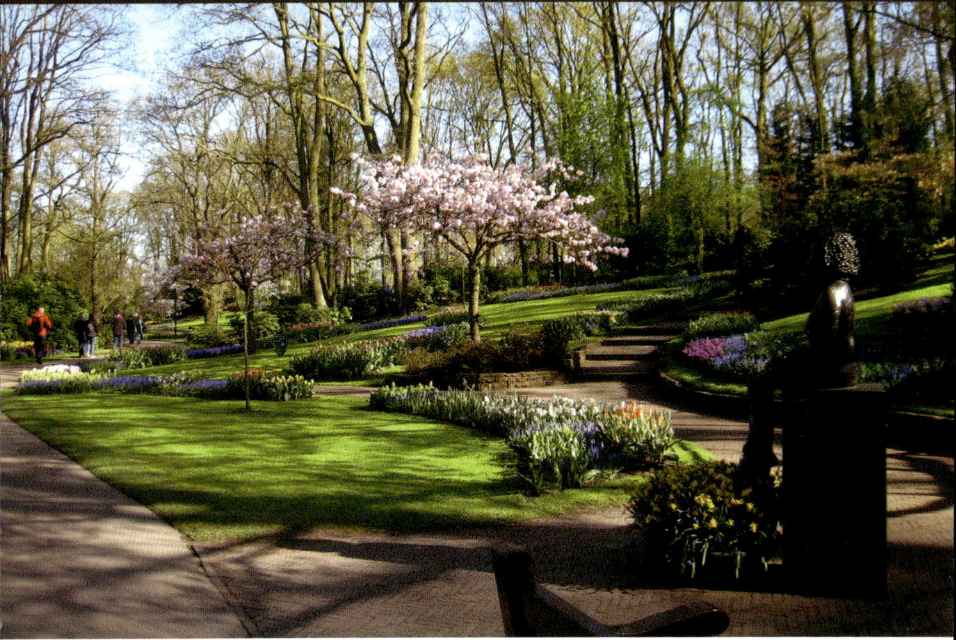

▲ *Scene in the Keukenhof Tulip Garden.* (Angela Youngman)

▼ *Flowering bulbs on display.* (Angela Youngman)

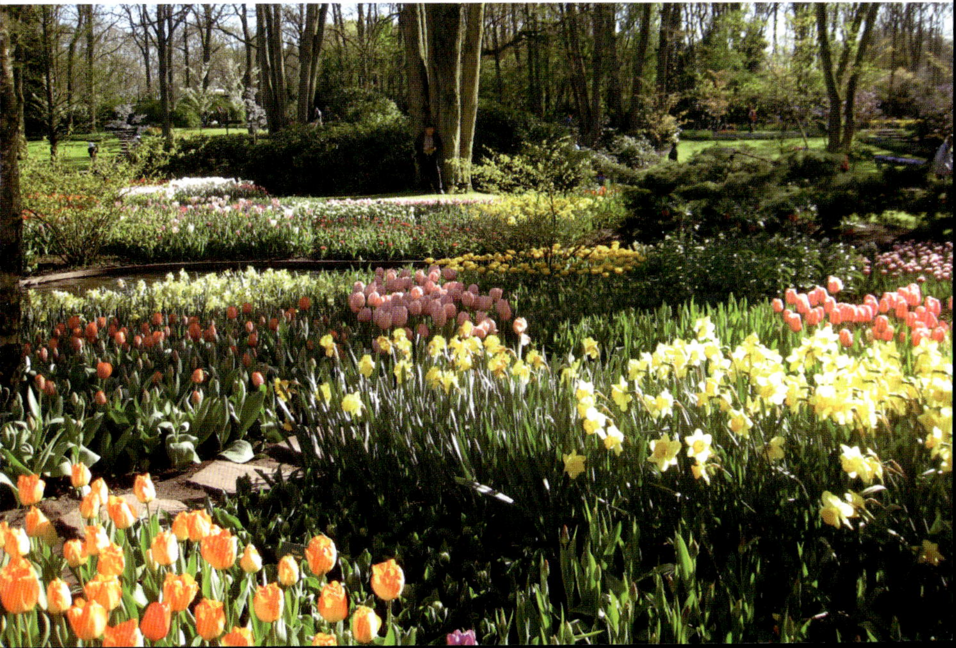

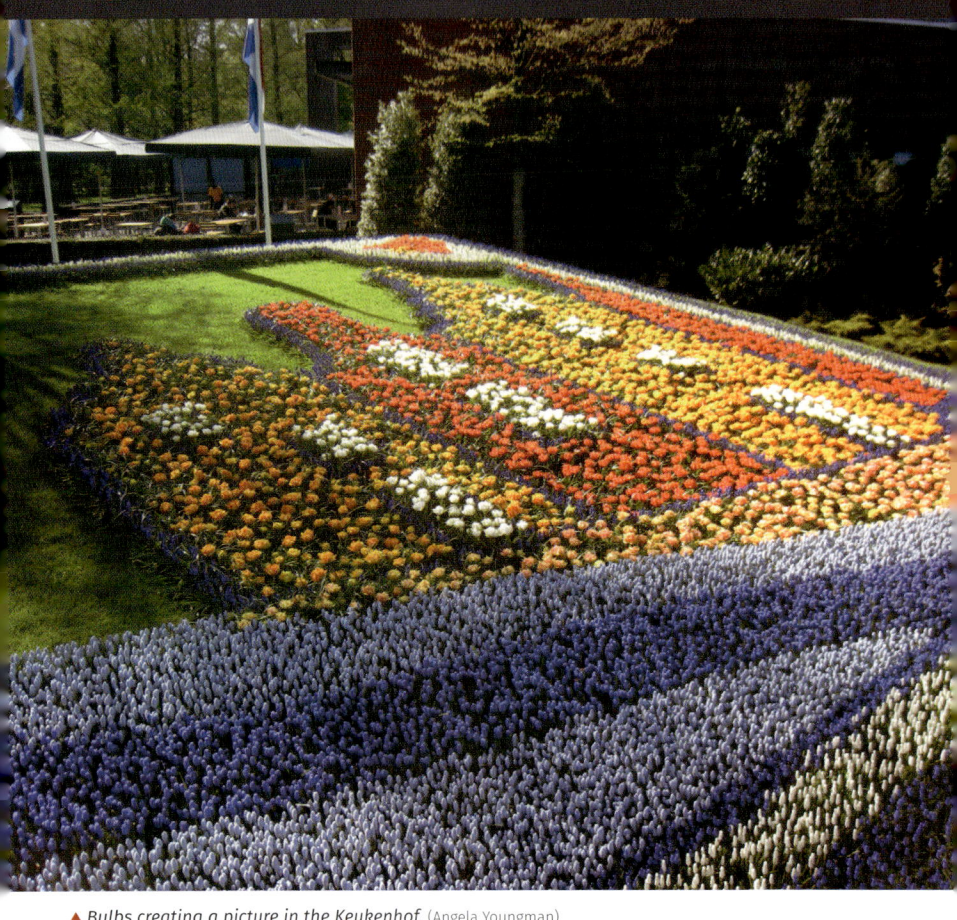

▲ *Bulbs creating a picture in the Keukenhof.* (Angela Youngman)

spring bulbs. The gardens contain 10 miles of paths offering glimpses of views across to the adjacent bulb fields. Guided pre-booked canal boat tours linked to the bulb fields are available.

More than 7 million bulbs are planted each autumn to create the displays. Many are planted in vast swathes to create rivers and beds of colour or in designs reflecting the chosen theme. A typical design for the Golden Age of Holland in 2016 showed a ship on the sea plus Amsterdam canal houses involving 100,000 tulips, grape hyacinths and crocuses.

Other displays have included a Delft Blue garden in which only white and blue flowers were used, together with pottery and tiles, a tea garden and replica of a Mondrian artwork.

Interspersed among the flowers are large sculptures and art. These include

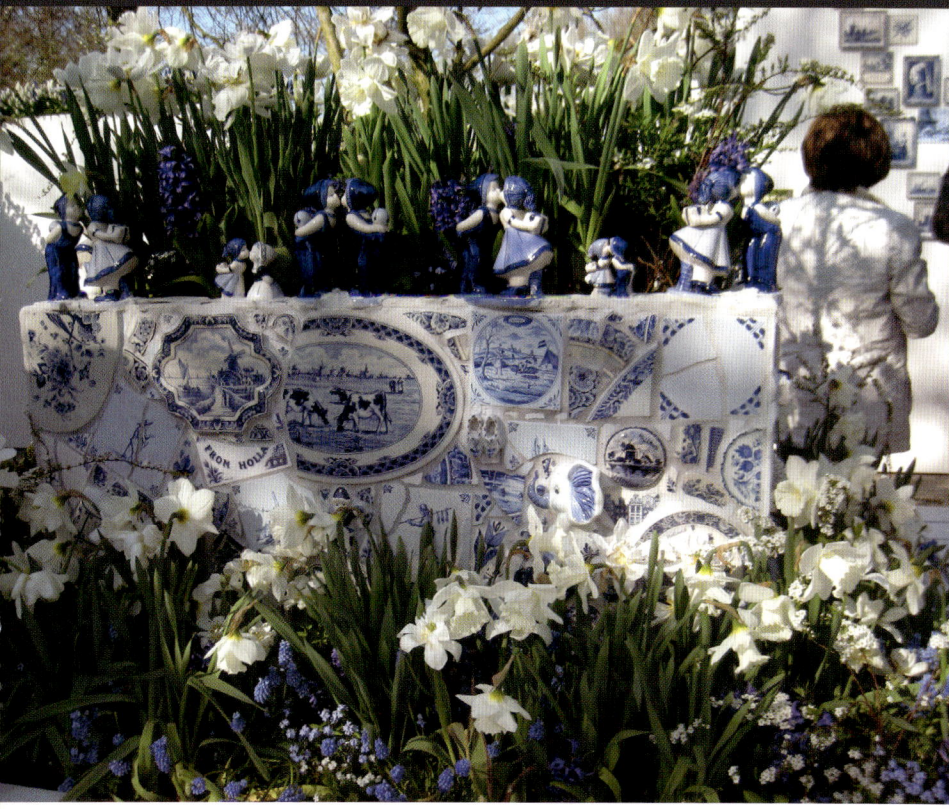

▲ *Delftware with flowers on display in the Delft Blue Garden, Keukenhof.* (Angela Youngman)

a giant White Horse and rider, which has been in the gardens since 1952, and a sculptured Tree of Life filled with birds.

Built in 1641, Keukenhof Castle contains portraits by Nicolaes Maes, a pupil of Rembrandt, and is accessible via guided tours. The castle interior is reminiscent of the Dutch Golden Age style in terms of décor and furnishings.

In spring, there are many buses to Keukenhof from central Amsterdam.

## Museum de Zwarte Tulp

Heereweg 219,
2161 BG Lisse
**www.museumdezwartetulp.nl**

This is the story of how the tulip has developed since its introduction in 1594. It covers the activities of bulb hunters, merchants and flower breeders and the search for a black tulip. There are many paintings, glass and furniture decorated with bulbs plus decorated hyacinth glasses, tulip vases and crocus pots.

## Maastricht

Maastricht is the oldest city in the Netherlands, dating back to Roman times, and is located in the southern province of Limburg, between Belgium and Germany. A cultural hub, it features contemporary art, Japanese prints, illusionary eighteenth-century ceilings, Dutch Golden art and medieval art.

By car using the A2, the journey is approximately 130 miles (212km) from Amsterdam. Trains from Amsterdam Centraal take two hours and forty minutes.

### Centre Ceramique

Avenue Ceramique 50,
6221 KV Maastricht
The Centre Ceramic contains an extensive collection of Japanese prints, school posters, glasswork and Maastricht pottery. The earthenware and porcelain created by the Maastricht Potteries, particularly Petrus Regout, are highly collectible.

### Castle Hoensbroek
**www.kasteelhoensbroek.nl**

One of the largest fourteenth-century castles in the Netherlands, it has an almost fairy tale ambiance. The ballroom contains eighteenth-century illusionistic ceiling paintings, gold-plated images of Countess van Hoensbroek and period furnishings.

### Bonnefanten Museum

Avenue Ceramique 250
6221 KX Maastricht
**www.bonnefanten.nl**

The Bonnefanten Museum contains a major collection of old masters and modern art including medieval sculptures from the Maas region, silverware, late medieval paintings from the Netherlands and work from the Dutch seventeenth century as well as early Italian paintings. Among the displays are works by Bruegel, van Dyck, Rubens, David Lynch and Grayson Perry.

▼ *The Bonnefanten Museum.*

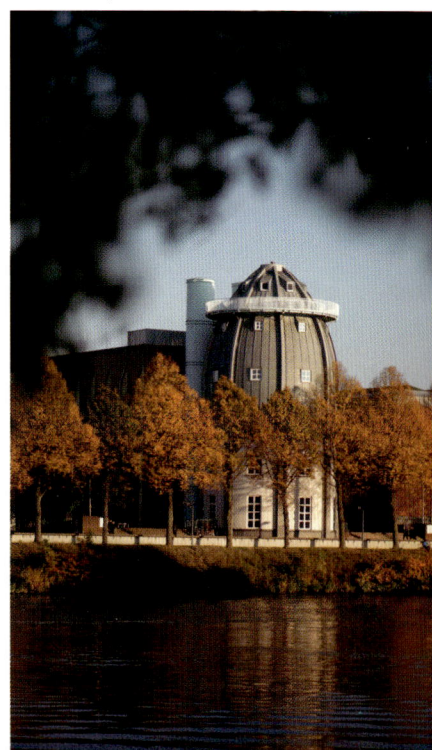

**Fotomuseum Aan Het Vrijthof**
Vrijthof 18,
6211 LD Maastricht
**www.fotomuseumaahetvrijthof.nl**

A private photography museum, temporary exhibitions cover themes including pop culture and entertainment. There is a permanent collection of silverware, clocks, ceramics and paintings from the city of Maastricht.

**Marres, House for Contemporary Culture**
Capucijnenstraat 98
6211 RT Maastricht
**www.marres.org/en**

An unusual cultural venue focusing on contemporary art including art walks, sensory workshops, collaborations with performers, perfumers and cooks. Exhibitions have included installations immersing visitors in a variety of changing sensory perspectives such as transforming the building into a jungle and a rooftop landscape.

**Museum of the Art of Printing**
Jodenstraat 22,
6211 EA Maastricht
**www.drukkunstmuseum.wordpress.com/english**

Explore the art of printing including Rembrandt's etchings and lithographic prints of Toulouse-Lautrec plus an exclusive collection of graphic art, drawings and objects by René Glaser.

**Museum of Illusions Maastricht**
Mosae Forum 18,
6221 DS Maastricht
**www.maastricht.museumofillusions.nl.en**

Nothing is as it seems in this museum of optical illusions where visitors can stand upside down in the reverse room and discover what it is like to be in a tilted room. Highly imaginative, it introduces some amazing visual art concepts.

**The Sphinx Passage**
Boschstraat 23b
Maastricht
**www.visitmaastricht.com**

At 120m long, this is the longest tile mosaic in the Netherlands. The historical story is told in twenty-six chapters with tableaus of family portraits, factory buildings, tableware decorations, advertisements and even toilet bowls. The passage links the Eiffel building with the Pathé cinema. The best route begins at the Penintentenpoort gate, ending at the Sphinxcour. Access is free and the passageway is open daily.

## Otterlo

A small village in Gelderland, Otterlo is the home of the Kröller-Müller Museum and art gallery.

Access to Otterlo by car is via the A1, 48 miles (78km) from Amsterdam. It is accessible by public transport from Amsterdam.

**Kroller-Muller Museum**
Otterlo
**www.krollermuller.nl**

Set within the beautiful surroundings of the De Hoge Veluwe National Park, this museum contains the second largest collection of works by Van Gogh worldwide. The founders of the museum were two collectors, Anton and Helene Kröller-Muller. Helene believed Van Gogh to be 'one of the great spirits of modern art'. They purchased ninety-one paintings and more than 180 works on paper between 1908 and 1929. Among the Van Gogh works owned by the museum are The Potato Eaters, Reaper, L'Arlésienne and Bridge at Arles.

Also on display are works by artists including Piet Mondrian, Barbara Hepworth and Johan Coenraad Altorf. The total collection houses more than 20,000 works of art.

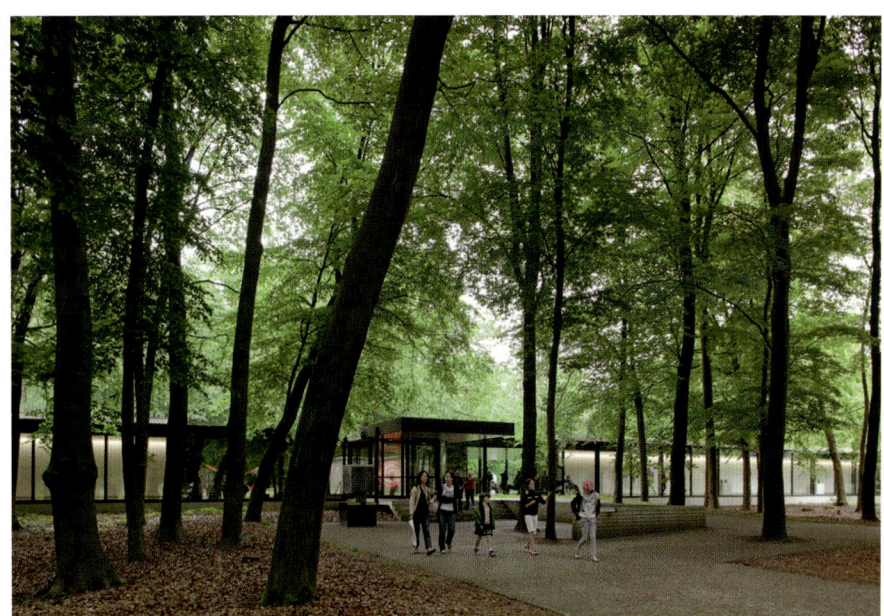

▲ *The Kroller-Muller Museum.* (Jannes Linders, Kroller-Muller Museum)

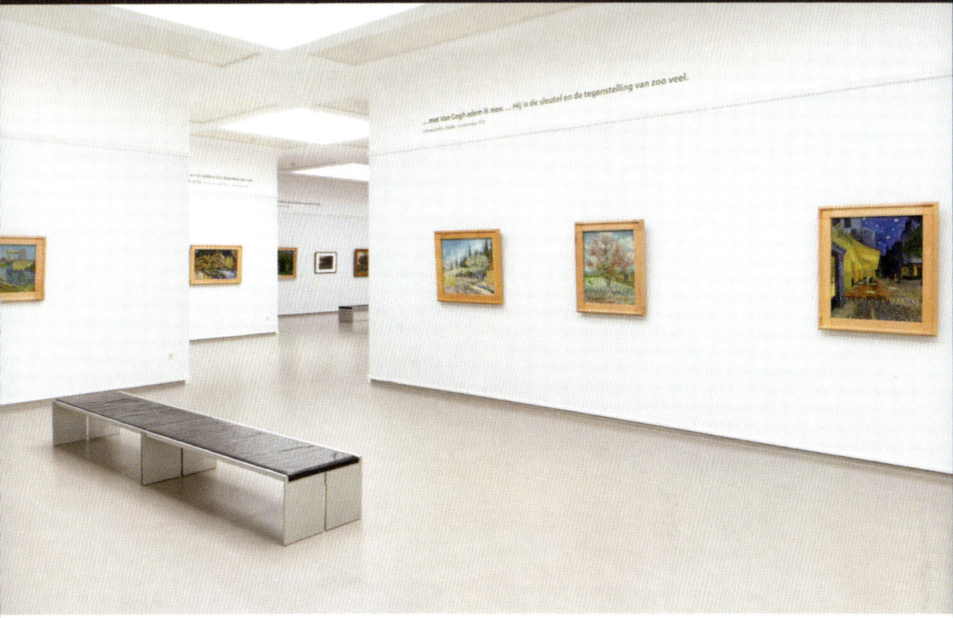

▲ *Van Gogh Gallery within the Kroller-Muller Museum.* (Marjon Gemmeke/Kroller-Muller Museum)

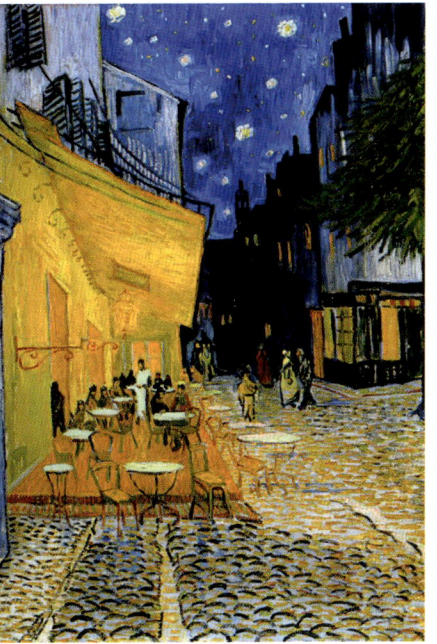

◄ *Vincent Van Gogh, Terrace of a Café at Night, circa 16 September 1888.* (Kroller-Muller Museum)

More than 160 works by iconic twentieth-century and contemporary artists are located in the sculpture garden.

## Rotterdam

Rotterdam is the largest seaport in Europe, and has an impressive artistic heritage. Fighting during the Second World War meant that the city had to be almost completely rebuilt, resulting in a skyline that in places resembles Manhattan. Contemporary art is very strong in Rotterdam, both in exhibition

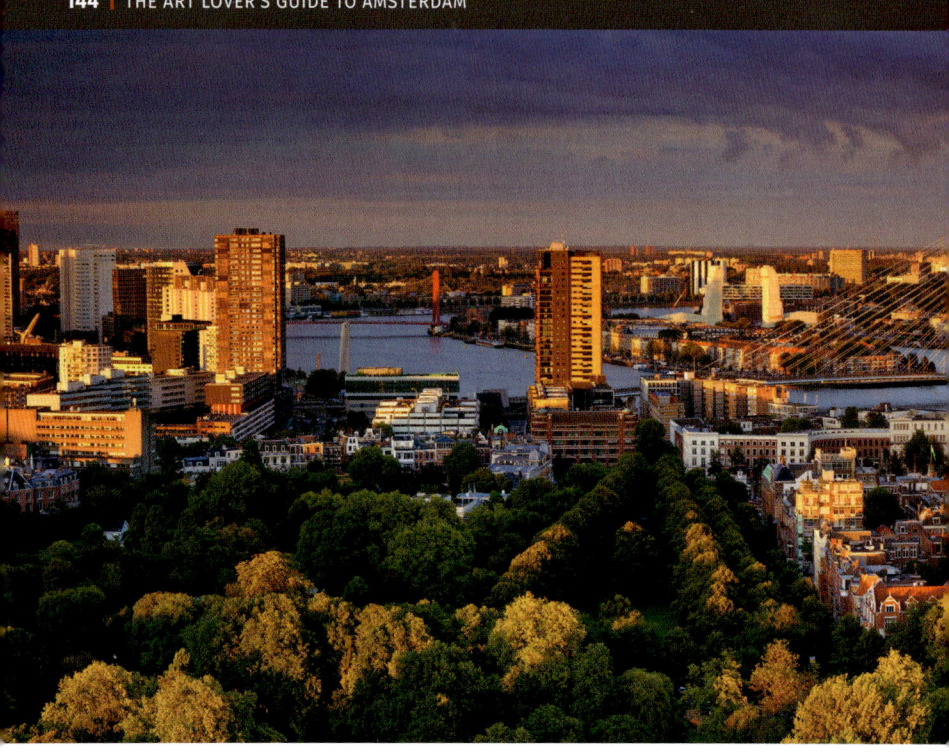

▲ *Panoramic image of Rotterdam.*

galleries and in terms of street art. It is home to the largest collection of works by Henrik Chabot, as well as a group of unique cubist-style houses. The Museum Boijmans van Beuningen contains an outstanding collection of art including works by Vincent Van Gogh, Rembrandt, Claude Monet, Peter Paul Rubens and Jacob Van Ruisdael, and is one of the most popular in the Netherlands.

Rotterdam is 48 miles (78km) south of Amsterdam, taking one hour via the A4. Direct trains from Amsterdam Centraal take approximately forty minutes.

**Art Cube Rotterdam**
Overblaak 70,
3011MH Rotterdam
**www.kubuswoning.nl/en**

Designed in a cubist style by Dutch architect Piet Blom, these distinctive, brightly coloured houses tilt at 45 degrees. The architect wanted 'an abstract forest, each triangular roof representing a treetop'. Inside, all the walls are slanted, and none are straight. One of the buildings has been turned into an Art Cube Museum while another cube house promotes the work of local artists.

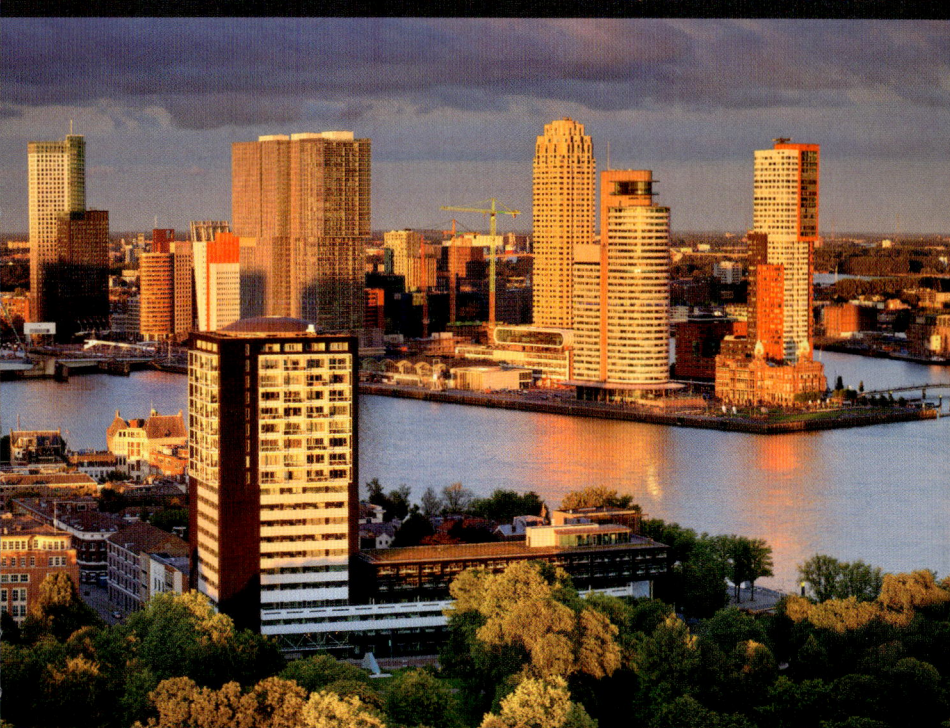

## Chabot Museum

Museumpark 11,
3015 CB Rotterdam
**www.chabotmuseum.nl**

Located in a modernist-style white villa, the Chabot Museum focuses on the work of Dutch expressionist Henrik Chabot (1894–1949). Artworks represent four categories: portraits, landscapes, figures and animals. Many scenes feature ordinary people, including Second World War refugees, prisoners and people in hiding.

It is a small museum, but filled with art. There are tours of the nearby former Van Nelle Factory that end at the Chabot Museum and explore modernist architecture and production processes.

## Garage Rotterdam

Goudsewagenstraat 27,
3011 RH Rotterdam
**www.garagerotterdam.nl**

Initially a Volkswagen showroom, Garage Rotterdam has become a contemporary art venue with exhibitions linking art with programmes of readings, films, talks, music and performance art. Artwork includes paintings, sculptures, videos, textiles and mixed media installations by artists such as Ghinwa Yassine, Kristina Benjocki and Cecilia Jonsson.

### Kunstinstituut Melly Art Gallery
Witte de Withstraat 50,
3012 BR Rotterdam
**www.kunstinstituutmelly.nl**

Founded in 1990, Kunstinstituut Melly is a contemporary art gallery displaying work, a publisher of contemporary art and an educational forum offering hybrid art and events including exhibitions by internationally acclaimed artists such as Ken Lum, Frederick Kiesler and Qiu Zhijie.

### Kunsthal Rotterdam,
Westzeedijk 341
3015 AA Rotterdam
**www.kunsthal.nl**

A popular art exhibition venue located within the Museumpark, it houses a changing programme of exhibitions, from old masters to contemporary art and photography. An unusual feature is the bright orange steel girder that sticks out over the edge of the roof.

▼ *Exterior of the Auditorium at the Kunsthal.*

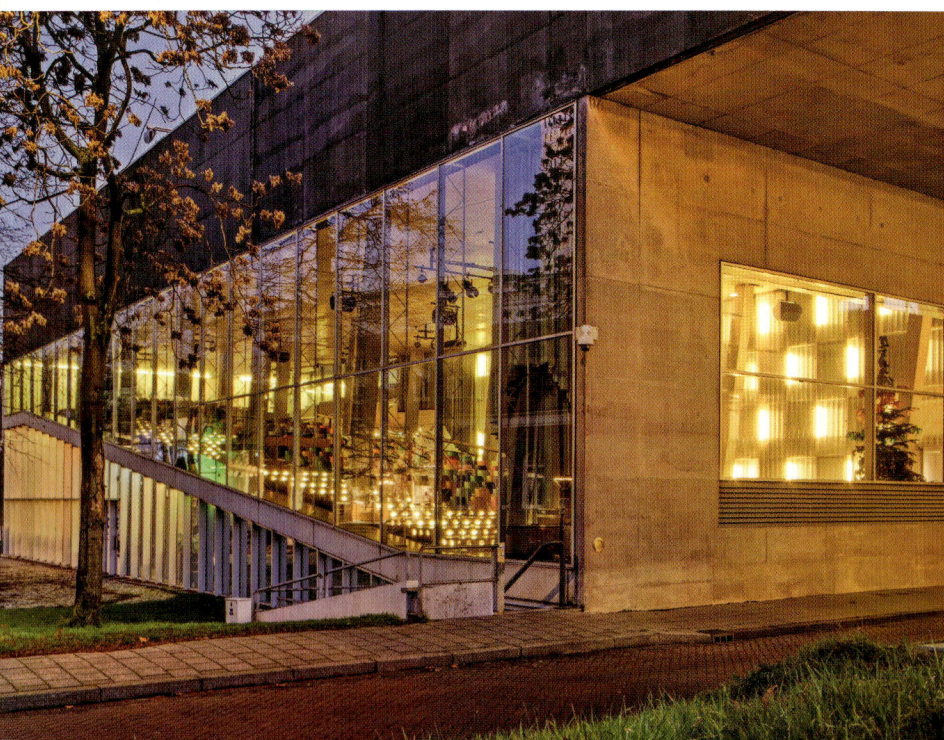

## Museum Boijmans van Beuningen
Museumpark,
18–20 Rotterdam
**www.boijmans.nl**

Opened in 1849, the Museum Boijmans van Beuningen is one of the most popular museums in the Netherlands. It contains the collections of Frans Jacob Otto Boijmans and Daniel George van Beuningen. It possesses more than 151,000 pieces of art covering all periods from medieval to contemporary art, including works by Rembrandt, Claude Monet, Vincent Van Gogh, Salvador Dali, Hieronymus Bosch, Edvard Munch, Paul Bruegel the Elder and Kandinsky. Typical paintings include Titus at his Desk by Rembrandt, Nest of Owls by Bosch, The 'Little' Tower of Babel by Bruegel the Elder, Portrait of Armand Roulin by Van Gogh, Hut of the Douaniers with Varengeville by Monet, The Face of War by Dali, The Wrath of Achilles by Rubens (part of the Achilles tapestry series) and the Renaissance Tulipcabinet by Herman Doomer featuring highly decorative motifs linked to the bulb industry. There are extensive collections of twentieth-century furniture, Oriental porcelain, medieval ceramics, drawings by Italian–Dutch sculptor Frederico Carasso and a unique library of surrealist works including monographs, catalogues and literature.

## Depot Boijmans van Beuningen

Opened by King Willem-Alexander in 2021, this is an accessible art storage facility and is located next to the Museum Boijmans van Beuningen within the Museumpark. It aims to make the museum's entire collection accessible to the public as well as providing behind-the-scenes glimpses highlighting the work of museums. Unlike a traditional museum, none of the artworks are stored by period or theme, but simply according to climate requirements. The seven-storey building contains separate sections for paintings, metal objects, organic and non-organic materials, black and white and colour photography. All are temperature and climate controlled. Visitors can enter specific sections accompanied by a guide.

The façade itself is outstanding, as it is a circular building covered in 1,664 mirrored panels that reflect the greenery and buildings within its vicinity. As a result, it blends into the landscape, especially since there is even a roof garden containing birch and pine trees. Entry tickets must be purchased in advance and online.

### Netherlands Photo Museum
Las Palmas, Statendam 1,
3072 MD Rotterdam

The museum possesses a unique collection of more than 5.6 million images related to the Netherlands. It hosts a changing exhibition programme covering all aspects of archive and modern Dutch photography such as a retrospective of the leading Dutch photographer Chas Gerretsen, who covered events such as the war in Vietnam as well as photographing celebrities including John Travolta.

### Street art and sculptures
www.rewriters010.nl

Rotterdam is a city filled with sculptures and giant murals created by national and international street artists including Rodin, Henry Moore and Picasso. The Rewriters App contains eleven routes that can be followed to explore all these different examples of art in public spaces. Among the routes on the app are walks around the Afrikaanderwijk neighbourhood, where there are works including a gallery of subway pillars by Foundation MESH and murals by Telmo Miel, Woes, Helen Proctor, Said Kinos and Danny Rumbi. The Central District includes works by Levi Jacobs, Tymon de Laat, Collin van der Sluijs and Venour, as well as the famous portrait of Rotterdam rapper Winne painted by Judith de Leeuw. In the Hall of Fame at the Schuttersveld, vast murals adorn the walls of buildings, while the Oude Western contains portraits of the Rotterdam jazz musicians who used to perform in the area, as well as door sticker street culture with works by Bier en Brood, Michiel Corver and Insane51.

Guided walks take place most days, while a map can be downloaded for self-guided tours.

### Street Art Museum
West-Kruiskade,
3014 AL Rotterdam
www.rotterdamstreetartmuseum.com

An unusual open air museum involving art projects within the streets around West-Kruiskade and 1e Middellandstraat. It was partly set up as a way of transforming urban streets better known for drug dealing and giving them a new ambience. It is now a busy multicultural area full of shops and artworks. The murals have been created by local artists, and reflect the multicultural nature of the area. Among the artworks to be seen are Insane51's Pulp Fiction 1950s-style character, an abstract mural complete with curves, calligraphy and dynamic shapes, and the manga-like figures created by Sharon van Dams. In total, there are eight murals to be found.

## Utrecht

Located in the eastern Netherlands, Utrecht is the fourth largest city in the country. Many buildings date back to the medieval period. Utrecht was the

▶ *Hendrick ter Brugghen, Sleeping, March 1629, Utrecht Caravaggists.* (Robert Oosterbroek/Utrecht Marketing)

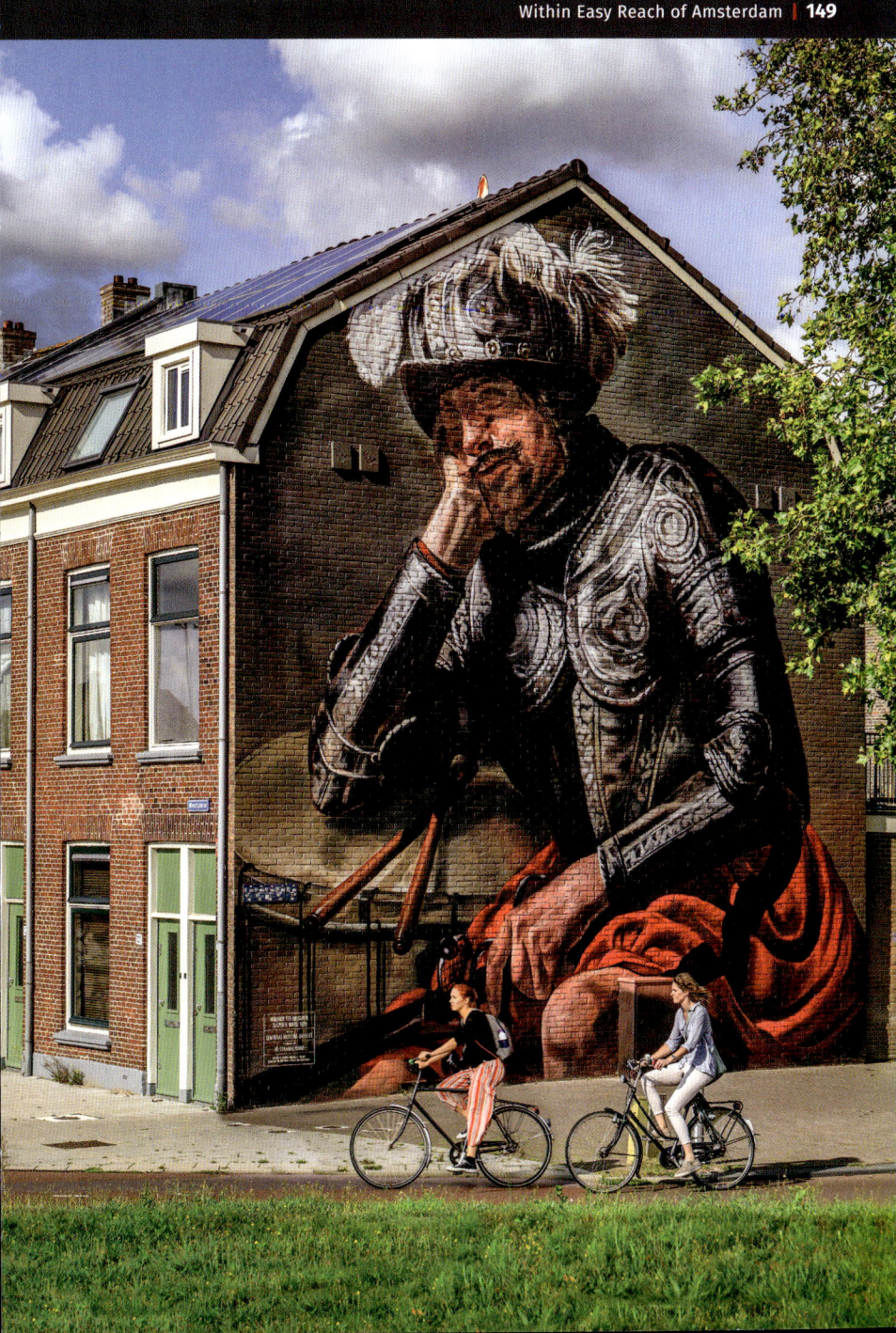

most important city in the Netherlands until the seventeenth century. Famous artists associated with Utrecht include the Utrecht Caravaggists group, Piet Mondrian and Dick Bruna.

Utrecht is just 30 miles (45km) from Amsterdam via the A2, and it is less than half an hour by train from Amsterdam Centraal.

## BAK
Pauwstraat 13A, Utrecht
**www.bakonline.org**

A venue for experimental and politically driven art, BAK holds a changing programme of art by contemporary artists. Many of the works aim to make statements on current issues, especially politics, the international scene and the environment. BAK sees itself as being a platform for research and art within the public sphere, and aims to work with communities involved in these sectors.

## The Centraal Museum
Agnietenstraat 1, Utrecht
**www.centraalmuseum.nl**

There has been a museum here since 1921 and it forms a group of buildings interlinked by a large interior courtyard. Inside the walls of the Centraal Museum, you can find artworks across the centuries from medieval sculptures

and the Utrecht Caravaggists to Dick Bruna. Other work on display includes that of Jan van Scorel, plus applied art such as the work of fashion designers Victor & Rolf.

The Centraal Museum contains the largest single collection of furniture created by the De Stijl-inspired designer Gerrit Rietveld. A special room is devoted to the work of Dick Bruna, creator of the children's character Miffy. Bruna lived in Utrecht, where he created Miffy as well as countless other illustrations and stories. His studio is now recreated within the museum, complete with numerous personal items used by the artist.

The Utrecht Caravaggists were a group of artists influenced by the work of Caravaggio. Utrecht-born artists including Dirck van Baburen, Hendrick ter Brugghen and Gerard van Honthorst went to Rome to explore Caravaggio's use of realism, drama and light, and the museum contains a number of the resulting works of art.

## Kunstliefde
Nobelstraat 12a, 3512 EN Utrecht
**www.kunstliefde.nl**

Kunstiefde is home to ten annual exhibitions covering all forms of visual art, from abstracts to ceramics. The exhibition topics are changing constantly, and the emphasis is very much on modern contemporary art.

## Miffy Square
1e Achterstraat,
3512 VL Utrecht

Named after the little white rabbit known as Miffy, who has become one of the most famous children's characters worldwide. At the heart of Miffy Square is a delightful statue of Miffy, created by Dick Bruna's son, Marc. Not far away there is a life-size Miffy to be seen on the Mariaplaats and a unique Miffy traffic light on the Vliestraat.

## Mondriaan House
Kortegracht 11, Amersfoort Utrecht
**www.mondraanhuis.nl**

Piet Mondrian was born in this house in 1872. He spent much of his childhood here, until his family left the area in 1892. It was not until 1994 that awareness of Mondrian's links with Utrecht began to be better known. Architect Leo Heijdenrijk and his wife Cis acquired the house and opened it to the public as a museum devoted to Mondrian's life and work. The rooms are decorated in Mondrian's style, and there is a full-size reconstruction of his studio in Paris. Many of Mondrian's early paintings are on display, enabling visitors to trace the development of his iconic art style.

## Museum Catharijne convent
Lange Nieuwstraat 38, Utrecht
**www.catharijneconvent.nl**

This medieval building was a Catholic convent. It contains a vast array of artworks focusing on the history of Christianity together with contemporary art. Among the works on display are paintings by Rembrandt, Jan Steen, Frans Hals, Pieter Saenredam and Jan van Scorel, video art by Guido van der Werve, medieval sculptures, and a stained glass window by Marc Mulders. Examples of the applied arts include ecclesiastical clothing, altarpieces, manuscripts and book-bindings with richly worked images. This is one of the largest collections of Catholic and Protestant art in the Netherlands, containing more than 65,000 items.

## Street Art
**www.discover-utrecht.com/collection**

Hunt the murals as you walk around Utrecht. These are magnificent, massive works with scenes covering everything from replicas of masterpieces by Dutch masters to a gigantic bookshelf and bird scenes. All the murals are located in very public positions covering the entire sides of buildings. On the Croeselaan is a gigantic 190 sq metre mural illustrating scenes from the 'Stories from the Dichterswijk'.

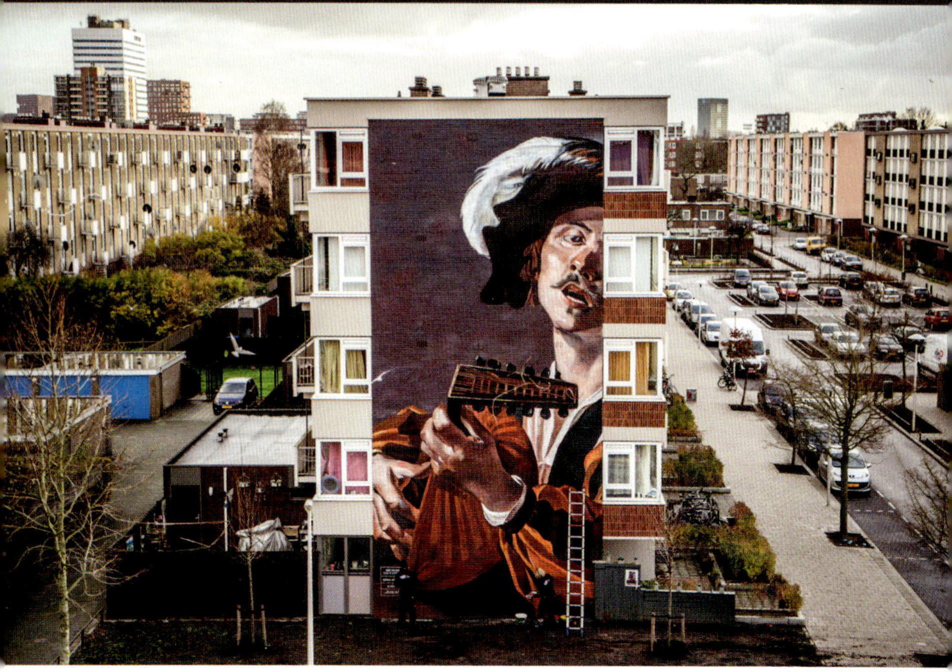

▲ *Dirck van Baburen, Lute Player.* (Robert Oosterbroek-De Strakke Hand/Utrecht Marketing)

▼ *Abraham Bloemaert's The Flute Player.* (Robert Oosterbroek-De Strakke Hand/Utrecht Marketing)

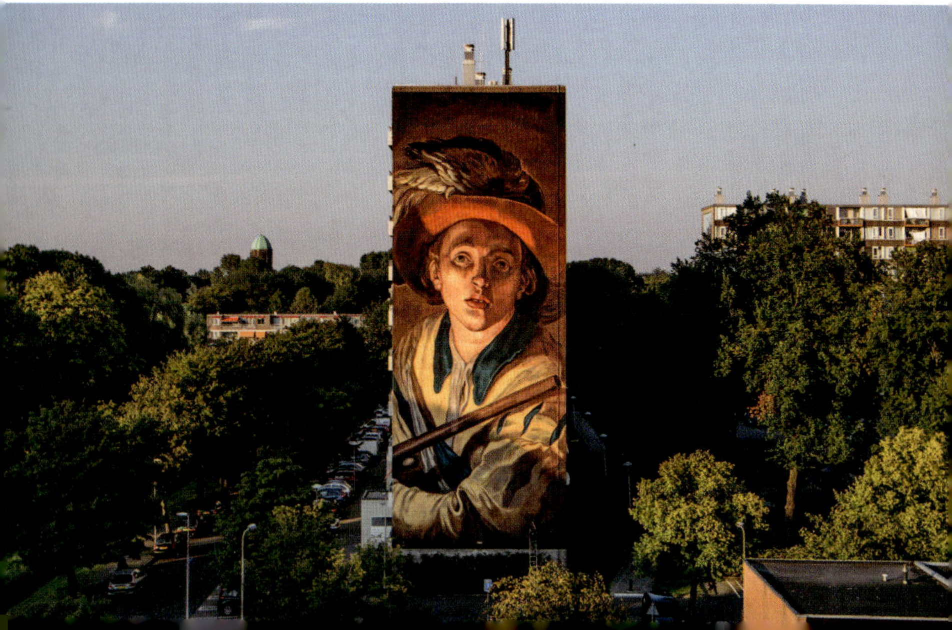

Among the most spectacular are three reproductions of works by seventeenth-century artists:

Dirck van Baburen, Lute Player, 1622, 14m high, on the Attleeplantsoen Kanaleneiland-North.

Hendrick ter Brugghen, Mars Asleep, 1629, 12m high, on the Westplein Lombok/Leidsweg.

Abraham Bloemaert, The Flute Player, 1621, 30m high, on the Dorbeendreef/Taagdreef.

These three murals were painted in 2018 and 2019 by the Utrecht painters' collective De Strakke Hand to promote the Utrecht, Caravaggio and Europe exhibition held in the Centraal Museum. The three paintings show people with a musical instrument and are known as 'Give Utrecht Masters a Face'.

## Utrecht Lumen
www.discover-utrecht.com/collection

This is art with a difference – it's light art, designed to illuminate and enchant, and involves more than twenty illuminations. Walking around the city of Utrecht at night, illuminated tales of the city are seen, giving insights into

▼ *Illuminated tunnel in Utrecht.*

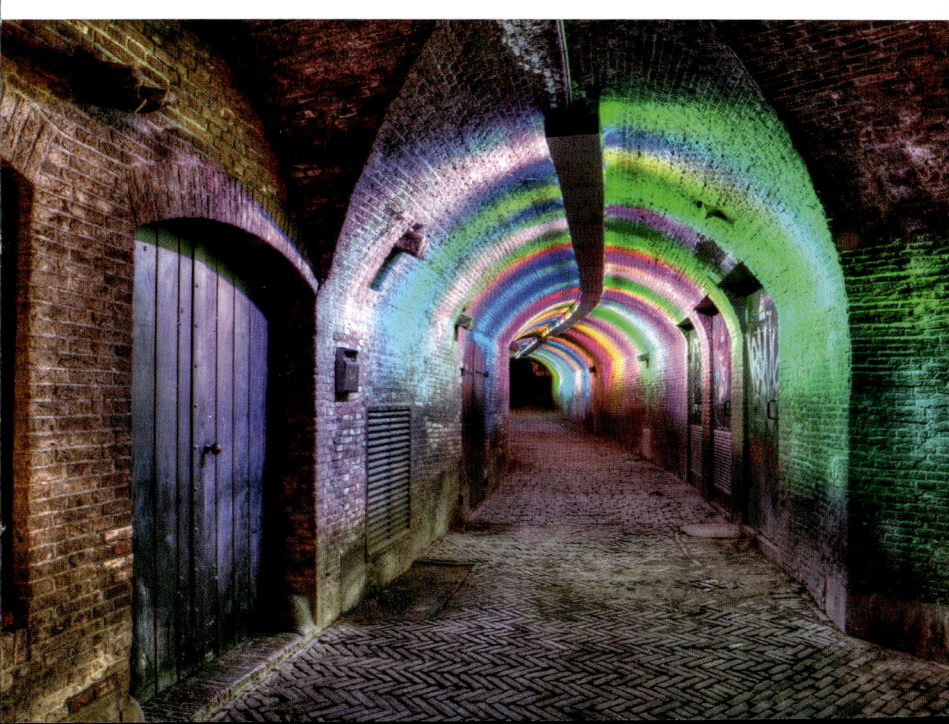

the story of a building. Tucked away in the Minrebroerderstraat 21 is the Sint-Willibrordkerk with a circular halo at night, while on the Domstraat is the line of a Roman fortress like a ghost from the past. There is a Mondrian-style beacon on Blitse Rading, and at Agnietenstraat 2, the world of Miffy comes alive on the exterior of the building every winter.

## Volendam

This is a traditional Dutch fishing village on the banks of Lake IJesselmeer. A very picturesque village, it is a popular tourist destination and can be very busy during the high season. It is worth visiting as the harbour is still reminiscent of traditional styles, and the colourful buildings are reminiscent of those found in countless paintings over the past few centuries. Visitors can take boat trips across the lake to the village of Marken with its countless wooden buildings.

Volendam is just twenty-three minutes by car along the N247 from Amsterdam, a journey of 12 miles (20km). There are no trains, but there are regular bus and coach trips available from Amsterdam.

▼ *Volendam seen from Lake IJesselmeer.*
(Angela Youngman)

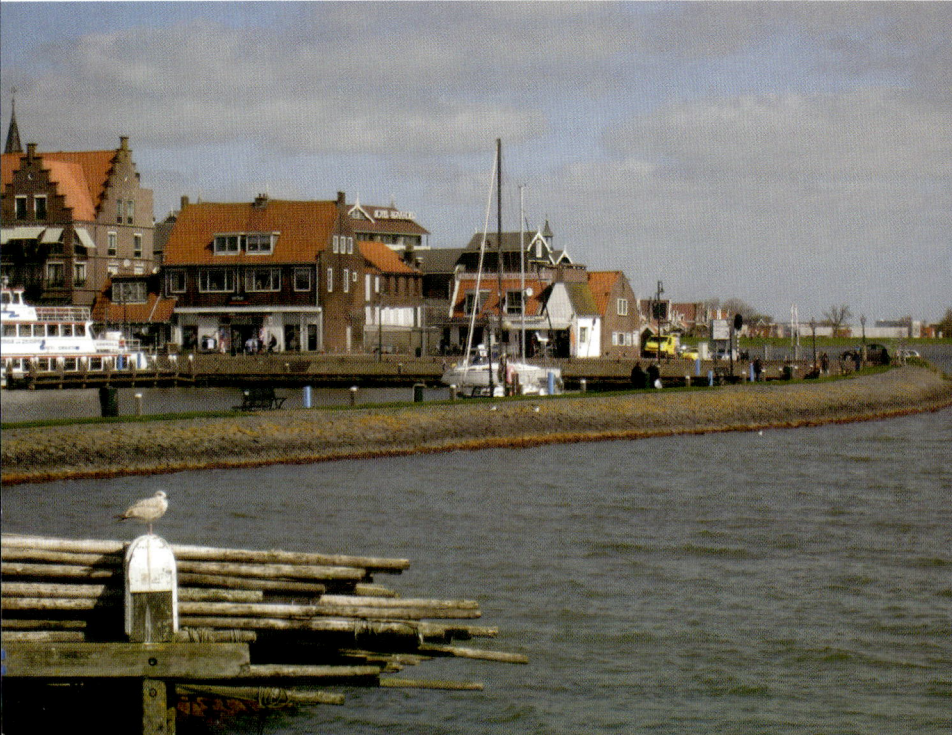

**Volendam Museum**
Zeestraat 41
1131 ZD Volendam
**www.volendamsmuseum.nl**

A small museum devoted to local history, particularly the period 1850–1950. There are permanent displays of traditional costumes and historical room interiors as well as paintings by artists like Henricus Rol and Edwin Austrin Abbey.

The Cigar Band House forms part of the museum, but is located in a separate building adjacent to the main museum. It contains a unique collection of mosaics made from 11 million cigar bands created by a former monk. Nicolaas Molenaar (1894–1964) was born in Volendam, but spent many years in a monastery before leaving it in the 1940s and marrying a former nun. He collected cigar bands and had the idea of turning them into mosaic art by cutting off the band edges, and using just the central medallions. Molenaar began the mosaics in 1947 by creating illustrations, which he housed in his attic. As the years progressed, his hobby took over the house and eventually covered walls as well as objects such as clogs and furniture. The images are wide ranging, from local scenes to famous buildings. Among the mosaics are iconic images such as Big Ben, St Peter's Basilica in Rome, the Statue of Liberty in New York and local buildings including the Water Tower in Sneek, scenes of windmills, the Basilica of Saint Servatius in Maastricht, the Martini Tower in Groningen and St Vincentius Church, Volendam. Other images include the Dutch Royal family, maps of the Netherlands and the Volendam football team. This mosaic collection has been registered in the Guinness Book of Records.

## Zaandam

A classic Dutch city complete with watery landscapes and close to numerous villages and windmills that have inspired many artists, particularly French impressionist Claude Monet. In 1871, Monet spent four months painting and sketching here. He wrote to his friend Pissarro that, 'Zaandam is rather remarkable, there is enough to paint for a lifetime. Houses in all colours, hundreds of mills and delightful boats.' Monet was fascinated by the Zaanse Schanse and painted many scenes on and around it. During this time, he created twenty-five paintings, including A Windmill at Zaandam, Bateaux en Hollande pres de Zaandam and Houses on the Achterzaan. In 1889 Whistler created etchings of the watery landscape.

Zaandam is located on the Zaan river and is approximately fifteen minutes from Amsterdam. Access is by road or by rail to one of the two railway stations in the city, Zaandam and Zaandam Kogerveld. There are boat connections from Amsterdam.

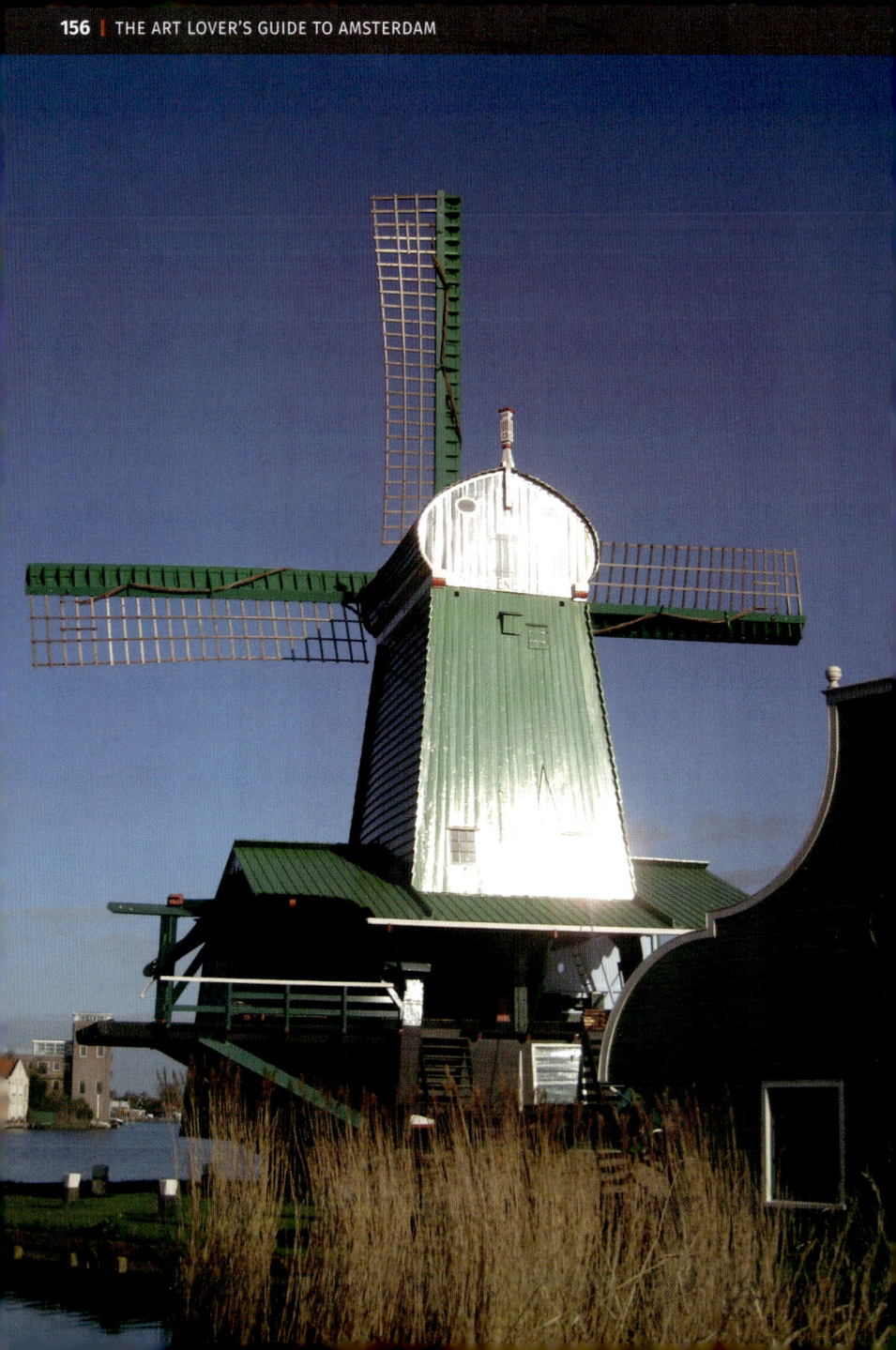

## Blue House,

Hogendijk 78,
1506 AJ Zaandam
This is the building that inspired Monet's painting The Blue House of Zandaam (1871). The building was repainted blue in 2014 following extensive colour research. It is not open to the public as it is a residential building but can be seen from the street. Since 1969 it has been a registered national monument.

## Monet Atelier

Westzijde 14g
1506 EE Zaandam
**www.monoetinzaandam**

At the Monet Atelier, visitors can see replicas of all Monet's twenty-five Zaandam paintings, many of which were made by Zaandam painters.

These paintings are highly important within Monet's work as they form the first large group of paintings that he created at one location over a continuous period of time. It marks the beginning of a technique that he later used to create his famous water lilies sequence at Giverny or the poplars on the River Epte. It shows how Zaandam and the Zaanse Schans influenced his work. There are frequent guided Monet walks available around the area, starting from the Monet Atelier. There are ferry links from the Atelier to the Zaanse Schans and the Zaans Museum.

◀ *Zaanse Schans.* (Angela Youngman)

## Windmill Museum

Kalverringdijk 30
1509 BT Zaandam
**www.zaanschemolen.nl**

Located on the Zaanse Schans, the museum includes an array of models, objects and paintings relating to the history and development of windmills, including the trade and culture that resulted. One of the most spectacular items is a large, 11m-wide painting that provides a panoramic view of all the windmills in the eastern part of Zaandam at the start of the nineteenth century.

## Zaans Museum

Schansend 7
1509 AW Zaandam
**www.zaansmuseum.nl**

The Zaans Museum explores the lifestyles of people living in the area during the past centuries. It owns a Monet painting, The Voorzaan and the Westerham, showing boats sailing on the water, with three windmills in the distance set against grey cloudy skies. The diverse collections on display include a range of paintings, clothing and factory materials. The Verkade Experience focuses on the production of biscuits and chocolates within the Verkade factory in the early years of the twentieth century.

**Zaanse Schans**
Schansend 7,
Zaandam
**www.dezaansechans.nl/en**

An area of spectacular windmills, traditional houses complete with wooden facades, many of which are painted green, as well as workshops and warehouses set alongside a long canal. The houses are still lived in, and businesses operate from the workshops. The windmills provide power to saw wood and mill oil, flour, spices and art pigments. Some of the mills are open to the public, for example the Windmill De Huisman situated on top of a spice warehouse.

▼ *Windmills at Zaanse Schans.* (Angela Youngman)

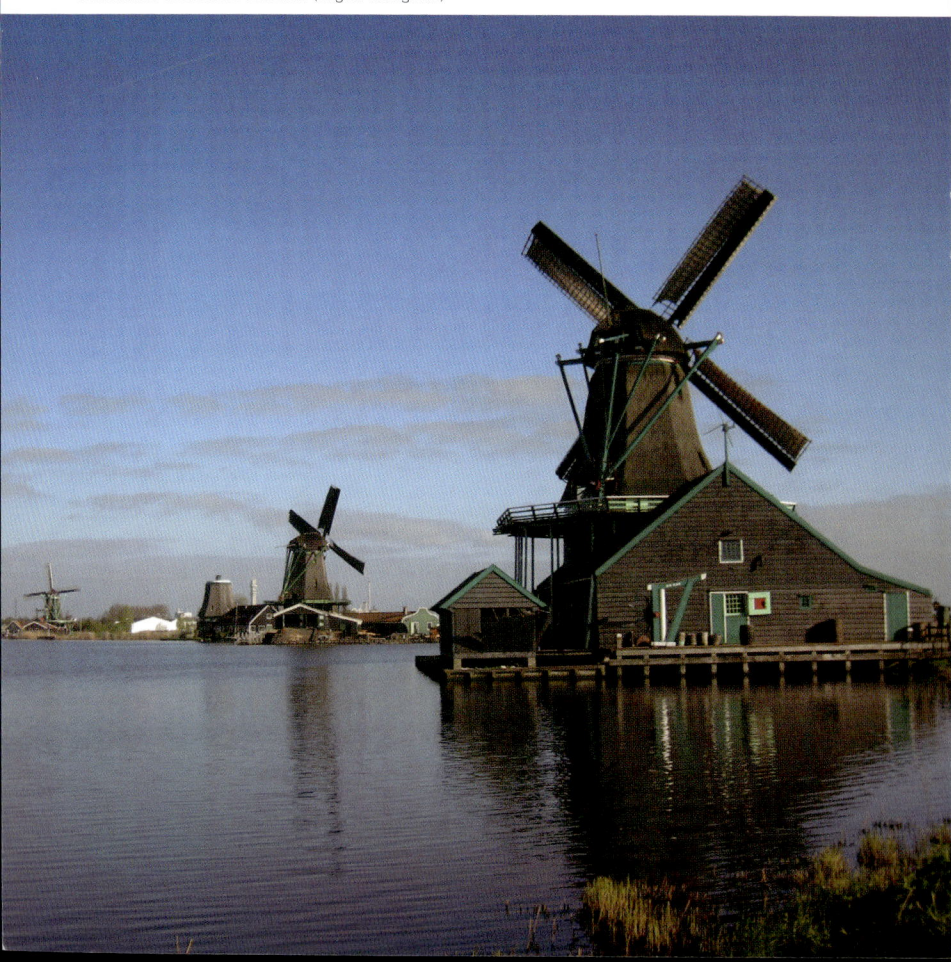

# FURTHER READING

Vermeer & the Delft School, Metropolitan Museum of Art, Yale University Press, 2001.

Netherlandish art in the Rijksmuseum 1400–1600, Henrick Vanos, Jan Piet Filedt Kok, Get Luijten and Frits Scholten, Waanders Publishers, Rijksmuseum, 2000.

Netherlandish Art 1600–1700 Rijksmuseum, Jan Piet Filedt Kok, Reinier Baarsen, Bart Cornelis, Wouter Klock, Frits Ícholten, Waanders Publishers, Rijksmuseum, 2001.

The Golden Age of Dutch Art, Judikje Kiers and Fieke Tissink, Thames & Hudson, 2000.